EXODUS POLITICS

Exodus Politics

Civil Rights and Leadership in African American
Literature and Culture

ROBERT J. PATTERSON

University of Virginia Press

CHARLOTTESVILLE AND LONDON

University of Virginia Press

First published 2013

9 8 7 6 5 4 3 2 1

LIBRARY OF CONGRESS CATALOGING-IN-PUBLICATION DATA

Patterson, Robert J., [date]
  Exodus politics : civil rights and leadership in African American literature and culture
/ Robert J. Patterson.
     pages cm
  Includes bibliographical references and index.
  ISBN 978-0-8139-3525-6 (cloth : acid-free paper)
  ISBN 978-0-8139-3526-3 (pbk. : acid-free paper)
  ISBN 978-0-8139-3527-0 (e-book)
  1. American literature—African American authors—History and criticism. 2. Civil
rights in literature. 3. Leadership in literature. I. Title.
PS153.N5P366 2013
810.9'896073—dc23

2013011900

THE
AMERICAN
LITERATURES
INITIATIVE

A book in the American Literatures Initiative (ALI), a collaborative
publishing project of NYU Press, Fordham University Press, Rutgers
University Press, Temple University Press, and the University of Virginia
Press. The Initiative is supported by The Andrew W. Mellon Foundation.
For more information, please visit www.americanliteratures.org.

For my first love, my greatest love
For Doris J. Patterson
For Marcilyn L. Patterson
For Bessie L. Patterson
For the love of music
For the children: the nieces, nephews, goddaughters, and godsons
For those who came before and those who will come after
For doing justly, loving mercy, and walking humbly
For life, love, laughter, grace, and the spirit of generosity
For one of many moments in time

CONTENTS

Acknowledgments

Exodus Politics came to fruition not simply as a result of my research, thinking, and writing. Thankfully, I also had friends and colleagues who provided intellectual spaces in which my ideas could grow. Equally important, I had friends and family who provided the emotional support necessary for me to succeed in this endeavor. And last but certainly not least, God and the Spirit were always present, helping me to keep my eyes on the prize—the finished product. Even though I often wrote this book while alone, I am joyous and grateful that I never was lonely when I wrote.

While writing a book, one incurs many debts—individual, personal, professional, and institutional—that cannot always be repaid. My acknowledgments, then, reflect my desire to credit all who invested in me, this project, and, in most instances, both.

My graduate education afforded me the skill set to write *Exodus Politics*, so I would like to acknowledge and thank my dissertation adviser Michael Awkward and committee members Rudolph Byrd and Dianne (Stewart) Diakité for their influences on my career. Not only did they help me conceptualize my project and force me to express my ideas precisely, they provided models of productivity and rigor that are worthy of emulation. Dr. Rudolph Byrd passed in 2011, but his commitment to scholarship, teaching, community activism, and institution building has left an enduring legacy. Mark A. Sanders, Regine O. Jackson, and Nagueyalti Warren gave me helpful insights and encouragement throughout my graduate education. I would also like to thank Kharen

Fulton and Theresa Cox-Kenney of the Laney Graduate School of Arts and Sciences for admitting me into the Graduate School (Kharen), for ensuring that my money was right (Theresa), and, most important, for always encouraging me and being invested in my success.

My colleagues at Florida State University played important roles in shaping this book. Elizabeth Spiller, Timothy Parrish, Maxine Montgomery, Jerrilyn McGregory, and Anne Coldiron not only provided excellent mentorship but also read my work and gave me useful feedback. More specifically, I thank Elizabeth, Timothy, and Maxine for reading this manuscript at different stages, and Jerrilyn for helping me develop the initial proposal that elicited an enthusiastic response from the University of Virginia Press. After my departure, Elizabeth and Maxine continued to be collegial and generous, providing insightful readings of my manuscript. Additionally, both the Council for Research and Creative Activity's First-Year Assistant Professor (FYAP) Summer Grant and the McKnight Junior Faculty Fellowship from the Florida Education Foundation (FEF) helped me advance this project. I appreciate each institution for committing financially to scholarly research.

My colleagues at Georgetown University entered this project at a critical stage, and I appreciate their advice, foresight, and assistance. More specifically, Angelyn Mitchell, as one of my faculty mentors, read drafts of the manuscript and gave me useful feedback for its revision. Angie always exhibits generosity, collegiality, and thoughtfulness in our scholarly conversations. Moreover, as the founding director of the African American Studies Program, she has played an instrumental role in building and institutionalizing African American studies at Georgetown. In this capacity, she also has provided many opportunities for me to engage in the interdisciplinary work that was crucial for writing this book. Another colleague, Noel Sugimura, has shown exceptional camaraderie in her willingness to read and respond to different drafts of the manuscript. I also extend gratitude to my colleagues Jennifer Natalya Fink, Brian Hochman, Gay Cima, Patricia O'Connor, Pam Fox, and Henry Schwarz for their publication advice and general support during my tenure at Georgetown. A Junior Faculty Research Fellowship from the Graduate School of Arts and Sciences and two summer grants from Dean Chester Gillis in the Georgetown College provided research opportunities that pushed this project to its final stages. Finally, my research assistants Regina Hamilton, Esther Owolabi, Khadijah Davis, and Meghan O'Hara gave me invaluable help as I completed *Exodus Politics*.

At the University of Virginia Press, Cathie Brettschneider, the humanities editor, is due special thanks for expressing interest in this project when it was in its early stages and remaining invested in it as I completed it. Ellen Satrom, the managing editor, provided much-appreciated assistance throughout the production process. My two anonymous readers gave important feedback, and *Exodus Politics* benefited from their insights. Tim Roberts, managing editor of the American Literatures Initiative, shepherded the book through production. Many thanks to Duke University Press for allowing me to include as chapter 1 of this book a longer, revised version of the essay "Rethinking Definitions and Expectations: Civil Rights and Civil Right Leadership in Ernest Gaines's *The Autobiography of Miss Jane Pittman*," which appeared in *South Atlantic Quarterly*, vol. 112, no. 2 (2013), pp. 339–64.

My friends who work at other institutions throughout the academic diaspora, particularly Brett Gadsden, Anjulet Tucker, Susana M. Morris, Aida Hussen, Yolande M. Tomlinson, and Soyica Diggs Colbert, have also helped me to develop the ideas I present here. After more than ten years of friendship, Anjulet remains one of the most energetic people I know, and her passion for scholarly inquiry helped me tease out many of the sociological and cultural questions that the project raises. My conversations with Brett have refined the book's historical analysis, and Susana's keen close-reading abilities brought fresh insights to the literary analyses. Aida's thoughtfulness and generosity in discussing my chapters and related conference papers have sharpened the book's clarity of thought and expression. Yolande has been another important interlocutor, and our numerous conversations have clarified my ideas. And Soyica, who introduced me to this profession, has been not only a perceptive and encouraging reader and comrade but also, since the time I first met her more than a decade ago, a role model for productivity, success, and cutting-edge scholarship.

I also have been fortunate to have generous mentors at other universities—Maurice O. Wallace, Christina Sharpe, Erica Edwards, and LaMonda Horton-Stallings—who have helped advance my career. Maurice graciously has given his time, talents, and humor to help me. Even while in graduate school, I benefited from his advice and scholarship (without ever having to live in Durham). Christina has to be one of the most conscientious people I have ever met. Her commitment to mentoring faculty of color in particular not only has helped diversify the professoriate but also has served as an inspiration to rising scholars. Erica's willingness to read drafts and to serve as an interlocutor has been important, and her interdisciplinary scholarship warrants emulation. I am also grateful to LaMonda Horton-Stallings for thoughtfully reading proposals for and earlier drafts of the book.

Friendship is not a term that I use loosely. I consider myself privileged and blessed to have *good* friends who have been important to *this* project. A host of people have been present from this book's beginning and have been remarkably supportive and exceptionally enthusiastic. While a few have read or provided instructive feedback on this manuscript, others have encouraged its production by consistently holding me accountable on my progress by asking me when the book was coming out and whether they could get a signed (free?) copy. For their consistent concern, interest, and excitement about my professional *and* personal successes, I thank Demetra Andrews, Crystal Brown, Carla Frett, Tiffany Craig Herring, Ramonda Horton, Shijuade Kadree, Nigel Kelly, Johnathan McGriff, Conitras Houston Moore, William Morris, Sherry Akande Nielsen, Fernando Porter, Anthony Powell, Christopher Powell, Brad Rahaman, Charles Shedrick, Jason Simmonds, Hattie B. Thornton, Ebony Walden, Michelle Wallace, and Wallrick Williams. I also extend special thanks to two lifelong best friends: Pauline Patterson, who, like many of my colleagues, read and commented upon various drafts of this project, and Karla Benson Rutten, who was equally kind.

My family has shaped this project by teaching me many of life's lessons, maintaining faith in my ability to succeed, and cultivating my spirit of independence. Two women in particular have held the responsibility and challenge of instilling in me the core values that are central to this project and my worldview. Not only have my mother, Doris J. Patterson, and my sister, Marcilyn L. Patterson, encouraged me throughout my entire life, but their own lives have testified to how opportunities, desires, and gifts can intersect to make a difference. I appreciate them not only for valuing education and instilling in me a thirst for knowledge and passion to succeed but also for being who they are; their concern and compassion for people amaze me as much as their generosity and goodwill inspire me. Their hearts are big, their smiles are wide, and their knowledge is vast.

Additionally, my aunts, Glenda F. Patterson and Shirley A. Williams, have been a source of encouragement and have played important roles in the village necessary to raise me. I thank them for their love, concern, and support. Last, but certainly not least, my grandmother, Bessie L. Patterson, who claimed me as "hers," taught me much about life and black culture before she transitioned on January 22, 2007. Her sayings were witty and replete with the intricacies of black culture. Each of these women—my mother, my sister, two aunts, and my grandmother—has in many ways exemplified what I came to learn about in graduate school as a "black feminist politic," including all of its possibilities and paradoxes.

For all these experiences and influences, I am who I am, and this book reflects the best of them all.

Introduction: Civil Rights, Leadership, and Exodus Politics

Without such [local] activists there can be no progressive politics. Yet state, regional, and national networks are also required for an effective progressive politics. That is why locally based collective (and especially multigendered) models of black leadership are needed. These models must shun the idea of one black national leader; they also should put a premium on critical dialogue and democratic accountability in black organizations.

—CORNEL WEST, *RACE MATTERS*

In *Race Matters* (1993), Cornel West argues that black leadership has entered a state of crisis because post–civil rights era black leaders do not possess "a collective and critical consciousness" for improving the plight of the black masses.[1] While romanticizing the commitment of pre–civil rights and civil rights era leaders to black communal enfranchisement, West rightfully illuminates how black politicians of the post–civil rights era might better serve black communities. West also, however, draws attention to a broader crisis of black leadership than just the lack of commitment to poor black communities among black politicians. As the epigraph reveals, he identifies the simultaneous masculinization and nationalization of black leadership as two phenomena that have thrown black leadership into crisis. By positing that black leadership models should be "multigendered" and that "the idea of one black national [male] leader" should be rejected, West challenges the dominance of black male leadership as necessary and desired for black political advancement. Similarly, by underscoring the need to develop "locally based" leadership that is connected to broader "national networks," he unsettles the notion that local leadership is less important than "national" leadership.

In West's analysis, the crisis of black leadership is connected to a crisis in civil rights attainment: his concerns about black leadership stem from its inability to ensure that the equality of opportunity that the civil rights movement demanded translates into material equality. His critique of black leadership, black political organization, and black political behavior then calls into question black communities' expectations for black leadership. He demands that black communities enlarge their definitions of civil rights and reexamine the goals of the civil rights movement to develop a progressive politics that improves black people's lives. West's book is one of several interventions in the new civil rights studies and studies of black leadership that emerged in the 1990s and have persisted into the twenty-first century.

In *Exodus Politics: Civil Rights and Leadership in African American Literature and Culture*, I theorize how African American literature intervenes in contemporary discourses about civil rights and black leadership by defamiliarizing definitions of "civil rights," expectations of civil rights leadership, and goals of the modern civil rights movement. *Defamiliarization* here refers to the invocation, by contemporary writers of African American literature, of seemingly familiar discourses, concepts, and events in such a way as to demonstrate that that familiarity is only partial. Defamiliarization draws attention to fields of knowledge that are uncommon, non-normative, and unpopular, thereby upsetting the normativity of hegemonic epistemologies. As social scientists, social movement theorists, and civil rights historians have revisited the civil rights movement to defamiliarize how popular and scholarly texts have represented, understood, and invoked it, a number of contemporary writers of African American literature have as well. These writers have called into question the cultural and historiographical tendencies to champion male leadership, to promote models of leadership that diminish the significance of mass mobilization, to conceptualize racial rights as disconnected from gender and sexual rights, and to restrict the modern civil rights movement to the years between 1953 and 1965. Each of these tendencies feeds into the crisis of black leadership and the crisis of civil rights attainment by producing what I theorize as "the paradoxes of exodus politics."

Exodus politics explains why normative trends have enshrined civil rights historiography and discourses in paradigms that do not adequately describe the movement's long-term and short-term vision for civil rights and empowerment. To begin, it is instructive to situate exodus politics within the context of the biblical Exodus narrative, since African Americans have long appropriated and typologically identified with this narrative to argue that their civil rights are God-given and divinely protected. Black freedom struggles, black leadership, and everyday black people historically have cited the Exodus narrative to argue that civil rights injustices contradict God's will for freedom. Yet, although African Americans have appropriated the Exodus narrative and other biblical "liberation" texts to contest racial oppression, they have been less inclined to conceptualize these narratives of "freedom" in terms that extend beyond "race." In other words, in the black political imagination, the Exodus narrative has not functioned as a rallying cry against all forms of political oppression that are related to identity politics—race, class, gender, and sexuality. To the contrary, some appropriations of the Exodus narrative not only justify heterosexism and heteronormativity but also excuse the gender and sexual oppressions of black women and LGBTQ communities.

One of exodus politics' main shortcomings emerges from appropriations of the biblical narrative that conclude, from Moses's being a man and God's choosing him, that God must have chosen Moses at least partly *because* he was a man—and that later emancipatory leaders must be male as well. This paradigm not only disallows the possibility of female leadership but also produces a gender hierarchy that prioritizes black men, black men's leadership, and black men's political interests. The oppression that black women, black gays, and black lesbians encounter remains illegible within this context because the paradigm does not conceptualize their experiences of disenfranchisement as civil rights violations.[2] Even when more progressive civil rights discourses acknowledge black women, black gays, and black lesbians' specific experiences of oppression as civil rights violations, they still place solving black men's political crises at the forefront of black communities' civil rights agendas.

One paradox that I examine is that exodus politics' reinforcement of heteronormative ideas has blocked the construction of a vision of empowerment for non-normative black subjects, or black subjects who are not heterosexual middle-class men. In an attempt to position black heteropatriarchy alongside white heteropatriarchy, exodus politics reinforces the notion that black men's empowerment as heads of their households will necessarily improve black communities. Although some black sociologists in the early twentieth century, including E. Franklin Frazier, claimed that "inverted" black familial structures contributed to black people's disenfranchisement, the publicizing of this thesis in the popularly named "Moynihan Report" resulted in its becoming one of the dominating discourses in black politics.[3] Not only does the report's conception of empowerment and civil rights fail to call into question the general ways that American patriarchy dysfunctions, it also neglects to consider how black people who are not heterosexual middle-class men would be empowered. Within the framework of exodus politics, civil rights are not an overlapping set of racial, gender, sexual, and economic rights that differ throughout black communities; instead, black communities are monolithic units that share the same political interests.

Another paradox of exodus politics that I examine is that its emphasis on messianic leadership, its characterization of leadership as a supernatural power available only to certain men, and its disregard for other types of leadership undermine the movement's long-term goals. By binding the movement's vision for empowerment to an individual man's leadership, exodus politics places the responsibility for the Herculean task of securing the group's civil rights on one person. Community members fail to see themselves as empowered leaders who can act in the absence of formal leadership to continue the quest for black freedom, which is still unfulfilled long after the passage of laws that granted access to America's institutions. Yet communities hold the responsibility of ensuring that the theoretical equality of opportunity translates into a material equality of outcome because neither one historical moment nor a few historical actors can gain civil rights. The civil rights movement offers both short-term and long-term visions for political empowerment, and each set of goals needs multiple leaders in order to succeed.

My theorization of exodus politics thus renders visible its paradoxes, demonstrating how the tendencies to be politically exclusive and politically hierarchical undermine the immediate and long-term goals of the civil rights movement, since neither exclusivity nor hierarchy provides an emancipatory politic that considers the varying political interests within black communities. In *Exodus Politics*, I analyze African American literature to identify three trends that exodus politics produces and that black political culture must disrupt if a more robust vision of black leadership and black politics is to be generated. First, exodus politics engenders and maintains hierarchies of oppression by not promoting the enfranchisement of black people who occupy non-normative gender, class, and sexual positions. Second, by masculinizing black leadership, exodus politics ignores how women, everyday people, and quotidian acts of resistance shape freedom struggles. Third, by conceptualizing the civil rights movement's short-term goals as its *only* goals, exodus politics creates leader-dependent communities that cannot enact a civil rights vision in the absence of the male leader. *Exodus Politics* argues that writers of African American literature upset this tendency to deify male (formal) leadership as desired and necessary for black freedom struggles to organize and to succeed. In this way, the literature functions as a call to action to develop a politic that is indeed emancipatory.

The Paradoxes of Exodus Politics and Disciplinary Concerns

To elucidate the paradoxes of exodus politics, this book draws upon the theoretical concepts of a variety of disciplines—emphasizing black feminism, civil rights historiography, literary studies, and cultural studies throughout, and black religious studies and, to a lesser degree, black queer studies as chapter-specific critical contexts. By challenging normative definitions of civil rights, expectations for civil rights leaders, and periodizations of the civil rights movement, *Exodus Politics* conceptualizes civil rights in paradigms that do not reproduce hierarchies of oppression. Beyond providing a critique of exodus politics' shortcomings, I explain how black cultural politics can develop models of leadership and civil rights that are more emancipatory for black communities. To do so, I analyze how the intersections of gender, sexual, class, and racial discourses make exodus politics paradoxical. That is to say, I uncover the implicit ideologies that undermine exodus politics' will to liberate. While the phrase "race, class, gender, and sexuality" has almost become a mantra in cultural studies and studies of identity politics, theorizations within black feminism and black queer studies of "intersectionality" as an analytic tool prove useful in demonstrating the degree to which these categories of identity remain imbricated. More specifically, *Exodus Politics* expands and elaborates upon the black feminist notion of intersectionality by foregrounding civil rights as a set of civil liberties that encompasses racial rights, gender rights, sexual rights, and economic rights.[4] An intersectional analysis not only refuses to single out and privilege any one category of identity over another but also, as black queer studies demands, "draw[s] attention to nonnormative sexual practice."[5]

Although early black feminist theory argued for a more complex notion of black subjectivity that would account for how gender and social class intersected with race to generate different political concerns within black communities, sexuality remained entrenched in heteronormative ideals. In her now-famous essay "Toward a Black Feminist Criticism," Barbara Smith aims to correct this tendency in black feminist literary criticism to be heteronormative, to "seldom use a consistent feminist analysis or write about black lesbian literature."[6] Her "queer" reading of Toni Morrison's *Sula* (1973) considers it a "lesbian text," "not because women are lovers, but because they are central figures, are positively portrayed and have pivotal relations with one another."[7] In other words, she examines how black women live outside the strictures of black heteropatriarchy to articulate a more expansive vision of black life. Her reading of *Sula* as a "lesbian text" engendered much debate, but her acknowledgment of black feminism's heteronormativity highlighted a critique of black feminism that was emerging within black lesbian-feminist politics. As Cheryl Clarke's essay "Lesbianism: An Act of Resistance" evidences, black (lesbian) feminists have foregrounded the (hetero)sexualization of racism and the racialization of (hetero)sexism throughout history in order to challenge the normativity of black heteropatriarchy and its related political concerns.[8]

While black feminism has begun to seriously engage heterosexism and heteronormativity in its intersectional theorizations, black queer studies has been particularly invested in analyzing the "(hetero)sexualization of racism" and how the mutually constitutive relationship of heterosexism and racism historically has undergirded and reinforced black oppression. Black queer studies conceptualizes black identity at the intersections of race, gender, class, and sexuality and claims that racialized discourses invoke black people's putative sexual deviance and gender nonconformity to justify their disenfranchisement in the United States (and across the African diaspora). As Aliyyah Abdur-Rahman argues, "Not only does sexuality fundamentally underlie racial logics, but, more to the point, racial identity is itself conceived, regulated, and disciplined through sexuality—through sexual practices, violations, and norms."[9] To this end, black queer studies historicizes the (hetero)sexualization of racism to examine the recuperative possibilities for non-normative genders and sexualities, what Darieck Scott theorizes as "abject blackness," or a "counterintuitive black power."[10] In light of these critical trends, I at times build upon the scholarship of Roderick Ferguson's *Aberrations in Black: Toward a Queer Color Critique* (2004), Sharon Holland's *Raising the Dead: Readings of Death and (Black) Subjectivity* (2000), Darieck Scott's *Extravagant Abjection: Blackness, Power, and Sexuality in the African American Literary Imagination* (2010), and Aliyyah Abdur-Rahman's *Against the Closet: Black Political Longing and the Erotics of Race* (2012) to explain how non-normative genders and sexualities support and/or challenge exodus politics as a master narrative of black political organization, activity, and thought.

My concern here, then, is to decode how implicit and explicit ideas about gender, class, and sexuality have become mapped onto the category "civil rights." The failure to make these ideas more explicit inhibits the development of an "antiracist" politics that considers the different and sometimes competing political interests of black communities.

As Devon Carbado has argued, antiracist politics that posit the black heterosexual male as "the black subject" dissociate civil rights activism from women's rights and gay and lesbian rights. In doing so, these discourses veil the fact that black gays, black lesbians, and black women have political concerns that differ from, and are sometimes antithetical to, those of black heterosexual men.[11] Whereas some black communities have disapproved of (white) feminist and (white) gay and lesbian movements appropriating the rhetoric of the civil rights movement to argue for their "civil rights," this disapproval ignores the reality of queer black subjects and black queer subjects (as Carbado and, elsewhere, Patricia Hill Collins suggest).[12]

From post-Reconstruction images that characterized the black male rapist as a threat to civilization, to protests during the 1950s and 1960s in which black men affirmed "I am a Man!," civil rights discourses always have been entrenched in racial, sexual, gender, and class ideologies.[13] By more explicitly articulating these relationships, I illuminate how discourses of exodus politics do not so much ignore the intersections of race, gender, class, and sexuality as collapse the categories in ways that inhibit communal empowerment. Both black feminism and black queer studies have provided theoretical paradigms that decenter the normative black subject as the representative black subject. By disentangling these collapsed, imbricated identities, black feminism and black queer studies have helped develop antiracist politics that resist the tendency to idealize the normative black subject. In the process, they have also clarified the interrelationships of race, gender, sexuality, and class. *Exodus Politics* therefore builds upon their theoretical insights, particularly their articulations of the relationship between identity politics and political praxis.

The texts that *Exodus Politics* examines add important layers to the paradoxical aspects of exodus politics—from *The Autobiography of Miss Jane Pittman*, which troubles the privileging of male formal leadership over what Belinda Robnett has described as women's "bridge leadership" (mobilization at the community level that raises individuals' awareness of social problems and helps them develop solutions in order to link individuals to a movement and their personal concerns to a broader strategic politics), to *Corregidora*, which emphasizes black women's rights to control their reproductive capacity as central to their freedom struggles. Both of these books historicize a vision of civil rights that constitutes the racial through the sexual and the gendered. As a result, they reconceptualize what civil rights are, as well as what constitutes civil rights leadership. Feminist historians, including Paula Giddings and Belinda

Robnett, have analyzed the masculinist and heteronormative discourses that at times have thwarted the civil rights movement's broader vision of liberation,[14] and womanist theologians, including Delores Williams, Irene Monroe, and Kelly Brown Douglas, have made similar arguments about cultural appropriations of the biblical Exodus narrative.[15] This analysis unites these areas of inquiry to demonstrate how exodus politics perpetuates hierarchies of oppression that frustrate the politics of gender and sexuality within black communities. More importantly, the novels that this book analyzes offer alternative models of civil rights and civil rights leadership that promote enfranchisement for normative and non-normative black subjects.

As the analyses of *The Autobiography of Miss Jane Pittman, Meridian,* and *Dreamer* elucidate, investment in the idea of one male messianic leader inhibits communities' abilities to act on their own behalf and generate indigenous leaders. In *The Autobiography of Miss Jane Pittman,* for example, I read the protagonist Jimmy's resistance to being "the One" as expressing Gaines's espousal of a more egalitarian notion of leadership. The participatory decision making that according to civil rights activist Ella Baker characterized the Student Nonviolent Coordinating Committee during the 1960s evidences a model of less hierarchical leadership that warrants further examination;[16] Baker contrasted it to the hierarchical leadership style in other civil rights organizations, including the Southern Christian Leadership Conference (SCLC), of which she was a member. As chapter 2 explains, Baker wanted a more egalitarian organizational structure, one that did not grant too much power to any individual and that cultivated a sense of empowerment and autonomy among members.

African American Literature and African American Politics

Exodus Politics situates its claims within long-standing debates in African American literary studies regarding the "value" of African American literature as a cultural source that reflects and shapes the political climate from which it emerges. Although literature is a force of political and cultural transformation, my argument does not reinforce a particular strand of black elite intellectualism that posits African American literature as best suited for (re)imagining black political possibilities.[17] To the contrary, despite the somewhat canonical status that specific African American literary texts and authors have earned, I think of how literature is an example of (popular) culture—of how it has been, in the words of Richard Iton, "an integral and important aspect of the making of politics throughout the pre–civil rights era and the civil rights era itself."[18] I resist making a *definitive* distinction between "pre–" and "post–" civil rights movement fiction when theorizing exodus politics because such a distinction buttresses a decisive split that needs to be reexamined; it sometimes disconnects post–civil rights movement fiction from the civil rights movement and thus helps produce the paradoxes of exodus politics.

Many scholars who have dealt seriously with literary representations of the civil rights movement, however, have made such a distinction. In "Revisiting the 1960s in Contemporary Fiction: 'Where Do We Go from Here?,'" for example, Sharon Monteith examines the formal and thematic concerns that differentiate civil rights from post–civil rights era texts: whereas civil rights texts are written during the 1960s within phase one of the movement, post–civil rights texts emerge after the 1970s and are within phase two. Monteith's strict dichotomy between civil rights and post–civil rights era fictions is not altogether persuasive. Yet she is right to suggest that "post–civil rights era fictions," including *The Autobiography of Miss Jane Pittman* (1971), "revisit and re-assert civil rights history."[19] In other words, texts such as *The Autobiography of Miss Jane Pittman*, as well as the other ones *Exodus Politics* examines, function as metanarratives about civil rights and civil rights leadership.

While Monteith argues that post–civil rights era fiction challenges dominant assumptions about black leadership, she maintains that this body of literature has yet to imagine a space for women's leadership. She asserts that "fictional interrogations of leadership models which incorporate women are yet to be imagined in post–civil rights fictions. Revisiting what was participatory about grassroots politics for both genders, and bridge leadership for women activists in the civil right[s] movement, would develop what is already an interrogative genre."[20] Monteith is right to demand a closer examination of literature's representations of the politics of gender and gender politics in "post"–civil rights texts. Yet she herself ignores how post–civil rights fictions do focus on "what was participatory about grassroots politics for both genders" and do "incorporate women" in order to demasculinize civil rights historiography. *Exodus Politics*, then, not only responds to Monteith's call by historicizing Ernest Gaines's *The Autobiography of Miss Jane Pittman* (1971), Gayl Jones's *Corregidora* (1975), Alice Walker's *Meridian* (1976), and Charles Johnson's *Dreamer* (1998) within their respective political, social, and literary contexts but also shows how they deprivilege the model of leadership by a single black male. To understand how they do this, it is instructive to situate them in the context of what civil rights historians theorize as a "long" civil rights movement.

Civil rights historian Jacquelyn Dowd Hall urges scholars to employ a "long civil rights movement" historical framework to analyze the continued significance of the black freedom struggle and thus to decenter the notion that the classical phase (phase one) emblematized *the* movement's long-term and short-term goals.[21] Hall argues that the tendency to confine the civil rights movement to the 1950s and 1960s produces two problematic notions. First, it suggests that the movement's only goal was to end de jure segregation. Second, it perpetuates the idea that the end of de jure segregation solved the problem of racial inequality. A "long" historical framework contests the absoluteness of these claims by expanding the vision of the civil rights movement's goals and by refuting the assertion that the civil rights movement eliminated racial inequality. Put another way, Hall's theory of a long civil rights movement challenges the historiographical tendencies to reproduce the paradoxes of exodus politics.

By employing a long historical framework, Hall connects the struggles for civil rights during the 1950s and 1960s to previous struggles to demonstrate the continuity between freedom movements. By foregrounding women's leadership and activism in earlier movements, she upsets the notion that only men led the movement. By demonstrating how women fought for black women's rights specifically in contemporary and earlier freedom struggles, she constructs a framework that links black women's gender and sexual rights to civil rights. By connecting contemporary post–civil rights era discrimination to earlier discrimination, she demonstrates that phase one was only one aspect of the civil rights movement and emphasizes the continuing significance of phase two. Neither the movement's historical and political scope nor its continued relevance can be apprehended from a focus on a narrow historical period, an exclusive list of male formal leaders, or an isolated set of legislative accomplishments.

The relationship between phase one and phase two, as the literary texts demonstrate, not only grounds struggles for civil rights within a larger historical trajectory but also reinforces the notion that civil rights struggles cannot be limited to a specific historical period (1953–68) or a specific set of legislative achievements (*Brown v. Board of Education*, the Civil Rights Acts of 1963, 1964, and 1968, and the Voting Rights Act of 1965). Whereas phase one of the civil rights movement aimed to end de jure segregation, the second phase attempted to eradicate the long-term aggregate effects of systemic discrimination. The literary texts that *Exodus Politics* analyzes consider ways to bridge the gap between the completion of phase one and the shift into phase two. During this transitional period, backlash against the movement, as well as crises of black leadership, increased African Americans' anxiety about whether the movement's legislative successes would translate the theoretical equality of opportunity into material equality. Civil rights advocates argued that the government needed to institute mechanisms, such as affirmative action, to ensure that the dream of integration would not dry up like a raisin in the sun and thereby make the material equality that was supposed to spring from it yet another dream deferred.[22]

A narrative privileging the legal end of segregation (*Brown*), the attainment of voting rights (Voting Rights Act of 1965), and the achievement of integration (King's "I Have a Dream" speech) as epitomizing the movement's primary goals leaves out the challenges that complicated these sometimes partial successes. Historians who are calling into question this tendency in civil rights studies to privilege phase one demonstrate why such a reading of the civil rights movement is politically dangerous: it divorces post-1970s civil rights struggles from the broader civil rights movement, while portraying African Americans' continued economic, social, and political disempowerment as consequences of their own shortcomings and as unrelated to institutionally imposed deprivation. If the classical phase did indeed grant equality, neither racism nor any of its interrelated "isms" can explain the persistent inequities African Americans still experience. And if African Americans are "equal," special programs such as affirmative action are unfair because they presuppose "inequality."[23]

Hall compellingly argues the political benefits of conceptualizing the civil rights movement within a long historical framework by thinking more robustly about the various people, events, and ideas that could be included in it. Yet the long analytical framework, as Christopher Metress observes, would benefit from considering how culturally rich sources such as African American literature also unsettle phase one's dominance in civil rights historiography. Building upon Hayden White's notion of emplotment, Metress remains concerned more with "how movement 'histories' operate as emplotted narratives" than with "how the movement narrative is being emplotted by historians."[24] Metress argues that literature demonstrates the impossibility of constructing a neat, prepackaged, containable history of progress about the civil rights movement, as literature's use of multiple narratives demonstrates the impossibility of attaining a fully knowable history. Building upon this thought, I assert that African American literature, in its engagement with the long civil rights movement, not only constitutes a body of texts that someday might be studied as "long civil rights movement narratives" but also "provides for a more expansive sense of the materials of civil rights history" and is "a valuable and an untapped legacy for enriching our understanding of the black freedom struggles of the mid-twentieth century."[25] In other words, civil rights era and post–civil rights era African American literature defamiliarizes historiographical accounts of the civil rights movement and thus adds an imaginative dimension to civil rights revisionist historiography that eludes historical studies.

My analysis of African American literature therefore invokes Robert Stepto's theory of intertextuality to argue that African American literature "responds" to civil rights historians' "call" to use a long historical framework and, by answering this call, upsets the cultural and political currency of exodus politics. In *From behind the Veil: A Study of Afro-American Narrative* (1991), Stepto argues that African American texts enter a call-and-response dialogic relationship: through formal and thematic tropes, they issue a "call" to which subsequent texts "respond." I would extend Stepto's idea to cultural texts more generally to suggest that texts do not exist simply in an isolated vertical relationship, "talking" only with other literary texts. Rather, they are also deeply entrenched in history and respond to historical texts, engaging in the revisionist historiographical recuperation that Toni Morrison explains in "The Site of Memory."[26]

Therefore, this book's argument draws upon literature that is set within phases one and two of the civil rights movement to consider how the literary texts respond to the previous cultural calls. While chapters 1 through 4 examine texts published between 1971 and 1998, I will briefly discuss here the engagement of exodus politics in some African American novels published as early as 1937. These literary texts are useful in that they frame the black freedom struggle in a "long" historical trajectory. If, as Iton contends, "political intention adheres to every cultural production," African American literary texts, as sources of cultural production, have practical value that extends beyond the politics of representation, which emphasized how writing itself evidenced African Americans' humanity and therefore deservedness of "civil rights."[27]

Exodus Politics further conceptualizes African American literary texts as cultural artifacts that directly and indirectly shape the movement for

African American civil enfranchisement. This argument exists alongside contemporary conversations in literary and cultural studies that theorize both the political value of African American literature and the political work it performs. In *Representing the Race: A New Political History of African American Literature* (2010), Gene Jarrett outlines the relationship of African American literature and politics. Jarrett's literary history "look[s] at African American literature's role in the political imagination, political action's role in the African American literary imagination, and, conversely, African American literature's role in political action, to the extent that it can facilitate social change."[28] Unearthing the specific political interventions African American literature has made throughout history, Jarrett asserts that it has in fact "helped African Americans secure or improve their representation in 'formal' realms of electoral voting, government intervention, public policy, and law, and not just in the 'informal' cultural realms where special portrayals of the 'black race' aim to affect social attitudes and attain racial justice."[29] Here Jarrett enters an at times contentious conversation within the fields of literary and cultural studies in order to clarify the role that African American literature performs within a broader cultural imaginary and political landscape.

Jarrett's analysis echoes Ralph Ellison's notion that "the novel at its best demands a complexity of vision which politics doesn't like" in order to underscore how literature complicates oversimplified ideas that circulate in political discourses.[30] The novel resists the temptation to reduce politics to empty sound bites and provides a discursive space to theorize the range of possibilities for politics. Literature's complexity of vision positions it as an arbiter in formal politics, using the medium of the informal to enact political change. In the context of exodus politics, the novel itself functions as a bridge between local (informal politics) and national (formal politics) realms. As bridge leadership and formal leadership mutually constitute each other, so too do formal and informal politics.[31] Jarrett's analysis articulates the political work that African American literature performs in the area of formal politics and ties that political work to the transformations it also enacts in informal politics.

While attentive to political scientist Adolph Reed's perturbation over literary critics' blurring of the distinction between "the history of social thought," which addresses "issues of legitimacy, justice obligation, the meaning of equality, or the nature of the polity," and "cultural history," which addresses the representation of such issues in the culture, Jarrett believes that Reed's ultimate "assumption that 'direct black political action' is more transformative than 'indirect cultural politics'" does not grasp how direct black political action and indirect cultural politics mutually constitute each other.[32] Jarrett proposes that a more fruitful analysis would examine how formal politics converges with informal politics to empower African American communities. Whereas *formal politics* "refers to the context of governmental activity, public policy, law, and social formations," *informal politics* "refers to the context of cultural media, representation, and subjectivity."[33] Bringing both sets of politics into dialogue, Jarrett specifies how African American literature, beyond its mere production, intervenes in African American politics both indirectly and directly. Again, these divisions between direct and indirect politics parallel the divisions between formal and informal politics and those between bridge leadership and formal leadership. More instructively, each division makes it difficult to fully understand the intricate processes that produce political change.

By theorizing the paradoxes of exodus politics as contemporary African American literature constitutes them, I contest, as Jarrett does, some of the guiding principles that have circumscribed African American literary criticism and cultural criticism, even though *Exodus Politics* does not purport to be a literary history per se. In *What Was African American Literature?* (2011), Kenneth Warren argues that the end of Jim Crow unsettles the African American literary tradition because without Jim Crow writers do not have a subject to "write against." Implicitly, Warren presupposes that "responding" to disenfranchisement is the sum total of African American literary production. Warren rightly suggests that the end of Jim Crow marks a shift in the political concerns that shape African American literary production, but his contention that African American literature has ended seems misguided. Warren further argues that "pointing out the persistence of racism is not to make a particularly profound social observation or to engage in trenchant political analysis,"[34] echoing Reed's concern that literary scholars are conflating cultural history and the history of social thought. Yet Warren's argument, like Reed's, ignores the broader discourses from which the texts emerge and in which they circulate. Critics and writers are not simply "pointing out the persistence of racism" (a phrase that itself suggests that writers and critics do not analyze, interpret, or theorize) and are not purporting to create manifestos of political analysis. Rather, they are considering how the persistence of racism, in the wake of the end of Jim and Jane Crow segregation, has altered African Americans' responses to this political problem. Whereas Warren seems inclined to overstate the degree to which the legal end of Jim Crow has improved African Americans' opportunities, African American writers call into question this narrative of progress that seems central to Warren's argument and civil rights discourse more generally. Like Valerie Smith, I am concerned with how literary texts use "the aftermath of the civil rights movement, the most obvious expressions of segregation and discrimination," to revisit the issue of civil rights and leadership.[35] I add to this discussion, however, in order to consider how the texts' engagement with not-so-obvious expressions of segregation and discrimination also helps develop more robust notions of civil rights and civil rights leadership in the context of how Jim and Jane Crow have changed.

African American literary texts have played an important yet understudied role in probing the nature of black leadership and civil rights in the wake of the achievements of the civil rights movement. An elucidation of the larger civil rights pattern that emerges in literary examinations of the civil rights movement after 1970 corrects this omission. African American authors up to 1970, including Zora Neale Hurston and James Baldwin, expose the paradoxes of exodus politics in order to call into question the efficacy of redemptive male leadership.[36] After 1970, and precisely because of the events of the previous decade, African American authors more explicitly foreground the paradoxes of exodus politics in relation to civil rights history. The civil rights movement, as a whole, becomes what French historian Pierre Nora would call a "lieu de memoire," a discursive site of memory that authors return to in order to defamiliarize reductionist definitions of civil rights, prescriptive expectations for civil rights leadership, and truncated periodizations of the movement.[37] I argue that African American literature engages with four primary questions that guide my examination of exodus politics in contemporary African American literature: (1) *What* liberties are to be included in the term *civil rights* when racial discourses implicitly and explicitly invoke the constructs of gender and sexuality to conceptualize "race," or, to put it another way, how does the inclusion of gender, sexual, and economic rights in the term *civil rights* reshape an understanding of its meaning? (2) *Who* will lead the movement, and how can leadership be redefined to include the work both men and women do to mobilize participants? (3) *What* paradigms of leadership—communal or individual—are African Americans employing to direct their efforts? and (4) *How* will society measure material and symbolic gains of the civil rights movement when the changing political landscape has made the remnants of Jim and Jane Crow practices more complicated to identify?

During the 1980s civil rights historians provided heuristics to examine the civil rights movement in phases, and in the early 1990s social movement theorists drew on civil rights historians' scholarship to distinguish among different types of black leadership and leadership roles within the civil rights movement. African American literature, however, grappled with these issues long before historical, sociological, and social scientific discourses did. While literature from and about the civil rights movement flourished during the 1970s, so did fictive examinations of chattel slavery, and it was the return to chattel slavery that garnered many critics' scholarly attention.

Several perceptive studies have emerged from this critical work, including Angelyn Mitchell's *The Freedom to Remember: Narrative, Slavery, and Gender in Contemporary Black Women's Fiction* (2002), Ashraf Rushdy's *Neo-Slave Narratives: Studies in the Social Logic of a Literary Form* (1999), Bernard Bell's *The Afro-American Novel and Its Tradition* (1987), and Arlene Keizer's *Black Subjects: Identity Formation in the Contemporary Narrative of Slavery* (2004). Studies have also focused on the Black Arts and Black Power movements, most notably Madhu Dubey's *Black Women Novelists and the Nationalist Aesthetic* (1991) and Rolland Murray's *Our Living Manhood: Literature, Black Power, and Masculine Ideology* (2007).

With the exception of Melissa Walker's *Down from the Mountaintop: Black Women's Novels in the Wake of the Civil Rights Movement, 1966–1989* (1991) and Brian Norman's *Neo-segregation Narratives: Jim Crow in Post–Civil Rights American Literature* (2010), the civil rights movement has yet to receive its due in literary studies. Yet the pervasiveness of the civil rights movement as both an implicit and explicit referent in African American literature makes it intellectually productive ground to enhance the work that social scientists and historians have begun. Even Norman's insightful analysis focuses more on the specific issue of segregation than on the movement itself. While Walker's, Dubey's and Murray's texts provide useful contexts for understanding *Exodus Politics*' arguments, Erica Edwards's *Charisma and the Fictions of Black Leadership* (2012) is its most immediate and relevant interlocutor;[38] its examination of leadership in African American literature intersects with several of the concerns that animate *Exodus Politics*. But *Exodus Politics*, unlike *Charisma*, is almost entirely dedicated to analyzing African American historical fiction about the long civil rights movement.

Edwards's interrogation of charismatic leadership in black literature and culture troubles the notion that "freedom is best achieved under the direction of a single charismatic leader," demonstrating the faulty logic in a concept that purports to be inclusive yet privileges "normative masculinity."[39] Edwards rightfully insists not only that the desire for charismatic leadership ignores the "undocumented efforts of ordinary women, men, and children to remake their social reality" but also that the concept itself is structured within a larger episteme of antidemocratic violence.[40] Edwards categorizes this violence in three trends that emerge in black culture and politics over the twentieth century: "the historical and historiographical violence of reducing a heterogeneous black freedom struggle to a top-down narrative of Great Man Leadership; the social violence of performing social change in the form of a fundamentally antidemocratic form of authority; and the epistemological violence of structuring knowledge of black political subjectivity and movement within a gendered hierarchy of political value that grants un-interrogated power to normative masculinity."[41] In her examinations of black expressive culture's restaging of the "charismatic scenario," Edwards not only demonstrates how the charismatic leader is a highly desired yet highly contested figure in black culture but also elucidates alternatives to the structures of violence that she theorizes as undergirding charismatic leadership. Edwards's desire to reframe black leadership in a way that attends to the multiplicities of black identity and the complexities of black leadership parallels my goal in this book to expose the paradoxes of exodus politics in order to develop a more emancipatory politic.

Exodus Politics in the Long Civil Rights African American Literary Tradition

Although *Exodus Politics* focuses primarily on engagements of the exodus politics trope in late twentieth-century African American literature, my simultaneous investment in a "long" civil rights movement periodization compels a brief exploration of just some of the ways this trope has been employed in a longer African American literary tradition. However vexed a motif exodus politics has been, African American literary texts have figured and refigured it, responding to the historical, cultural, political, and economic circumstances that both necessitated the trope's use and rendered it problematic.

While pre-twentieth-century artists celebrate exodus politics without much explicit angst about its paradoxes, twentieth-century artists have been more skeptical about its efficacy as a strategy for enfranchisement. Unlike the spiritual "Go Down, Moses" and Frances Ellen Watkins

Harper's poem "Moses: A Story of the Nile" (1869), texts such as James Baldwin's *Go Tell It on the Mountain* (1953) and Zora Neale Hurston's *Moses, Man of the Mountain* (1939) deploy the exodus politics trope to propose paradigms for civil rights and black leadership that do not reproduce exodus politics' paradoxes;[42] they conceptualize civil rights as simultaneously constituting race, gender, class, and sexual rights, and they unsettle notions of the idealized black male leader as necessary for civil rights attainment. These two texts are important because they exemplify African American literature's implicit and explicit responses to the cultural phenomenon of exodus politics.

Moses constructs a narrative that foregrounds the biblical Exodus narrative as its discursive point of departure to call into question leadership and civil rights hierarchies that African American appropriations of the narrative reinscribe, whereas *Go Tell It* only implicitly alludes to the Exodus narrative through its construction of familial and social relationships. Yet exodus politics seems central to Baldwin's engagement of the politics of gender in African American communities, and Baldwin links gender politics to the discursive power of exodus politics. Exodus politics, therefore, pervades notions of leadership, and its hierarchies are mapped onto institutions like the family and the church as well as explicitly "political" domains. All these contexts demonstrate how exodus politics erodes collective progress.

Although Hurston and Baldwin are two of the main writers who criticize the paradoxes that exodus politics produces, their engagement with Christian imagery and tropes fits within a broader trend in mid-twentieth-century African Americans letters. In *Religious Idiom and the African American Novel, 1950–1998* (2007), Tuire Valkeakari argues that post–World War II African American writers challenged the ways earlier generations of African American writers typically had invoked Christianity. Although Richard Wright, in the "Blueprint for Negro Writing," insisted that religion diminished African Americans' ability to be politically active, a long-standing African American literary tradition had appropriated Christian rhetoric and biblical typologies to engage in "social analysis and protest" and to argue that social and political injustices contradicted God's will for freedom.[43]

Post–World War II African American writers, according to Valkeakari, positioned themselves within this tradition but creatively reshaped it by "signifying on the sacred." The publication of Ralph Ellison's *Invisible Man* (1952) was a turning point: "Ellison's parodic play with Christological and messianic discourse combined literary subtlety with profanatory boldness in a way that was unprecedented in African American novelists' treatment of Christian influences."[44] Instead of simply rejecting the usefulness of religion, as Wright had done, postwar writers "re-envisioned" it as a way of simultaneously exploring its emancipatory possibilities and examining its discourses critically. In particular, they reconfigured the discourse of messianism to contest the idea that a political messiah was capable of securing African Americans their civil rights. *Exodus Politics* extends Valkeakari's argument to examine how, as the civil rights movement gained increasing visibility, African American literary texts made the movement itself an object of scrutiny and linked the shortcomings of messianic discourses to modern crises in civil rights attainment and black leadership.

Baldwin's *Go Tell It on the Mountain* demonstrates not only how African Americans' appropriations of the Exodus narrative circumscribe discourses on civil rights and leadership in black political contexts but also how exodus politics' gender and sexual ideologies frustrate interpersonal relationships. As the novel tells the story of the protagonist, John Grimes, coming of age in a conservative black Pentecostal church, it illuminates how his stepfather, Gabriel Grimes, becomes the patriarchal authority in his family and church. Gabriel emblematizes the potential dangers that emerge when communities confer on black masculine leaders the right to dominate women, children, and gays and lesbians. Baldwin not only links Gabriel's authority to his manhood (gender) and role as a minister (God's chosen status) but also demonstrates how black culture collectively champions black masculine authority.[45] One consequence of privileging black masculine authority is that communities treat black men's political concerns as the most important, while subordinating other political interests within the community.

Baldwin situates Grimes's patriarchal authority within the context of his sister Florence's terminal illness and decline to argue that black communities' preferential treatment of black men does not improve the collective conditions of black communities. As a child, Florence lives in Gabriel's shadow because "Gabriel was the apple of his mother's eye" (67). As the narrator further notes, "With the birth of Gabriel, which occurred when she was five, her future was swallowed up. There was only one future in that house, and it was Gabriel's—to which, since Gabriel was a man-child, all else must be sacrificed" (67). Within their mother's logic, Florence, as a woman, will have the opportunity to marry and thus improve her life. Gabriel, by contrast, needs all of the opportunities that will allow him to embody patriarchal authority. Both of these ideas ignore, as Roderick Ferguson spells out in "Nightmares of the Hetero-normative: *Go Tell It on the Mountain* versus *An American Dilemma*," the specific material circumstances that have made the heteronormative patriarchal ideal especially challenging for African Americans because of their vexed relationship to the state and capital.[46] Nevertheless, Gabriel capitalizes on both his mother's and society's investment in cultivating black masculine leadership and uses his role as a minister to enact power and to demand respect. He sees himself as *the* manifestation of God's power on earth, deeming it his duty to "make low" anyone, especially women and children, who will not submit to his authority.

Florence refuses to submit to Gabriel's power because she understands that such a submission would reinforce the notion that his maleness gives him the authority to restrict her choices. While facing death, Florence thinks, "If Gabriel was the Lord's anointed, she would rather die and endure Hell for all eternity than bow before His altar" (60). Florence denies that Gabriel's maleness or his chosenness as the "Lord's anointed" gives him permission to enact unchecked power. In this way, I read Gabriel as a metonym for God's chosen people in the biblical Exodus story, and I frame Florence's lamentation as a womanist theological critique of uncritical deployment of this narrative. As the next section of this introduction explains, another reason to be skeptical of the Exodus narrative's use as an exemplar of liberation is that it ends with the decimation of the Canaanites. A reading that only celebrates the narrative reinforces the idea that one group is empowered by another group's disempowerment. Such an understanding of the Exodus narrative reinscribes hierarchies of oppression that antagonize gender politics within African American communities.[47]

The juxtaposition of Florence's physical decline against Gabriel's flourishing life in the context of the black church highlights the ways that religion and patriarchy intersect to confer his authority and expect her submission. As Rolland Murray contends, "The novel frames Gabriel's entitlement as a male heir and future patriarch as necessarily contingent upon Florence's truncated life chances, so that while Gabriel and his mother seek to create a 'royal' patriarchal line to redeem their peasant origins, the novel disrupts such a project by telling the story of Florence's bid for autonomy. With an unusual incisiveness, this text provides a discursive map of how patriarchal entitlement is linked to women's subordination."[48] Murray's suggestion about a royal redemptive line reveals how African American writers are calling into question the tenability of messianic discourses. Although one might object that Gabriel Grimes is an extreme case, that he exemplifies the appropriation of exodus politics gone awry, Baldwin casts Gabriel as representative of a common black cultural icon—the black patriarch. Baldwin's representation frames his discussion of gender and black male leadership within a broader conversation about black identity and civil rights in the mid-twentieth century.

Fourteen years before Baldwin's novel became one of the most important and widely read works in African American letters, Zora Neale Hurston foregrounded similar concerns in *Moses, Man of the Mountain* (1939), which renders visible the crippling power of the exodus *event* in African American cultural-political thought. Hurston's *Moses* examines how discourses about nationalism, gender, and identity politics intersect and argues that the paradoxes of exodus politics obscure the complex relationships among these ideas. As the title of the book intimates, *Moses* revisits the biblical Exodus narrative to reimagine how the politics of gender informs the story and to unsettle cultural practices that justify the preference for black masculine authority. Hurston's skepticism toward black male leadership emerges from the paradoxes that exodus politics produces, which include prioritizing black men and their political concerns, disconnecting black women's rights from civil rights, and privileging formal leadership over bridge leadership.

Moses examines the fictional Moses's sometimes reluctant and other times tyrannical leadership, demonstrating how his rise to power suppresses his sister Miriam's voice. Moses, like Jimmy in *The Autobiography of Miss Jane Pittman*, initially resists the responsibility of leading "his people," but the allure of patriarchal power extends his ambitions. Hurston demonstrates how this authority becomes detrimental for communal progress even when community members want a patriarchal leader. As Moses internally debates whether to become the "deliverer," Hurston upsets the notion that God called Moses to his leadership position: she casts Moses's father-in-law, Jethro, as a conjurer who coerces the burning bush to "call" Moses. If, in the biblical Exodus narrative, the burning bush is a sign that God calls Moses to be the leader, Hurston's farcical rendering of this scene makes an important point: God does not in fact call Moses, and it is instead Moses's cultural context that shapes his leadership role. This intervention in the biblical story destabilizes related arguments that ground hierarchies of oppression in a "call by God."

Moses's increasing impatience with the Israelites' inability to understand the responsibilities of citizenship grows with his increasing investment in what he sees as his God-ordained authority. As he ponders toward the narrative's end, "If their representatives saw the benefits and not the difficulties, then Israel was ready for Canaan. If they saw the difficulties bigger than the benefits, they were unfit for citizenship and he would have to draw back and try again in another generation" (244). Although the Israelites' complaints and idolatry directly defy the covenant they made with God, Moses's frustration with them completely discounts their misgivings: they are as disconcerted by Moses's antidemocratic leadership as he is by their disobedience. Moreover, as Miriam and Moses interact, Moses clarifies that he disregards Miriam's leadership style and ideas *because* she is a woman.

After Moses has attempted to silence Miriam by allowing her to communicate only through Aaron (who does not have as much power as Moses does even within the patriarchal hierarchy), she breaks this silence to reassert her voice. In a heated exchange that epitomizes Hurston's cultural intervention into the politics of gender in African American religious-political discourses, Aaron admonishes Moses: "You act like you're the boss of everything. God didn't call you, and you only, you know. . . . He called me and Miriam too. All three of us is supposed to be on a equal balance" (244). Not only does Aaron signify on the possibility that Moses was not called at all. By foregrounding the "multiplicity" of the call, he also unsettles Moses's status as the only leader for the group. "He didn't call you and you can't be on balance with me," Moses retorts (244). This debate reinforces how the superordination of one person over a group becomes detrimental to the group's overall progress toward empowerment because such a paradigm entrusts one person with too much power. It also wrongly assumes that the leader will be mindful of all of the group's differing political interests.

Miriam challenges Moses's status as the group's leader to argue that models of individual leadership ignore the plurality of leadership styles and diversity of political concerns that constitute the community. Responding to Moses's attempt to silence her, Miriam counters, "The Lord did call us just as much as he did Moses and it's about time we took our stand in front of the people. I was a prophetess in Israel while he was herding sheep in Midian" (245). By repositioning herself and Aaron in the forefront of the freedom struggle, Miriam disrupts Moses's hegemonic rule and emphasizes the importance of shared leadership. By referring to her position as a silenced prophetess, she censures the Mosaic paradigm of leadership; insofar as exodus politics presumes that Moses's maleness makes his decisions, priorities, and concerns right and more pressing than those of others, the paradigm elides political differences and thus creates a singular political agenda.

Moses cautions readers against simply celebrating the Exodus narrative without questioning the political implications of its gendering for black freedom struggles, and in giving this admonition it demonstrates the insufficiency of exodus politics' strategies for political enfranchisement. Erica R. Edwards argues that Hurston "rewrites the political romance of Exodus as a horror fiction, a satirical cautionary tale about the gendered violence that often founds charismatic leadership, writing the story as a gothic tale rather than as a romance" in order to upset the cultural practices that celebrate the narrative as a model for liberation.[49] In the vein of womanist theologians, she illuminates how the romanticization of the biblical Exodus narrative as a model for redemption, salvation, and enfranchisement has ignored the fact that "Miriam's story in *Moses, Man of the Mountain*, is a story of a martyr whose exposure of the masculinist bias of the charismatic model of leadership is punishable by death."[50] If, in fact, "Miriam's death marks a turning point for Hurston's Exodus," as does Florence's death for Baldwin's "royal line," questions emerge: What is the significance of women having to die in order for certain cultural paradigms to live? How might it elucidate the limitations of exodus politics as a mobilizing force for black political empowerment?[51]

Both Hurston and Baldwin suggest that insofar as exodus politics undermines women's authority and subordinates women's political concerns, exodus politics must die, lest it continue to deaden communal liberation efforts. Deborah McDowell, like Edwards, notes, "In telling the story of a people's deliverance into a new nation state— A Fatherland, if you will—Hurston says much about the relations between nationalism and masculinity and how, for both, the presence of the feminine is a problem."[52] Hurston is showing how patriarchal leadership models silence women in particular, and, I would add, all non-normative black subjects. It is significant that Hurston writes *Moses* at this particular moment in world history, when Nazism, Fascism, and American racism were escalating global and domestic tensions. As Barbara Johnson explains in "Moses and Intertextuality: Sigmund Freud, Zora Neale Hurston, and the Bible," Hurston understood the dangerous uses to which "territorialist" readings of the Exodus narrative might be put: she realized that being God's chosen people came at the literal and figurative expense of other groups.[53]

How does exodus politics engender these paradoxes? To answer this question, I turn now to the biblical Exodus narrative itself in light of black theological and historical critiques.

The Exodus Narrative and African American Exodus Politics

Long before the term *civil rights* entered American political discourses, and long before black liberation theology formally theorized the relationship of black religion to black politics, African American religious and political thought invoked exodus politics to proclaim that God was justice seeking: that, to use the words of black liberation theologian James Cone in his landmark work *God of the Oppressed* (1975), God was on the side of the oppressed.[54] Unprotected by law, beaten, lacking rights to their own children or control over their own reproduction, and dispossessed of their earned wages, enslaved African Americans in particular found biblical narratives of freedom, justice, and reparation resonant. While disenfranchised African Americans typologically identified with several biblical narratives that exemplified God's liberating power, the experience of chattel slavery made the Exodus story especially popular.

As political theorist Michael Walzer argues, "Wherever people know the Bible and experience oppression, the Exodus has sustained their spirits and (sometimes) inspired their resistance."[55] Zora Neale Hurston similarly asserts that "this worship of Moses as the greatest one of magic is not confined to Africa. Wherever the children of Africa have been scattered by slavery, there is the acceptance of Moses as the fountain of mystic powers. This is not confined to Negroes. In America there are countless people of other races depending upon mystic symbols and seals and syllables said to have been used by Moses to work his wonders."[56] Hurston illuminates how the Exodus narrative has shaped freedom movements globally, underscoring how it animates the desire for freedom.

As the historian of American religion Eddie S. Glaude Jr. explains, the Exodus story not only inspired African Americans to become empowered but also provided a model for political agitation and leadership. Exodus politics helped them to situate themselves within the context of a nation that had built itself on their exclusion from the body politic. As Glaude explains, "Exodus is a metaphor for a conception of nation that begins with the common social heritage of slavery and the insult of discrimination—the psychical and physical violence of white supremacy in the United States—and evolves into a set of responses on the part of a people acting for themselves to alleviate their condition."[57] Glaude maintains that blacks conceptualized themselves as a nation in order to overcome white supremacy; they bonded with each other through the "common social heritage of slavery" in order to become collectively empowered. Their "set of responses," exodus politics, however, has not always provided a model for liberation. I therefore return to Glaude toward the end of this section to call into question the implications of this homogeneous group identification—this "common social heritage." The uncommon elements of the social heritage complicate exodus politics' ability to enfranchise black communities.

By identifying with the chosen Israelites, African Americans conceptualized God as a liberator of the oppressed, one who championed the cause of the politically, economically, socially, and culturally disenfranchised. In this strain of political thought, God orchestrates African Americans' struggles for political rights insofar as he sends a Moses/Jesus/messianic figure to lead them. Identifying solely with the aspects of the Exodus story that emphasized deliverance and empowerment, African American communities have ignored the less politically empowering aspects of the narrative. The destruction of the Canaanites, for example, calls into question the narrative's status as a model for liberation and further illuminates how appropriations of this story reinscribe the paradoxes of exodus politics. What are the political, cultural, and social implications of appropriating a story that sanctions the genocide of one group (the Canaanites) as part of the liberation of another? How has the male identity of the "chosen" figure contributed to the proliferation of sexist, homophobic, and heteronormative political discourses in African American political thought and praxis? How has the Exodus narrative in turn justified these practices? If a chosen leader is necessary for civil rights attainment, how are groups to achieve or sustain their liberation in the absence of the leader? These questions are central to exodus politics' paradoxes because they illuminate the direct and indirect, implicit and explicit ways that discourses on civil rights and leadership have privileged black heteropatriarchy. Moreover, the questions suggest that an emphasis on formal leadership and a deification of male leadership undermine the creation of empowered, self-sustaining communities, which are necessary if civil rights are to be preserved over the long term.

Because the Exodus narrative historically has embedded masculine privilege, appropriations of it have justified male privilege, female exploitation, and heterosexual domination. While black liberation theologians and church historians have amply explained the history and significance of the Exodus narrative in African American culture, womanist theologians have challenged liberation theologians to employ what Delores Williams calls "a womanist hermeneutic of identification-ascertainment" to contest the normative uses of the Exodus narrative in black religious and political contexts.[58] Williams argues that normative appropriations of the Exodus narrative isolate the liberation of the Israelites from the decimation of the Canaanites. As Williams suggests, an examination of this event within the context of the entire Exodus story demonstrates how the story functions as a narrative of both political empowerment and political dispossession:

> This kind of usage [treating the exodus as an event and not a story] has prohibited the community from seeing that the end result of the biblical exodus event, begun in the book of Exodus, was the violent destruction of a whole nation of people, the Canaanites, described in the book of Joshua. Black liberation theologians today should reconceptualize what it means to lift up uncritically the biblical exodus event as a major paradigm for black theological reflection. To respond to the current issues in the black community, theologians should reflect upon exodus from Egypt as *holistic story* rather than *event*. This would allow the community to see the exodus as an extensive reality involving several kinds of events before its completion in the genocide of the Canaanites and the taking of their land. The community would see the violence involved in a liberation struggle superintended by God.[59]

Williams's reading of the Exodus narrative not only complicates any rendering of the exodus event as solely empowering but also reveals that the story's core values promote hierarchies of oppression that obstruct the development of equality within black communities and American society. Collectively, womanist theologians assert the impossibility of developing antiracist politics by simply adopting traditional celebratory appropriations of the Exodus narrative; African Americans must instead return to this narrative to trouble it and decode its embedded oppressive ideologies if they are to create a politics of empowerment that does not replicate internally the persecution and violence that others have inflicted upon them.

In her groundbreaking *Sexuality and the Black Church* (1999), Kelly Brown Douglas historicizes the anxieties of sexuality in black culture in the context of white racism and demands a similar queering of the biblical exodus event. Whereas Williams focuses on appropriations of the Exodus narrative that justify sexism, Douglas extends this discussion by focusing on justifications for homophobia and heteronormativity. Like other queer theorists, Douglas is, in the words of Roderick Ferguson, "retheorizing culture so that it [will] reflect a gender and sexual disruption to heteropatriarchy and inspire practices and formulations that [are] alternatives to nationalism."[60] *Nationalism* here refers to invocations of the Exodus narrative that seek to create a unified black community whose subjects possess a common set of political interests. Echoing Cone's notion that God is on the side of the oppressed, Douglas employs the phrase "authentic black faith" to explain black faith's central tenet: the will to eradicate oppression and champion liberty. However, she maintains that heterosexism, homophobia, and sexism contradict authentic black faith insofar as these practices "terrorize other human beings."[61]

Douglas urges the adoption of a "hermeneutics of suspicion" toward any biblical justifications of sexism, heterosexism, and homophobia, within and outside of black communities, because such practices undermine authentic black faith. She therefore urges biblical scholars to queer their deployment of paradigmatic liberatory texts, such as the book of Exodus, by considering if and how they might address the liberation of non-normative black subjects. She asserts, "Biblical scholars are challenged to advance the discussion of the Bible and homosexuality by employing the canon that has become authoritative for Black people. The Exodus event, for example, will have to be interpreted and understood in light of the experience of Black gay and lesbian persons."[62]

Building upon Douglas's notion that heterosexism runs counter to authentic black faith, Irene Monroe offers one of the most compelling analyses of the Exodus story as an urtext for black male privilege by asserting that it underwrites the modern notion of the "endangered black male."[63] Her analysis of the story precedes the adult life of Moses leading the Israelites out of Egypt, going back to Moses's childhood, when his mother saved him from Pharaoh's death edict. Whereas authors such as Zora Neale Hurston and Frances Ellen Watkins Harper return to Moses's birth as a way to reposition women and their roles in African American freedom struggles, Monroe argues that ignoring these roles represents a larger cultural tendency to neglect women's political interests: "In the African American Christian and Muslim communities Exodus 1:22 is the legitimate biblical sanction for heterosexism, expressed in terms of the 'endangered black male.' When interpreted within the patriarchal constraints of the African American experience the Exodus narrative tells African American women that only their men's lives are endangered."[64] Her analysis of Moses as the representative endangered black male explains and contextualizes biblical justifications for idolizing the black heterosexual male subject as leader and viewing his political concerns as representative of the entire community's. Black culture expects black women to subordinate their concerns so that their men may gain their rights and embody a "manhood" that may not benefit women.[65]

The portrayal of black men as uniquely endangered institutes hierarchies of oppression and suggests that restoring men to their rightful social positions will alleviate the problems of African American communities. Together, Monroe, Douglas, and Williams elucidate and complicate the biblical context from which exodus politics emerges and offer compelling evidence about the pitfalls of the Exodus narrative. They also strategize about employing the Exodus narrative in new ways, without reproducing its paradoxes. Whether the narrative is indeed salvageable remains open for discussion. However, I think an unwillingness, in African American political culture and religious thought, to engage the womanist theological exegesis of the narrative reinforces the very paradoxes that many appropriations produce.

Glaude's pioneering analysis of the Exodus trope in *Exodus! Religion, Race, and Nation in Early Nineteenth-Century Black America* (2000) offers a comprehensive examination of the Exodus narrative in black culture that considers its specific gendered use as a metaphor for nation building, leadership, and civil rights in nineteenth-century America. Glaude analyzes the narrative's significance for black political organization, articulating the strategic ways African Americans invoked the exodus *event* in the nineteenth century to argue for their civil rights. By examining these usages, he captures how the political organization around this metaphor has specifically focused on men's leadership and thus exposes exodus politics' deep gendered roots in African American political culture. Unlike womanist theologians, Glaude forgives exodus politics for instituting gender and sexual hierarchies in African American culture: that is, he stops short, acknowledging only that African Americans use racial solidarity to elide the significance of their gender differences.

For Glaude, the appropriation of this model to privilege male leadership, exclude women's leadership, and suppress gender and class differences is not a problem. Rather, it is a strategic move that African Americans employ to mobilize politically. Emphasizing racial solidarity, in Glaude's estimation, "simply isolates a problem that confronts some of us in such a way as to lead to a subordination of some values and the superordination of others (choosing to speak at that moment to the issue of race as opposed to that of gender or class)."[66] Glaude's contention not only implies that there are ways to degender, declass, and desexualize racial identity but also assumes the existence of an imagined racial community.

In the nineteenth century many African Americans, particularly women, were calling into question the idea of a homogeneous black community by highlighting gender, class, and sexual differences among African Americans. Maria Stewart, for example, was a black woman who dared to speak in a culture that marginalized black people's and women's voices. Given that, as Carla Peterson contends, "oratory was deemed to be a specifically masculine genre and public speaking an activity only proper to men," Stewart's lectures in Boston in the early 1830s unsettled the expectations that black men, white men, and white women had for black women's proper roles within society.[67] As Frances Smith Foster argues, Stewart's "militant Christianity" fueled her belief "that women had the responsibility of speaking out and into history."[68] Moreover, even though Stewart addressed a variety of "promiscuous audiences" (that is, audiences composed of both women and men), she grounded her lectures in her gender as an integral and yet distinguishable aspect of her racial experience, specifically referring to her sisters, "ye daughters of Africa," and describing herself as "a female of a darker hue." Her entrance into the public sphere, however brief, disrupted the normativity of black masculine leadership and upset the related notion that black men's political concerns represented all black people's interests.[69]

Whether in Stewart's public lectures and written essays, Sojourner Truth's famous "Ain't I a Woman" (1851) speech ("Woman's Rights"), or Harriet Jacobs's emancipatory narrative *Incidents in the Life of a Slave Girl, Written by Herself* (1861), African American women contest a general notion of African American homogeneity by foregrounding specific markers of gender, class, and sexual difference.[70] And in religious discourse more specifically, works like Jarena Lee's *Religious Experience and Journal of Mrs. Jarena Lee, Giving an Account of Her Call to Preach the Gospel* (1842) and Anna Julia Cooper's exposition on the church and black men in "Womanhood a Vital Element in the Regeneration and Progress of a Race" (1892) unsettle the use of biblical narratives that have justified black women's exclusion or limited their participation in African American leadership and the American body politic.

While Glaude contends that African Americans have emphasized their racial identity over other aspects of their identity, the presence of these discourses indicates a not-so-subtle resistance to the elision of difference, the language of sameness that has functioned to disenfranchise black women. These writings, moreover, are precursors to the many similar arguments black feminists have made during and in the wake of the modern civil rights and Black Power movements, when it again became increasingly clear that the language of men's rights meant exactly that: the rights of men to be empowered and to (sometimes) oppress women. That Glaude, in the phrase "speak at that *moment* to the issue of race," temporalizes the superordination of rights also suggests that black cultural politics will at some later *moment* address subordinated gender, class, and sexuality issues. Such a formulation, however, assumes that the newly empowered (black men) will use their increased political capital to uplift those who remain disenfranchised—black women, black gays and black lesbians, poor black men, and so forth. While it is clear that there is a "crisis" of black manhood, given the percentages of African American men who are incarcerated, unemployed, and undereducated, one should be wary of assuming that black men are *more* oppressed than black women: after all, black women not only face challenges similar to those of black men but must contend with other social, cultural, and political obstacles as well. The superordination of race tends to reinforce hierarchies of oppression by privileging one identity over the others. This practice impedes efforts to develop political strategies that will help to empower the sometimes competing constituencies within black communities. Whereas Glaude renders the Exodus narrative in a way that allows for the possibility of recuperating the gender (and even sexual) hierarchies that emerge from it, this potential can be actualized only by upsetting, as *Exodus Politics* does, the trope's normative usages. By the end of *Exodus Politics*, readers may remain skeptical of exodus politics' potential to be inclusive and nonhierarchical, but they will have clearer insights as to why exodus politics must be challenged.

Plan of This Book

Chapter 1 of *Exodus Politics* argues that Miss Jane's role as bridge leader in Ernest Gaines's *The Autobiography of Miss Jane Pittman* challenges the primacy of formal leadership, which has circumscribed the definitions of civil rights activism and leadership, and calls into question the politics of gender central to civil rights struggles. Accordingly, it also challenges the notion of redemptive patriarchal leadership and the framework of exodus politics. By focusing on bridge leadership and the quotidian acts of ordinary black people, Gaines encourages African

Americans to renounce the external search for male messianic leaders to lead their struggles to secure civil rights. He also foregrounds cross-cutting political issues that the other texts engage. Building upon chapter 1's argument, chapter 2 examines how Alice Walker's *Meridian* foregrounds the character Meridian as an example of a civil rights leader who extends the interrogation of the limitations of patriarchal leadership that begins in *Miss Pittman*. Moreover, it shows that Walker, by focusing on Meridian's leadership and activism, demonstrates how the civil rights movement morphed during the 1970s to respond to the achievements of the 1960s and expanded its goals beyond ending de jure segregation. In championing a "long" view of the civil rights movement, *Meridian* emphasizes that bridge leaders and communities must themselves advance the civil rights movement by ensuring that the theoretical equality of opportunity will translate into an equality of outcome. By emphasizing Meridian's role as a grassroots bridge leader, Walker displaces the male formal leader from the center of civil rights discourses and underscores how empowering communities to be self-sufficient is central to any civil rights campaign.

Whereas the end of chapter 1 and the majority of chapter 2 focus on redefining leadership as it relates to civil rights struggles, chapter 3 focuses on redefining "civil rights" as inclusive of gender rights and sexual rights. Disrupting the idea that the normative black subject is *the* black subject, and the related idea that his political concerns represent those of black communities, my analysis of Gayl Jones's *Corregidora* considers how the Corregidora women's mission to "make generations" and Ursa's blues performances function as forms of civil rights activism and leadership that counter masculine and heteronormative civil rights discourses. It foregrounds gender and sexuality as always entangled in discourses about race, and it reflexively situates the text's discussion of reproduction in the context of *Roe v. Wade*. This argument challenges definitions of civil rights that idealize men and masculine forms of leadership as exemplars, while considering the contributions of black women blues performers to the civil rights movement.

Finally, in chapter 4, I turn to Charles Johnson's *Dreamer*, which was written at the turn of the twenty-first century, because its historical perspective on the preceding thirty years captures the political shifts that have occurred in civil rights and civil rights leadership discourses and the stagnation that has resulted. In this chapter, I argue that *Dreamer*, by vacillating between contesting and reinscribing the paradoxes of exodus politics, shows how difficult the project of unsettling this paradigm in

African American politics and culture really is. I juxtapose Johnson's expressed desire to be historically accurate against the palpable absence in his novel of the women bridge and formal leaders who actually worked in the historical movement between 1965 and 1968.[71] This analysis examines the implications of Johnson's attempt to provide a more inclusive historiography of the civil rights movement without engaging women's leadership and specific civil rights concerns. While *Dreamer* repositions social class as central to civil rights discourses and questions the long-term consequences of privileging male formal leadership, it ignores black women's civil rights leadership, oppression, and specific political concerns altogether. Finally, the brief epilogue discusses the significance of *Exodus Politics* in contemporary black politics by situating my analysis of exodus politics within the contexts of messianism and charisma, contemporary black political trends, and the long African American literary tradition.

In its broadest aims, then, *Exodus Politics* unsettles notions of normative blackness by foregrounding how race, gender, sexual, and class discourses intersect to constitute black subjectivity. It contests the primacy of formal leadership by arguing for the centrality of bridge leadership in civil rights movement successes, and it suggests that civil rights still unattained will be won through quotidian and (non)-exemplary instances of bridge leadership. Finally, *Exodus Politics* underscores the urgent need to contest any model of leadership and any definition of civil rights that do not grapple with, however uneasily, developing modes of liberation that are in fact empowering to the whole person and the whole community.

1 / "Is He the One?": Civil Rights Activism and Leadership in Ernest Gaines's *The Autobiography of Miss Jane Pittman*

The lesson she had learned from her sixty years a slave and ten years free: that there was no bad luck in the world but white people. "They don't know when to stop," she said, and returned to her bed, pulled up the quilt and left them to hold that thought forever.

—TONI MORRISON, *BELOVED*

The publication of *The Autobiography of Miss Jane Pittman* (1971) defined Ernest Gaines's position as a national and international literary historian,[1] for the text makes a self-conscious effort to record African American women's and men's leadership in civil rights struggles from Emancipation to the middle of the civil rights movement. Like other fiction that emerges between the mid-1960s and the late 1970s, *The Autobiography of Miss Jane Pittman* employs a "long" civil rights historical framework to establish a continuous, ongoing history of black freedom struggles in the New World and to emphasize that the civil rights movement occurring in the 1950s and 1960s did not emerge in a vacuum.[2] This engagement with historical events and leaders that have shaped black freedom struggles has earned its classification as a historical novel.[3] Yet unlike most historical novels *The Autobiography of Miss Jane Pittman* is not a mere fictionalized re-creation of history; instead, it diverges from master narratives to explore in new ways the roles of black men and women in events like the Spanish-American War of 1898 and the 1963 March on Washington. Historiographies of the Spanish-American War of 1898 have not fully examined how African American men's participation in that war altered black people's attitudes toward civil rights. Relatedly, historiographies of the civil rights movement have not fully addressed how black women's leadership in the movement reconstituted the movement's goals. By defamiliarizing these events, Gaines uncovers significant moments that shape civil rights discourses.

Whereas master narratives of black civil rights struggles that emerged in the late 1960s and flourished into the 1980s reinforced the paradoxes of exodus politics by suggesting that only black men had fought and won the black freedom struggle, Gaines brings nuance to the politics of gender in historiographies of the civil rights movement. Not only does he call into question the efficacy of male formal leadership that social movement theorists have privileged in evaluating the success of the movement's organizational and mobilization tactics, but he disrupts the related notion that normative black men's political interests are those of the entire community.[4] At a time when black nationalism's emphasis on black unification contributed to the proliferation of discourses that promulgated sameness, Gaines's text foregrounds difference, underscoring the need for a liberatory politics that will consider black community members' sometimes competing political interests. In making this choice, he exemplifies the beginnings of a post–civil rights era development in black politics and culture later described by Cathy Cohen as the shift from an emphasis on "consensus issues construed as having an equal impact on all those sharing a primary identity based on race" to an increasing exploration of "cross-cutting issues structured around and built on the social, political, and economic cleavages that tear at the perceived unity and shared identity of group members."[5]

Black studies, black feminist studies, and black queer studies have taken cross-cutting issues as their disciplinary points of departure and have spent the late twentieth century theorizing the discontinuities within black identities in order to foreground the multiplicity of black political concerns.[6] When Gaines published *The Autobiography of Miss Jane Pittman*, however, he entered territory that had been of particular interest primarily to black feminist critics and cultural producers. Around that same time, Toni Morrison's *The Bluest Eye* (1970) and *Sula* (1973) and Alice Walker's *The Third Life of Grange Copeland* (1970) were upsetting black aestheticians' notion that black art would best serve black politics and civil rights attainment by depicting positive (and idealistic) images of black life and family;[7] but even more important, they were demonstrating how a political agenda that privileged the normative black subject's concern to regain his putatively rightful position as the head of the black household undermined the struggle to collectively enfranchise black communities. During this black women's literary renaissance, black women writers depicted black heteropatriarchy as an institution that created as much conflict and division between men and women as white heteropatriarchy did by subordinating black women and refusing to recognize or value their specific experiences of oppression. Black women writers thought about ways to develop political agendas that did not require black women to be subjugated in order for black men to be enfranchised.

For some black male critics, however, these representations were complicit with white assaults on black manhood: Ishmael Reed and Addison Gayle, among others, excoriated black women writers (and cultural producers more generally) for conspiring to decenter political concerns that, in their view, should take precedence on black communities' public agendas.[8] The controversy shows how difficult it is to disrupt monolithic notions of black subjectivity and politics. Gaines's text, which at times struggles to foreground Miss Jane's voice, importantly diverges from this pervasive trend among black male cultural producers. Critics thus have praised *The Autobiography of Miss Jane Pittman* for developing a multidimensional black female character who has a distinctly "feminine" voice."[9]

Gaines remains attentive to the historical and cultural processes that have rightfully made black men like Frederick Douglass, Booker T. Washington, and Dr. Martin Luther King Jr. especially prominent in black civil rights historiography. Yet he also examines how lesser-known people, especially black women, and more quotidian acts of resistance contributed to civil rights successes. His exploration troubles the arbitrary boundaries historiographers and everyday people have erected between leadership and activism, as well as between civil rights and other social movements. Gaines's desire to center Miss Jane's story gestures toward a larger cultural movement with the goal of disrupting masculinist civil rights discourse and articulating new discourses that will be more broadly emancipatory, conceiving of civil rights as encompassing not just racial rights but the gender rights, sexual rights, and economic rights with which they intersect.

In this chapter, I argue that by foregrounding Miss Jane's story as exemplary of black women's leadership across decades of black freedom struggles, Gaines decenters exodus politics as *the* political model of black leadership. He emphasizes the complementary and mutually constitutive aspects of black women's and black men's leadership (in terms of both formal and bridge leadership) and demonstrates that sole dependence on a male leader keeps communities from recognizing their own empowering role in freedom struggles. Gaines challenges communities to discard their messianic hopes (which privilege formal leadership over bridge leadership) and instead to view political change as an ongoing process in which their participation remains necessary. My analysis of exodus politics in this chapter is especially concerned with how Gaines engages two of the four questions that I raised in the Introduction: (2) *Who* will lead the movement, and how can leadership be redefined to include the work both men and women do to mobilize participants? and (3) *What* paradigms of leadership—communal or individual—should African Americans adopt?

The Autobiography of Miss Jane Pittman, which I will subsequently refer to as *Miss Pittman,* chronicles the triumphs, trials, and tribulations of a 110-year-old protagonist, Miss Jane, whose life extends from slavery through the contemporary civil rights movement. Although this time frame makes African American civil rights attainment the telos of a century-long struggle, it resists the notion that the history of this period has shown a linear trajectory of progress. Encompassing both individual and communal transformations, *Miss Pittman* reveals the processes by which the African American masses come to, in the words of Keith Byerman, "a consciousness of their role in history" and demonstrates the leadership activities that help create this awareness.[10] It also shows how the characters' understanding of civil rights and leadership evolves through changing historical, economic, political, and cultural contexts. In particular, the characters grow to understand civil rights, activism, and leadership in terms that exceed gender norms that would otherwise limit their political achievements and access.[11] Gaines's presentation of male and female leadership roles in the civil rights movement is central to his book and is especially nuanced and complex, in ways that are best illuminated by an exploration of formal and bridge leadership in that movement.

Bridge Leadership and Formal Leadership

Male formal leaders have been the face of the civil rights movement in the political imagination and civil rights historiography.[12] As Robnett states, they held the titled positions, "usually provide[d] the press statements[,] and [were] responsible for decision making regarding organization tactics, goals, and strategies."[13] It was men therefore who came to dominate civil rights leadership discourses. Yet it is ironic that a small group of visibly public men would come to symbolize the movement's leadership when the majority of leaders were actually women. In her groundbreaking *How Long, How Long? African-American Women in the Struggle for Civil Rights* (1997), Robnett discovered, from interviews with black women who had been active in the civil rights movement, that many women who were excluded from formal leadership positions exerted a less visible but just as influential form of grassroots leadership. While male formal leaders used their access to national media outlets and government institutions to agitate for civil rights, female bridge leaders grounded themselves in communities where, using one-on-one interactions and formal and informal meetings, they linked individuals to the broader movement. If formal leaders could be thought of as macro-mobilizers, bridge leaders might be seen as micro-mobilizers who catalyzed the macro-movement, using what Robnett called "prefigurative strategies" (strategies aimed at changing individual consciousness and identity) to spur political action. As an often neglected and understudied group in the movement, bridge leaders typically secured movement followers and sustained the movement over the long term. In foregrounding their contributions and conceptualizing their activities as leadership, Robnett not only contested the primacy of male formal leadership but provided a more comprehensive and nuanced way of understanding, evaluating, and *valuing* the types of leadership positions that women typically held.

Bridge leaders' main role inside communities was to raise consciousness and make legible the goals of the civil rights movement so that individuals would see themselves as essential agents in the movement's success. As Robnett explained, bridge leaders used "frame bridging," or "providing those already predisposed to one's cause with information sufficient to induce them to join the movement"; "frame amplification," or "convincing individuals that their participation is crucial and that the movement's goals can be achieved"; "frame extension," or "incorporating concerns not originally part of the movement's goals but valuable as a means of expanding support"; and "frame transformation," or "the process whereby individually held frames are altered . . . to achieve consensus with the movement's goals."[14] They engaged in these activities, Robnett wrote, "to foster ties between the social movement and community and between prefigurative strategies (aimed at individual change, identity, and consciousness) and political strategies (aimed at organizational tactics designed to challenge the existing relationships with the state and other societal institutions). Indeed, the activities of bridge leaders in the civil rights movement were the stepping stones necessary for potential constituents and adherents to cross formidable barriers between their personal lives and the political life of civil rights movement organizations."[15] The different types of "frame" activities that

Robnett listed collectively illustrate the various points on the spectrum of political consciousness in which bridge leaders found potential adherents and the differing tactics necessary to integrate those members into the movement. It is significant that the term *frame* modifies each of the bridging activities because the word emphasizes how the activities aim to alter, or reframe, potential adherents' understanding of their agency, their relationship to the movement, and the movement's relationship to them.

Robnett's description of how bridge leaders connected "prefigurative" to "political" strategies is important because it elucidates how women's activism and leadership—at the grassroots level—integrally molded the civil rights movement's national achievements as women developed and implemented local programs and activities that engendered support for the broader movement. Consider, for example, the leadership philosophy of Septima Clark, a teacher and longtime activist who established the Citizenship Schools, which taught reading to adults across the Deep South. Clark believed that "direct action [w]as a distraction from the more substantive process of local leadership development and education" and preferred "face-to-face contact which drew people into activities until they were immersed in a movement culture that altered consciousness and impelled action."[16] Although Clark did not altogether dismiss the importance of direct action, or of male formal leadership, she insisted that communities needed to develop, train, and sustain their own leaders and constituents/followers. By accentuating the roles bridge leaders held and the strategies they employed, Clark also subverted the "Great Man" theory of leadership that has been so persistent in the black political imagination. Clark foregrounded consciousness-raising as necessary to "local leadership development and education" and thus as crucial to the continuation of black freedom struggles.

Although Robnett maintained that the majority of bridge leaders were women while the majority of formal leaders were men, she did not place the two types of leadership in binary opposition; she pointed out that some men were in fact bridge leaders, while some women were formal leaders, and claimed that both types of leadership were necessary and that they complemented and reinforced each other. Her work, along with that of other revisionist historiographers exploring the transformative influence of female bridge leaders on the long civil rights movement, has thus provided a broader discursive context to theorize black leadership generally and to challenge the priorities of exodus politics.[17] Female bridge leaders did more than mobilize support for the civil rights agenda: they reshaped that agenda by formulating specific initiatives and programs and by foregrounding cross-cutting issues. Their prefigurative strategies not only brought the movement new supporters but helped broaden the movement's scope. Without this grassroots activity, it would be difficult, if not impossible, to mobilize and sustain a movement or to enable it to grow and change.

Gaines's novel is a powerful precursor to these theoretical developments, destabilizing the traditional narrative of the civil rights movement and assumptions about the relationship between the movement's leaders and its participants. It depicts men and women functioning as both bridge and formal leaders and employing both prefigurative and political strategies. Miss Jane, Big Laura, Ned, and Jimmy all act outside their socially constructed gender roles of (female) bridge and (male) formal leaders, thereby frustrating the paradoxes of exodus politics while simultaneously complicating their own statuses as leaders in civil rights struggles. Readers see how a movement develops in local communities and how local concerns and struggles are bridged to a broader movement for the long term. Activities like teaching black people how to read and encouraging them to overcome their fear of random white violence emerge as an important foundation for increased black political activity. *Miss Pittman* emphasizes in particular how bridge leaders transform individuals who in turn transform others to further build their communities. This accomplishment, which is no small feat, forms a marked contrast to an exodus politics in which communities become disillusioned, disaffected, and immobilized in the absence of a formal leader.

Like Gaines's *Miss Pittman*, Andrea Lee's novel *Sarah Phillips* explores how black people experienced these feelings more intensely following King's death—at a time when they were wondering about the future of black leadership and of the black freedom struggle more generally. In a provocative reading of the novel, Aida Hussen concludes, "King's assassination . . . is a fundamentally disorienting event because it signals the symbolic loss of the figure of the leader who once lent organization and intelligibility to both loyal identificatory impulses and rebellious, disidentificatory impulses."[18] Her argument illuminates some of the consequences of aligning a movement too closely with its formal leadership: African American writers such as Lee warn against letting the loss of one formal leader signify the end of, or a disruption in, black freedom struggles. They eschew singular models of political organization and leadership because such models do not produce self-empowered and self-led communities. These writers conceptualize ways to develop bridge and formal leaders who fulfill multiple roles within their communities; they aim to produce highly functional leaders who continuously train the next generation of leaders, thereby keeping the political movements alive.

Much literary criticism has ignored Miss Jane's leadership roles or argued that her assumption of these roles is implausible. Such arguments rely upon masculinist formulations of leadership that exclude the more subtle forms of leadership that Gaines so carefully traces. For example, Byerman—in an otherwise persuasive analysis of *Miss Pittman*—argues that the plot's development does not logically allow Miss Jane to become a formal leader:

> Her survival to tell the story to the history teacher, who interviews her and establishes the novel's frame, implies that she has escaped the fate of all previous rebels. At the time of the telling, she is still on the plantation, though Samson had threatened to evict anyone who disobeyed him. Although Gaines prepares us for such a conclusion by having Jimmy argue that Miss Jane could be the parish's Rosa Parks, the book does not offer adequate motivation for her playing such a role. Neither the transcendence nor the success of her act is grounded in the patterns elucidated by the narrative. While she had engaged in small acts of resistance and kept alive the stories of greater ones, she had primarily been the character in the middle and the recorder of stories of the suffering that accompanies such courageous acts. Therefore, she violates her function and her wisdom in order to become the unpunished radical we see at the end.[19]

Byerman's analysis, however suggestive, depends on a narrow understanding of the relationship between bridge leadership and formal leadership; the ways movements mobilize communities; and the ways individuals mobilize movements. More problematically, this reading conceptualizes Miss Jane's "*small* acts of resistance" as insignificant moments of defiance that do not connect to a larger political process and movement.

The narrative does, however, show adequate motivation for this role—a motivation that begins with Miss Jane's assertion that her name is Jane, not Ticey, and that continues as acts of bridge leadership by others raise Miss Jane's awareness and spur her to acts of resistance that will subsequently influence others. The novel recounts a progression in which various events cultivate Miss Jane's capacities to undertake more sustained bridge and formal leadership roles. Byerman is right in stating that Miss Jane records the stories of Ned and Jimmy, and Gaines himself lends credibility to this claim when he observes, "The book's about those four men [Ned, Jimmy, Joe Pittman, and Tee Bob], really, as much as it is about Miss Jane herself."[20] But Miss Jane is not merely a "recorder." Such a classification of her role parallels the historiographical tendency to characterize women's leadership roles in the civil rights movement as "activism" and thus to diminish their importance.

By devaluing the significance of Miss Jane's acts of resistance—by not considering those acts as instances of bridge leadership that are integral to the movement's overall success—readings like Byerman's reinforce masculinist definitions of civil rights leadership; they idealize black men as civil rights leaders and define only particular actions as "leadership." Since men have held titled positions and have been most visible in public spheres, society accepts and imagines the movement as male. Byerman's failure to recognize Miss Jane's leadership makes her an exception to his own overarching claim that the book shows black people becoming conscious of their role in history, for Miss Jane becomes an increasingly empowered black woman and develops in a profound way over the course of the narrative.

By conceptualizing black women's acts as "smaller acts of resistance" and not as prefigurative strategies aimed at individual transformation, Byerman confines examples of civil rights leadership to the normative, formal leadership that was most visible in the public sphere. His objection illuminates the difficulties Gaines faced at this particular moment in history, when he himself struggled between defamiliarization and reinscription. Readers wonder, how does Gaines tell the struggles of Miss Jane and the men without allowing the men's narratives to dominate her story? This question acquires additional meaning when they realize that Gaines wants to show how public and private spheres are gendered in specific ways. If readers believe that the men's stories assume a primacy in the narrative and are somehow more important than Miss Jane's own story, might not that belief be related to their own understanding of whose roles are more important and more highly valued in the text?

William Andrews's analysis of Miss Jane's character development argues that her social and political perspectives evolve, suggesting that the raising of her consciousness prepares readers for her expanded leadership roles. As Andrews explains: "The climactic synthesis of Gaines's dialectic of progress emerges through Miss Jane's assumption of leadership in the march on Bayonne. Her psychological development through the book has prepared her for this ultimate act of self-assertion, the unprecedented yoking of the faraway and evanescent ideal of socio-political progress."[21] While Andrews rightly identifies Miss Jane's final action as an example of leadership, her leadership actually emerges before that moment in Bayonne in numerous, less prominent ways. As Miss Jane later tells Jimmy, who is struggling to organize a scared community, "People and time bring forth leaders, Jimmy, people and time" (241). While it is true that "movements mobilize leaders as much as leaders mobilize movements," Miss Jane's remark unsettles the pervasive notion of top-down leadership, which, according to historians such as Robin D. G. Kelley, inadequately grasps the relationship between leaders and (potential) constituents.[22] The notion of a (divine) male leader who possesses the power to attract, organize, and lead participants must be set aside if communities are to understand the processes by which political organization and change occur. That Miss Jane's transformation occurs over time reminds the reader of the particular challenges bridge leaders (and even formal leaders) face in garnering, building, and maintaining support, while at the same time preparing self-sufficient indigenous leaders.

Rising and Finding a Voice:
Miss Jane from Emancipation to 1901

By framing the opening of *Miss Pittman* with Miss Jane's name change, Gaines demonstrates how seemingly "small acts of resistance" reflect, in significant ways, the positive effects of the prefigurative strategy of consciousness-raising that bridge leaders employ, not simply to gain "followers," but also to connect the individual to a broader movement, where she or he can lead as well. Miss Jane's name change awakens her consciousness about racialized gender injustice and gendered racialized justice. It also foreshadows the continued character growth that ultimately propels her into her final role as a formal leader. In one of the text's earliest scenes, Miss Jane grapples with the fact that slavery has stripped her and other enslaved African Americans of basic prerogatives, molding their view of the world as a set of eclipsed opportunities. They experience their lives as circumscribed not only by the abject conditions of slavery, as DuBois famously analyzes, but also by the control owners exert, including their ability to name and thereby categorize their property.[23] In what Kimberly Benston persuasively calls an act of "genealogical revision," one that subverts the slave owner's attempts to "fix the named as irreversibly other," the union soldier changes Miss Jane's name from "Ticey" to "Jane."[24] The name change not only signifies her impending movement from enslavement to enfranchisement, from object to subject, but also marks the beginning of Miss Jane's political journey: her evolution toward bridge and formal leadership roles.[25] If, as Valerie Babb proposes, the significance of this name change is that "for the first time in her life Jane has the option of deciding whether or not she will retain it," this incident underscores the importance of individuals buying into a movement's broader goals (abolition and emancipation) as they move from a state of oppression to one of liberation.[26]

This early episode, then, establishes the basis on which Miss Jane's political awareness evolves and demonstrates how Miss Jane, a beneficiary of consciousness-raising, becomes instrumental in raising consciousness in others. The name change is a decisive moment that transforms Miss Jane's life, when she refuses to let white racism completely define her life choices and when she decides that she cannot simply wait for a man to liberate her but must herself resist being dominated (even though she later will push the male characters into the publicly visible leadership roles).[27]

Big Laura, whose leadership Miss Jane witnesses immediately following this self-assertion, further shapes Miss Jane's developing political consciousnesses. Gaines fashions her in the image of Sojourner Truth to disrupt the normativity of black male leadership and recall black women's historical roles as civil rights leaders. Big Laura establishes a "genealogy" of black women's civil rights leadership to which Miss Jane can claim ownership and also displaces male formal leadership as ideal and necessary for black people's collective empowerment. Gaines's allusion to Truth is important given Truth's role in nineteenth-century politics and culture, and the role of her speeches and politics in shaping black feminist thought. Claiming Truth as a grandmother for contemporary black feminism, black feminist critics have applauded her for considering the politics of gender and sexuality alongside that of race.[28] By casting Big Laura as a literary cousin to the historical figure of Truth, Gaines allows readers to consider Big Laura as a female leader who leaves a lasting impression on Miss Jane's political consciousness, as well as her attitudes toward leadership. In later years, Miss Jane will articulate ideas about the intersections of race, class, gender, and sexuality that inform her understanding of oppression. However implicitly, Gaines links this political development to Big Laura.

Although Big Laura is present only briefly before white rebels murder her, she defies nineteenth-century gender norms and leadership expectations for black women. She serves as the local formal and bridge leader for the group of formerly enslaved African Americans of which she is a part. Big Laura leads the group toward "freedom," instructs the mixed-gender group in behaviors appropriate for "free" individuals, and physically defends herself against unprovoked white violence. As this scene represents the men, they are woefully incompetent to lead the group; it is Big Laura who takes charge, providing the blueprint by which the group is to thrive. If as Mary Ellen Doyle contends, Big Laura models "true power, dignity, and leadership in a black woman," her presence provides yet another example of Gaines's attempt to undermine exodus politics' tendency to privilege male formal leadership.[29] By ignoring the significance of Big Laura's leadership, readers overlook how quotidian acts of resistance sustain a larger civil rights movement by motivating those who witness such behavior to act similarly.

In 1971, the same year that Gaines published *Miss Pittman*, Mary Helen Washington criticized the masculinization of African Americans' political histories by calling into question the representational politics that excluded women from civil rights accounts. She asked, "Why is the fugitive slave, the fiery orator, the political activist, the abolitionist always represented as a black man? How does the heroic voice and heroic image of the black woman get suppressed in a culture that depended on her heroism for its survival?"[30] These questions were not meant to be rhetorical. Washington asserted that when historiographies cast men as the main or only civil rights leaders and activists, they suggest that women are not leaders—or, just as problematically, that their only work is behind the scenes.

By framing the origins of *Miss Pittman* in the context of a history teacher's desire to provide students a more accurate representation of civil rights history, Gaines foregrounds his own role in upsetting the masculinization of civil rights history. The fictional teacher interviews Miss Jane because the history books he uses in the classroom have omitted black women's history,[31] and her "life's story can help [him] explain things to [his] students" (v). Her life as a civil rights leader, then, complicates reductionist notions that replicate heteronormative idealizations of black men as the only and true "leaders."

Thus the early incidents that connect Miss Jane to larger social movements prefigure the later transformations in consciousness, thought, and action that readers observe in her character. By emphasizing a dialectical relationship between "being bridged," "bridging," and formal "leading," Gaines demonstrates the shifts that individuals and communities undergo as they move from outside the movement to inside it. He also illuminates how formal and bridge leadership constitute each other. *Miss Pittman* shows how women and men of the civil rights movement shifted between the two types of leadership, though men's gender privilege gave them access to public platforms for protest and reform, such as state institutions, that women did not possess. Miss Jane ultimately becomes a formal leader, but she cannot move as fluidly from one leadership role to another as the men do; unlike Ned, for example, she does not have the cultural capital to build a school. While her more limited opportunities illustrate the gender politics central to exodus politics and the time period, her roles as a leader and activist also challenge that gender politics, and her participation shapes her own and eventually others' evolving political consciousness.

For instance, Miss Jane unarguably contributes to Ned's success by the choices she affords him, much as Charmian's decision to save Moses's life in "Moses: A Story of the Nile" lays the foundation for Moses to become a formal leader. Yet to read Miss Jane primarily as a supportive, strong maternal figure oversimplifies her complex role in the struggle that Ned leads by ignoring how his bridge leadership raises her political consciousness. Her role of maternal nurturer is significant because it reveals much about the cultural context of black politics and leadership, as well as the limitations society imposed upon black women at the turn of the twentieth century and afterward. As the historian Kevin Gaines has argued, "a middle-class ideology of racial uplift that measured race progress in terms of civilization, manhood, and patriarchal authority" ultimately excluded black women activists and leaders, including Anna Julia Cooper, from civil rights historiographies.[32] Yet these women, who challenged "the male dominated character of black leadership," were leaders in their own right, and their vision of civil rights often reflected a gender consciousness and included cross-cutting issues that disrupted the centrality of the normative black subject in civil rights discourses and political agendas. Their history further contextualizes why Miss Jane's leadership status remains contested in the text; insofar as she does not merely champion "manhood" or "patriarchal authority," her leadership roles do not conform to the established protocols of male formal leadership.

Whereas Ned acts sometimes as a formal leader and other times as a bridge leader, he primarily wants to work at the grassroots level as a bridge leader to transform individuals through consciousness-raising because he sees such work as crucial for empowering black communities in their quest for civil rights. Miss Jane witnesses and internalizes the political values he imparts (just as she does through her interactions with Big Laura). Although her role in Ned's campaign for African Americans' full citizenship is less pronounced than it will be fifty years later when she works with Jimmy, she does undergo significant transformation through her membership and participation in this community. She is no longer disconnected from the social changes that are occurring around her. Rather, by listening to Ned speak with (not lecture at) the children, grasping the significance of his work and views for her and others in the community, and realizing that she ultimately will have to act in order to live as a free subject, Miss Jane becomes "bridged." Her transformation reminds readers that bridging can be active and passive, implicit and explicit, simultaneously.

The Foundation Has Been Laid:
Negotiating Bridge and Formal Leadership Roles

Gaines draws on the historical period that frames Ned's story, which extends from Emancipation to the turn of the twentieth century, to underscore the institutional practices and policies that prevented blacks from achieving full citizenship, the rise to formal authority of black male officeholders in government during Reconstruction, and debates among blacks over how they could further their own cause. As historical referents, both Kansas (as a physical place) and the Spanish-American War of 1898 (as an event) enhance the reader's understandings of Ned's perspective on black enfranchisement; they situate his desires to build a school, educate black citizens, empower black communities, affirm black subjectivity, and upset white hegemony within a broader discursive context of late nineteenth-century American culture and politics.

Events between Emancipation and the turn of the twentieth century, such as the end of Reconstruction, the institutionalization of white supremacy by Jim and Jane Crow segregation, the rise in lynching by the Ku Klux Klan, and a general antiblack sentiment, led historian Rayford Logan to term this period the "nadir" of American race relations.[33] During it, African Americans increasingly began to wonder whether they would ever obtain their full citizenship rights in America. Having lived in the state of Kansas before his military service in the Spanish-American War, Ned has an understanding of civil enfranchisement and a self-assuredness that contrasts with the docility Jim and Jane Crow segregated societies depended on and expected black men to exhibit.[34] This enforcement of docility contextualizes why the problematic quest to "restore manhood" became so deeply entrenched in civil rights discourses for black empowerment.

Kansas, for some African Americans, marked a "promised land," a space free from white violence, where they might enjoy full citizenship rights and responsibilities. The exodus from the South to Kansas, which Benjamin "Pap" Singleton led, suggested that many blacks saw freedom in the South as impossible to achieve, since residing there demanded a constant deferral of civil rights. Urging African Americans to migrate, Sojourner Truth declared, "I have prayed so long that my people would go to Kansas, that God would make straight the way before them. This colored people is going to be a people. Do you think God has them robbed and scourged all the days of their lives for nothing?"[35] Truth's notion of a promised land reiterated African Americans' belief that God was on the side of the oppressed, guaranteed their civil rights, and would ensure their entrance into the American body politic. While this idea of chosenness involves the problems that I detail in the Introduction, Ned's ability to build schools for African Americans to attend while living in Kansas shows that African Americans enjoyed a greater sense of freedom there than in places like Louisiana.

If Ned's experience in Kansas gives him glimpses into the possibilities for what black enfranchisement might look like, his participation in the Spanish-American War of 1898 expresses his hope that America will honor its commitment to granting civil rights to all of her citizens. Indeed, black male participation in the United States' international military conflicts has always embodied the paradox that they are upholding ideals of citizenship and civil rights they themselves do not enjoy. Nevertheless, from the Revolutionary War to the war in Iraq, black men have hoped that their participation in military conflict might once and for all prove their investment in democratic principles and deservedness of civil rights. Yet, as Chandan Reddy argues persuasively in *Freedom with Violence: Race, Sexuality and the US State* (2012), the civil rights accomplishments that followed American international military conflicts sprang more from America's need to defend its image abroad as a fair, democratic world power than from a newfound belief in equality for African Americans. As Reddy suggests for the post–World War II period:

State reform incorporated and attempted to absorb African Americans' social movements that targeted the symbolic and material racial disparities of US society at midcentury through a Cold War–era liberal framework of universal rights. . . . Civil rights legislation and court decisions were less the effects of the successful transformation of state meanings by ethical, moral, and political worldviews organizing the black freedom movement, and more the outcomes of the US Cold War initiatives to be globally hegemonic after the implosion of the European empires on their own continent. . . . The liberal reformist state narrated its delegitimation of white supremacy as protections against arbitrary local violence. Arbitrary violence became the terrain upon which the state attempted to settle the meaning of US racial projects in the context of competing and at times conflicting interests of US postwar geopolitics and policies.[36]

While perhaps pessimistic, Reddy's view brings out the irony of black participation in military conflict: paradoxically, black men are mobilized to fight against international evils that remain largely unaddressed domestically. Yet even if the motives for enacting political change are suspect, black men's participation in military conflict makes them more aware of the domestic conditions that require transformation to render black participation less ironic. Gaines's portrayal of Ned's military service illuminates these complexities. Although Ned never speaks directly about how the war has shaped his views about domestic race relations, Gaines implies this relationship by showing Ned as wearing his army uniform whenever he discusses civil rights with African Americans. Wearing the uniform suggests not only Ned's pride in his military service but also his belief that his and other black men's participation in the war, even under the military's separate-but-equal doctrine institutionalized by *Plessy v. Ferguson* less than a decade earlier, marks a new era of citizenship, rights, and responsibilities for African Americans. However, what Reddy observed at the end of the twentieth century is true for American history generally: "The inclusion of race in the juridical and institutional forms of egalitarian freedom creates the inverse: . . . racial inclusion in the form of the US state has in important ways expanded and made more complex racial and racialized gendered inequalities."[37]

Gaines has Ned invoke the accommodation-integration debate that animated the political careers of Booker T. Washington and Frederick

Douglass (and W. E. B. DuBois) in the late nineteenth century as a way to differentiate Ned's leadership from the formal leadership roles that were central to Washington's and Douglass's perspectives. Although Ned believes, like Douglass and DuBois, that immediate political empowerment and integration are necessary if black people are to ever enjoy equality, he is unlike Washington and DuBois in that he primarily works to transform local communities rather than institutions. Douglass's general political stance on integration and his opposition to migration further explain his significance for Ned's civil rights vision.

Douglass did not believe that migrating to Kansas, the West, or any other place, would remove the threat of white terrorism from the daily lives of African Americans. As he declared: "The country would be told of the hundreds who go to Kansas, but not of the thousands who stay in Mississippi, they would be told of the destitute who require material aid, but not of the multitude who are bravely sustaining themselves where they are. If the people of this country cannot be protected where they are in every state of the Union, the sovereignty of the nation is an empty one, and the power in individual states is greater than the power of the United States."[38] Whereas Douglass here astutely captures the larger philosophical questions of sovereignty that migration undermines, both he and Ned underestimate the South's resistance toward having its racial, economic, and social order challenged, a realization that DuBois came to before he renounced his citizenship.

In this context, Ned engrosses himself within his communities out of a sense of responsibility for raising consciousness about what civil rights are and why African Americans should desire them. He believes that removing the psychic yoke that white racism has placed on African Americans is the first step in removing them from "the corner," a spatial metaphor that emphasizes how segregation compresses and closes off African Americans' opportunities. That Ned goes back and forth between bridge and formal leadership as he imagines the future of African American enfranchisement is important because this movement foregrounds bridge leadership as pivotal to long-term communal change. As a bridge leader, Ned uses his relationship with his community to foster ties to a larger political discourse, exemplifying how bridge leaders close the gap between macropolitical movements—which Douglass, Washington, and DuBois lead—and micropolitical movements—like the one Ned leads—that begin in, and emerge from, local communities.

Even though readers can commend Ned for modeling bridge leadership in a way that disrupts the normativity of male formal leadership, they must not ignore the paradox of exodus politics that emerges when Ned indicates that he wants his children (a crowd that consists of boys and girls) "to be men." Ned's use of the term *men* to address a heterogeneous crowd mirrors exodus politics' substitution of "black men" for "black subjects." A century of black leaders have issued this call "to be men," from organizers like the fictional Ned to minister Louis Farrakhan, who asked black men to participate in the Million Man March as a way of showing their commitment to assuming their rightful patriarchal positions.[39] This problematic conflation of gender and race continues to impede civil rights struggles, producing insufficiently complex political agendas that purport to serve a "black community" while actually serving only the interests of a very narrow portion of black communities.

While Ned's access to larger state institutions might define him as a formal leader, Gaines purposefully emphasizes his bridge leadership activities in order to unsettle investments in exodus politics that idealize men's formal leadership and, however unintentionally and implicitly, valorize their deaths. While the presence of a white man patrolling the river as Ned speaks, Miss Jane's preoccupation with the possibility of his being killed, and Ned's own admission that he is going to die all foreshadow Ned's impending death, Gaines resists letting his readers champion him as an exemplary formal leader whose death redeems America. Such a reading would counter Gaines's desire to contest patriarchal formal leadership's cultural currency in black freedom struggles and to assert the significance of quotidian instances of leadership that emerge from self-empowered and self-sustainable communities. Instead, by focusing on how Ned empowers individuals, Gaines destabilizes the paradox of exodus politics that emerges when communities rely on political messiahs and therefore do not develop politically active, self-sustaining communities.

Although the African American sociopolitical imagination sometimes exalts the martyrdoms of male formal leaders as exemplary instances of civil rights leadership and sacrifice, *Miss Pittman* criticizes this tendency both because it assumes that deaths are necessary to redeem America and because these deaths may not in fact "redeem" America. Yet the reality that civil rights leaders and activists have died while participating in black freedom struggles, and the subsequent deification of these leaders, have contributed to a mythology in which African Americans need a political savior, who, by biblical and historical examples, will necessarily die. This "messiah complex," as Cone explains it, "is a danger that pervades the leadership expectations of the African-American community;

for African Americans this complex involves looking forward to the coming of a 'modern Moses' or a Christlike figure who will deliver them from the bondage of white racism. When we make Black Messiahs out of Martin and Malcolm, as if they alone knew how to achieve black freedom, we will not be encouraged to complete their unfinished task but rather to wait for another savior to come and liberate us."[40] Such an exodus politics, resting on a reliance on divinely sent male leaders, limits how communities participate in their own transformation. The tendency to look outwards prevents them from seeing themselves as change agents. Relatedly, the messiah complex has helped keep leadership discourses entrenched in masculinist ideologies. The bridge leadership depicted in Gaines's book disrupts the tendency to privilege male formal leadership and reinforce the messiah complex, thereby provoking the shift necessary to conceive of leadership and activism beyond the limited expectations of exodus politics.

This argument is not meant to diminish the significance of Ned's death or the deaths of actual male formal leaders such as Dr. Martin Luther King Jr. and Malik El-Shabazz (Malcolm X) during the civil rights movement in the 1960s. Rather, it is meant to draw attention to questions about leadership and the future of black freedom struggles that their deaths raised and that persist still in African American communities. Who, for example, will lead the movement when assassins murder its most visible formal leaders? Does the murder of one person, or a few people, mark the end of a movement that gained its momentum from a much broader constituency? Writing a narrative that is so self-consciously concerned with these issues within the decade that many people conceptualize as the "end" of the civil rights movement, Gaines shows how quotidian acts of everyday people, when combined with the micromobilization that bridge leaders provide, sustain a movement's legacy and momentum.

Within this context, Gaines refuses to let the reader memorialize Ned's death as an exemplary instance of civil rights martyrdom. Instead, he demands that readers commemorate Ned as a man who taught self-empowerment, valued education, took a stand for integration, and understood the importance of each of these for African American enfranchisement struggles. Gaines therefore emphasizes the core values that are central to Ned's instances of bridge leadership; Ned died as a consequence of his bridge leadership that aimed to alter his community members' consciousness by encouraging them to see themselves as subjects who deserved rights and were willing to fight for them. It is his "challenging" of the system that, if anything, has the potential to redeem America, and Gaines, like Walker in *Meridian* and Johnson in *Dreamer*, seriously questions whether America can be redeemed.

Although theologians have argued for the redemptive value of unmerited suffering, as King did when he eulogized the four girls killed in the Sixteenth Street Baptist Church bombing in Birmingham in 1963, Stephanie Mitchem, a womanist theologian, provocatively claims that unmerited suffering is not necessarily redemptive: "Suffering in itself is not salvific. It is redemptive only in that it may lead to critical rethinking of meaning or purpose, as might any life process."[41] Miss Jane makes this point when she acerbically recalls the community members who "didn't want to go near [Ned] when he was living, but when they heard he was dead they cried like children" (122). Her tone suggests that the dramatic reaction to this death, this desire to possess "a piece of lumber with his blood on it," is misguided (122): the energy would have been better spent following his teaching and espousing his cause. Unless the community fundamentally alters its understanding of itself in relation to the broader body politic, and unless the broader body politic confers citizenship rights upon black subjects and ensures that those rights are honored, the death will possess limited, if any, political significance.

The lesson of Ned's death, then, lies in the significance of bridge leaders' role in empowering local communities and connecting them to larger movements. The extension of Ned's struggle to Jimmy's in the civil rights movement of the 1950s and 1960s not only elaborates upon this point but also demonstrates how Miss Jane, observing where the community failed itself, incorporates her understanding of Ned's values into her growing political consciousness. To think of Ned's death as necessary for his vision to come to fruition, however, is to confound the end with the means. Further, African Americans are not suddenly empowered nor are white racists suddenly disempowered after Ned's death; Ned's life is significant for the accomplishments that his vision of civil rights made possible.

The Transformation Continues:
Miss Jane as Bridge and Formal Leader

Between Ned's death in 1901 and Jimmy's birth in 1937, *Miss Pittman* does not chronicle anything that might be characterized as an explicitly politicized civil rights agenda, and perhaps this is one reason why some critics have claimed that Miss Jane's final act of formal leadership as head of the protest in Bayonne after Jimmy's death emerges from nowhere and is incongruous with the text's development. It is during this period, however, that Miss Jane's consciousness develops most profoundly, enabling her to move from political awareness to her final act of leadership and resistance. Miss Jane's initial investment in black male leadership, and by extension exodus politics, complicates any reading that would try to categorize her as an unabashed early black "feminist." Yet her political consciousness reflects some aspects of black feminist thought, particularly her critique of the failure of exodus politics to make black women's oppression central to civil rights struggles and to consider black women's leadership as central to civil rights progress.

Early black feminist thought developed over the period spanned by *Miss Pittman*, so one way readers can understand how Miss Jane's black feminist consciousness emerges is by situating her within this genealogy. Frances Beale's theory of double jeopardy, which articulated the specific contours of black female oppression in the context of racism, sexism, and classism, extends Truth's early notions of black women's civil rights and lays the groundwork for more recent black feminist theories: multiple consciousness (Deborah King), standpoint theory (Patricia Hill Collins), and intersectionality (Kimberlé Crenshaw). Although Barbara Smith outlines valid shortcomings of black feminism's intersectional theories that failed to "queer" heteronormativity, these theorists do initiate a conversation about a politics of gender that both intersects with and diverges from racial politics. They begin to address cross-cutting issues by conceptualizing black women's gender rights *as* civil rights. As Miss Jane encounters and participates in events that exemplify the interrelatedness of race, gender, sexuality, and class issues, her consciousness becomes more complex, reflecting the processes that black feminist theorists describe.

Seeing the inequities that both disenfranchised blacks and poor whites suffer, Miss Jane draws parallels between their experiences. Her intersectional analysis of cross-cutting issues adds social class to conversations about racial enfranchisement and complicates monolithic notions of racial oppression. In a discussion about Huey Long's death, for example, Miss Jane expresses a keen awareness of the complexities of systemic disenfranchisement. Rather than suggesting erroneously that class oppression is equal to or has the same effects as racial oppression, she exposes racism and classism as an interwoven system of forces that truncate people's life opportunities.

By complicating notions of what constitutes "oppression," Miss Jane, along with her black feminist interlocutors, forces herself and her community to think differently about what solutions will eradicate oppression. Addressing racism without attending to how capitalism shapes (overdetermines) it would prove inadequate as an antiracist strategy, and critical race theorists have argued this point over the last two decades. This portion of the narrative shows how much bridge leadership has transformed Miss Jane and raised her consciousness, thus preparing her for the final experience of formal leadership.

If Miss Jane's comments on Huey Long demonstrate her understanding of the relationship between racial and class politics, her discussion of the tragedy of Tee Bob and Mary Agnes reveals her understanding of how sexuality and gender intersect with racial and class identities and complicate identity politics even further. When Tee Bob commits suicide because he, as a white man, is unable in his society's hierarchy to have a consensual relationship with a black woman, Miss Jane clarifies that it is not simply racism that prohibits this relationship but also the sexualization of racism and the racialization of sexism. Although a white neighbor, Jules Raynard, speaks much of the dialogue in the scene, Gaines frames Miss Jane as an active participant who absorbs, supports, and processes Raynard's assertions.

While the scene rightfully connects Tee Bob's decision to commit suicide to his inability to admit how his white privilege thrives upon the exploitation of black female sexuality, Jules Raynard concludes that his suicide has the potential to redeem their society: "One day he had to. For our sins" (206). Whereas Miss Jane up until this point has agreed with Raynard, she diverges from his conclusion, asking with skepticism, "He was bound to kill himself anyhow?" (206). Although Tee Bob is neither a bridge nor a formal leader, Miss Jane's resistance to reading his death as redemptive is in line with her earlier reaction to Ned's death. Death cannot redeem this society if the communities refuse to conceptualize the intersections of race, gender, class, and sexuality in ways that defy society's norms and allow black subjects to obtain their civil rights. Revisiting this particular issue thirty years after Ned's death, Gaines uses these instances to demonstrate further how Miss Jane's political consciousness has evolved in the context of her increased understanding of oppression, injustice, and political empowerment.

While the reader witnesses a transformation in Miss Jane's attitude toward political mobilization, the community remains, to its detriment, deeply invested in exodus politics' notion of a political messiah, who by definition must be male. Even Miss Jane, who has developed more complicated notions of freedom and leadership, does not completely eschew the problematic gender ideologies of exodus politics. Yet, unlike the community at large, she begins to conceive of exodus politics as culturally constructed sets of values and norms that can be undone. Therefore, when Jimmy—whom the community refers to as "the One"—is born in 1937, his community expects him to lead them to freedom, but Miss Jane, as a politically aware and transformed member of the community, has a more nuanced view of what the attainment of that freedom requires.

Whereas the beginning of *Miss Pittman* details the events that raise Miss Jane's consciousness, the middle of the novel shows the effects, and the final section the enactment, of that raised consciousness. While Jimmy wants Miss Jane to be a formal leader and challenge the notion that she, and women more generally, cannot be at the forefront of a movement, Miss Jane wants Jimmy to understand that a community must be mobilized—that is, bridged—before it can be led. Both of these individuals must change the gendered expectations for leadership if they are to be effective in helping their communities secure civil rights. Whereas Gaines emphasizes how the community members' beliefs overdetermine Jimmy's role and truncate the community's vision for political enfranchisement, Jimmy's resistance to his role, and Miss Jane's evolving understanding of her position, challenge normative politics of gender as they relate to black leadership.

Gaines juxtaposes the community's desire for Jimmy to be their formal leader with Jimmy's demand that Miss Jane be their leader, thereby unsettling the gender norms and expectations that frame exodus politics as the privileged model of leadership in the community. That since 1901 the community has been searching for another male leader—one they believe will obtain their rights for them—reinforces how dependency on a formal leader discourages communities from acting. Since community members have adopted the messiah complex, they do not conceptualize themselves as leaders or ordinary citizens who have the power to enact social and political change. *Miss Pittman*, although to a lesser extent than the other texts this study examines, reminds readers that through these localized acts black freedom struggles gain and sustain momentum.

While the community views Jimmy's birth in messianic terms that reveal an investment in exodus politics, male formal leadership, and the messiah complex, Gaines simultaneously shows that they actively construct his leadership by *selecting* and *grooming* him for his role. Gaines does so for three reasons: to dislodge the centrality of exodus politics as the main model for African American leadership, to emphasize the important role bridge leaders play in communities, and to divorce formal leadership from maleness. Each of these actions aids the development of more complicated expectations for civil rights leadership, primarily because each one implodes the idea that male formal leaders are the only leaders qualified to lead. As Miss Jane explains, "Lena was the first one to ask if he was the One, then we started wondering if he was the One. That was long before he had any idea what we wanted out of him. . . . Why did we pick him? Well, why do you pick anybody? We picked him because we needed somebody. We could 'a' picked one of Strut Hawkins's boys or one of Joe Simon's boys . . . —but we picked him" (212). Ironically, the community believes that the Lord has sent them someone whom they actually have chosen.

Miss Jane's reflection demonstrates the community's yearning not only for a leader but specifically for a male leader. Like Ned's use of the term *men* in "sermon on the river," her use of the term *boys* here cannot be dismissed as gender neutral. Rather, Miss Jane specifies that the community keeps an eye out for boys who will eventually become their male formal leaders. That she does not mention daughters or girls resonates with Mary Helen Washington's earlier poignant question pondering why, and how, civil rights discourses exclude black women despite the roles they have held. Here the exodus politics model writes women out of civil rights historiographies, rendering their political activities invisible.

The choice—on the part of the community and Miss Jane—to select Jimmy as an exemplar of civil rights activism reflects Gaines's own decision, as fictional historiographer, to depict how communities groom men to be formal leaders, to become the face of the movement. Although the text is less explicit about how societies groom women for their leadership roles, it is clear that certain communities view only men as leaders and only certain activities as examples of true leadership. But by showing Miss Jane's, Ned's, and Jimmy's actual leadership roles and how and why some roles have been elevated while others have been suppressed, the text resists these narrow prescriptive conceptualizations of leadership.

Even if communities presumably groomed women to function as bridge leaders, normative definitions of leadership would exclude their behaviors, thoughts, and activities. As Robnett and Giddings have demonstrated, analyses of the movement tend to categorize women's leadership as "organizing," with the result that their work is regarded as less important than men's "leadership." While Gaines significantly (though perhaps too implicitly) interrogates this "stratification" within leadership discourses, his contemporaries, such as Alice Walker in *Meridian* and Toni Cade Bambara in *The Salt Eaters*, consider more explicitly the ramifications of masculinizing civil rights and civil rights history during and after the civil rights movement.

The community actively grooms Jimmy for leadership by compelling him to "get religion" at the same age "the master does," preventing him from socializing with children whose paths seem wayward, and forcing him to excel academically. Yet Gaines counters any notion that Jimmy, by biological or divine mandate, predeterminedly occupies this role, despite the community's insistence that the one fulfilling this role must be male. This final section offers Gaines's most explicit critique of exodus politics. Because the community members believe God is an active agent in humans' political affairs (to paraphrase James Cone) and because they interpret the events of their lives through Afro-Protestant symbolism (as Byerman rightfully suggests), they draw on an exodus typology to articulate their desire for a messianic leader.[42] By articulating their political desire through this paradigm, they are participating in the African American tradition of *actively* appropriating biblical narratives that defy oppression to support their claims that oppression counters the will of God for black people's freedom; in the words of Qiana Whitted, they are "spur[ring] human activity by emphasizing the earthly obligations of humanity to work against individuals and systemic structures that cause evil."[43] However, this tradition, by limiting the scope of black people's oppression to focus on race and not its intersections with gender and sexuality, and by treating the normative black subject as the primary black subject, falls short of creating a liberatory politic and foregrounding cross-cutting issues.

Despite the community's efforts to situate Jimmy within the discourses of exodus politics, Jimmy resists becoming either a Mosaic or Christlike messianic figure or a King-like formal leader. He refuses to use the pulpit to galvanize support for civil rights because he understands that communal mobilization must fuel the movement for civil rights and that top-down male formal leadership may not be the best model for political enfranchisement. Jimmy's political consciousness, which matures in 1954, "the same year they passed that law in Washington," situates him squarely within a discourse of civil rights leadership that—like the *Brown v. Board of Education* case—demands judicial redress for racial inequalities (229).

To lead his community effectively, Jimmy must unsettle their monolithic view of leadership by disrupting their expectations for him and themselves. Whereas he wants to complicate the triangular relationship among exodus politics, maleness, and leadership, his ability to possibly lead is intricately tied to this triad. Not only do the community members refuse to see themselves as leaders, a phenomenon he must counteract through bridge leadership itself, but they see only men as leaders. The juxtaposition between Jimmy's wish to see himself outside that paradigm and the community's readiness to fix him within it foreshadows the later difficulty he faces when he attempts to solicit the community to participate in its own liberation struggle.

By viewing civil rights leadership as a communal responsibility, Jimmy challenges how community members understand their own leadership. He also highlights how exodus politics ultimately undermines the long-term continuation of civil rights gains by leaving communities inadequately prepared to lead in the absence of male formal leaders. Jimmy realizes that to be an effective formal leader he must first function as a bridge leader, so he enlists Miss Jane's bridge leadership to help raise the community's consciousness about the urgency of "civil rights." He does so, not simply because he "is not strong enough to stand out there all by [him]self," but because he understands that without the people there is no movement (237).

Jimmy's desire to debunk the hierarchies of formal leadership in which the community members are invested illuminates the challenges bridge leaders face when they try to incorporate potential adherents into the movement and also reminds the reader that movements falter when they lack indigenous leaders. As is the case with Ned's community, the black people in Jimmy's community are reluctant to participate because they rightfully fear white retaliatory violence. The growing list of slain civil rights leaders in the historical civil rights movement contextualizes their fear and confirms that violence is always an immediate threat. Throughout this final section, Gaines highlights the chasm between prefigurative strategies aimed at individual transformation and the actual changes in consciousness. Yet the fact that members ultimately join the movement underscores that neither the prefigurative strategies nor the people to whom they are directed remain static.

Miss Jane's comment that "people's always looking for somebody to come lead them" grounds "the people" as the necessary catalysts for change, even when they themselves do not recognize it: "People and time bring forth leaders, Jimmy. People and time bring forth leaders. Leaders don't bring forth people. The people and time brought King; King didn't bring the people. What Miss Rosa Parks did everybody wanted to do.

They just needed one person to do it first because they all couldn't do it at the same time; then they needed King to show them what to do next. But King couldn't do a thing before Miss Rosa Parks refused to give that white man her seat" (241). Ironically and tellingly, Miss Jane also does not see herself as one of these leaders, as a local Rosa Parks. Yet the presence of Rosa Parks in the novel—and, by extension, the historical Parks, who linked race, gender, and sexuality to civil rights issues—supports the contention that Miss Jane's consciousness is developing in the context of a burgeoning black feminist theory. Aside from the historical Rosa Parks's well-known role in the Montgomery bus boycott, scholarship has only recently investigated her leadership in working to secure justice for black women whose white rapists the law refused to prosecute. As Danielle McGuire details in *At the Dark End of the Street: Black Women, Rape and Resistance—A New History of the Civil Rights Movement from Rosa Parks to the Rise of Black Power* (2010), Parks's role in the civil rights movement encompassed a struggle to obtain black women's civil rights. In her vision of social justice, gender rights were indeed civil rights.

Miss Jane's status as the oldest member of the community, her embodiment of historical memory, and her ability to mediate between different segments of the community all contribute to her effectiveness as a bridge leader. Moreover, her longevity in the community positions her as an indigenous leader who can influence community members to join the movement. These same qualities, Jimmy argues, make her an ideal formal leader. To Jimmy's mind, Miss Jane will be able to use mass participation and support to compel state institutions to implement legal changes. His belief also acknowledges the reality that women bridge leaders have historically occupied formal leadership positions, however temporarily, in the absence of male formal leaders. More suggestively, Miss Jane's ability to overcome her own fear and motivate community members to do the same indicates an important prefigurative consciousness-raising strategy that ultimately will connect the constituents to a larger movement.

Jimmy's death on the morning that the civil rights demonstration at the courthouse is scheduled marks Miss Jane's transition from bridge leader to formal leader. In his absence, the community proceeds, with Miss Jane declaring, "Just a piece of him is dead. The rest of him is waiting for us in Bayonne" (259). By saying "us," Miss Jane acknowledges her desire to participate and accepts her role as a formal leader in the civil rights movement. Even if her leadership at this moment is only temporary, it demonstrates a profound transformation from the woman who in 1937, and even 1954, looked for the "One" who would bring her rights. In some respects, Jimmy's presence does help Miss Jane to secure rights: his leadership further shepherds Miss Jane into her own political consciousness and makes her an active participant in securing her rights and those of the community. Miss Jane's final confrontation with Robert Samson, the white man who owns the land upon which she lives and works, confirms this. Before she left for Bayonne, Miss Jane notes, "Me and Robert looked at each other there a long time, then I went by" (259). That she "went by" parallels the earlier moment when Miss Jane asserted that she was "Jane Brown" and not "Ticey." If the first scene instantiates her black consciousness, this final encounter with Samson reveals a full actualization of that consciousness.

This encounter suggests that Miss Jane and her fellow community members will not defer to Samson's threat to remove them from the "plantation" for participating in the demonstration, or to the broader institutional practices and ideologies that sanction this violence and intimidation. That they still reside on the "plantation" when Miss Jane tells her life story to the history teacher evidences the success of her action. The reader is left to imagine Miss Jane serving as a formal leader of the demonstration that concludes the book.[44] As Doyle observes: "Her final lesson learned, Jane can teach again. By readiness to risk all she has and to be moved away, she undertakes the culminating experience of her long life. She becomes Big Laura, moving ahead, leading the people."[45] Although Doyle rightfully asserts the genuineness of Miss Jane's role as a formal leader, Miss Jane has actually been learning, teaching, and leading throughout her entire life. In the end, at Bayonne, Miss Jane synthesizes a life of bridge leadership with an opportunity to be a formal leader.

To read *Miss Pittman*, or the modern civil rights movement, as a story of conclusive triumph only perpetuates the notion that African American political leadership models rooted in a narrative of exodus politics always empower and liberate. As *Miss Pittman* demonstrates, however, an exodus model, with its embedded gender hierarchy, while purporting to emancipate, further disenfranchises women by not considering the specific forms of discrimination and oppression that they experience as result of their racial and gender (and other) identities. Miss Jane's attention to cross-cutting political issues demonstrates an awareness of the complexities of identity politics and their relationship to political empowerment.

Even in the twenty-first century, when the existence and meaning of "race" are contested, the idea that the normative black subject's political concerns must take precedence in black communities persists: diverse black subjectivities are conflated into a singular black subject with one set of political circumstances, opportunities, goals, and desires. But solutions to the problems that African Americans face must be multiple and equally diverse: cross-cutting issues must lie at the heart of black political agendas. The failure to make this paradigm shift will leave people wondering, as Miss Jane's community does about Jimmy, "Is he the One?" In reality, there is no "One"; rather, *she* is one of many.

The next chapter's examination of *Meridian* shifts attention from the century of leadership leading up to the middle of the civil rights movement to the decade that extends from the high point of the civil rights movement to its transition into phase two. Whereas *Miss Pittman* examines issues of leadership in the context of African Americans trying to obtain legal rights, *Meridian* shows what leadership and the movement look like once these legal rights have been enacted.

2 / "The Refusal of Christ to Accept Crucifixion": Bridge Leadership in Alice Walker's *Meridian*

> *"Now, before we proceed," Velma said, "we need to be clear, all of us, about the nature of the work. About how things have gotten done in the past and why that pattern has to change."*
>
> *"Don't be so damn polite," Ruby interrupted. "It boils down to this. You jokers, and especially you," cutting her eyes at Lonnie, "never want to take any responsibility for getting down. Mr. Reilly excepted. Now, what that has meant in the past is that we women have been expected to carry the load."*
>
> —TONI CADE BAMBARA, *THE SALT EATERS*

Claims that the civil rights movement began to decline in 1965, with the passage of the Voting Rights Act of 1965, and ended in 1968, with the death of Dr. King, declare a decisive break in history marked by the end of that movement, the rise of the Black Power movement, and the onset of a post–civil rights era.[1] Even more problematically, they bind the movement's goals to the passing of legislative acts and its lifetime to the life spans of a few exemplary male formal leaders. This narrative of historical "progress" elides the fact that neither social movements nor historical periods decisively break and further ignores the enduring significance of the civil rights movement. Alice Walker's second novel, *Meridian* (1976), demonstrates why civil rights historians' call for a "long" historical framework to analyze the civil rights movement proves useful; through this perspective readers can see how the civil rights movement to enfranchise African Americans persisted beyond the 1960s. That is, a "long" view connects contemporary experiences of political disempowerment to a broader history of oppression, while upsetting the notion that the legislative achievements of the 1960s eradicated all of society's inequities. Although ending legal segregation was at the heart of the judicial fight that the movement waged, *Meridian*, like other cultural texts, admonishes against misinterpreting the laws against segregation and the attainment of the legal right to vote as evidence that the movement has succeeded or ended.

Although the movement's legislative successes produced political, economic, and cultural gains, they were not, in and of themselves, sufficient to "establish equality." Dr. King criticizes the view that the laws aimed to end de jure segregation and discrimination mark an ending rather than a beginning: "I am appalled that some people feel that the Civil Rights struggle is over because we have a Civil Rights bill with ten titles and a voting rights bill. Over and over again people ask, What else do you want? They feel that everything is all right. Well, let them look around at our big cities."[2] As King suggests, the end of de jure segregation did not transform the reality that inequality continued to circumscribe African Americans' life chances. Moreover, as the reference to the "big cities" suggests, the civil rights movement had only begun to address de facto segregation, which, while not legally enforced, truncated African Americans' access to equal opportunities.

As King notes, the mere removal of the legal obstructions to equality could not fix racial inequities. The absence of significant material improvement in the areas of education, finance, housing, and employment evidenced this claim in both the North and the South. Whereas King's comment signaled his civil rights campaign's shift in focus to racial inequities in urban areas, Walker remains focused on the same inequities in the rural South. But like King, she suggests that following phase one of the civil rights movement popular activism and governmental reform must collaboratively ensure that the foundational work of phase one comes to fruition during phase two.

Meridian, then, employs the concept of phases of the movement that civil rights historians would later use, one of agitation culminating in legal victories and one of implementation to actually enforce and consolidate legislative gains and to produce in reality the equality that legislation promises.[3] The book contests the ideas that the civil rights movement's history spanned only fifteen years, that ending de jure segregation was its only goal, and that formal leadership was necessary to advance the movement. Walker's situating of the civil rights movement in a "long" periodization reframes the movement's goals to include not only removing legal obstructions to equal rights but also ensuring that equality of opportunity translates into equality of outcome. Walker's periodization foregrounds the strategies bridge leaders use and the philosophies they invoke to combat changing forms of discrimination that emerged in the wake of the political possibilities the civil rights movement made possible.

Meridian's view of the goals of phase two of the civil rights movement underscores bridge leaders' role in training communities to develop indigenous leaders who will sustain civil rights gains over the long term.

The book reflects the shift in the movement's focus when, as the activist Bayard Rustin described it early on, "the single-issue demands of the movement's classical stage [namely integration] gave way to the 'package deal,'" or demands for the eradication of housing, employment, and economic disparities that were preventing African Americans from achieving equality.[4] The empowering of black communities, however, as Senator Daniel Patrick Moynihan suggests in his controversial report *The Negro Family: A Case for National Action*, could not be achieved only by the efforts of black people. The government would need to institute structural changes to American society that would help produce "equality—in terms of group results."[5] *Meridian*, like the other literary texts this book examines, challenges readers to think about what specific markers—more schools, better jobs, fewer prisons, increased entrance into the middle class—would be tangible evidence that equality of opportunity had effectively been translated into equality of outcome. (More painstakingly, a text such as *Dreamer* calls into question the very possibility of this premise, particularly in a capitalistic society, where economic success is predicated on the exploitation of non-normative groups' labor.)

Unlike *Miss Pittman*, which concludes in the early 1960s, before the passage of both the Civil Rights Act of 1964 and the Voting Rights Act of 1965, *Meridian* develops precisely during this moment and beyond. Walker focuses on a "long" civil rights movement not only to emphasize a mutually constitutive relationship between the civil rights and Black Power movements but to show that even as the civil rights movement has moved into phase two, it remains bound to phase one. The protagonist, Meridian Hill, is initially conflicted between the violent strategies that the Black Power movement proposes and the nonviolent direct action strategies that the civil rights movement promotes. By juxtaposing Meridian's initial uncertainty as to whether she would be able to kill for the revolution with her later certainty that she would not, Walker questions the efficacy of making a hasty transition from the civil rights movement to the Black Power movement.[6]

While Meridian's vision of political activism builds upon the discourses of both of these movements, it also implicitly draws on black feminist thought in that it seeks justice for all people within black communities and does not privilege the political concerns of the normative black subject. As Thadious Davis has compellingly argued, Meridian "searches for causes in which to enact her faith in expansive rights for all, and most particularly for black people still discriminated against in the South,"[7] and her political consciousness, her understanding of leadership and civil rights, evolves in light of the legal victories that phase one made possible. As this chapter will show, her implicit and explicit rejection of gender norms enhances her conceptualization of civil rights, civil rights leadership, and social justice. Further, the new forms of Jane and Jim Crow that appear in the late civil rights era, and the failure of equal rights to translate into material gains, engender Meridian's critique of exodus politics and the paradoxes that exodus politics produces.

In this chapter, I argue that this critique takes two main forms. By framing her examination of the civil rights movement in the context of phase two, Walker contests the tendency of exodus politics to treat phase one as *the* civil rights movement. And by underscoring the roles of bridge leaders in phase two, Walker reinforces the idea that communities can sustain their civil rights gains only by developing a network of leaders—and not by relying on individual (male) formal leaders. Walker also employs iconic civil rights referents, including the Student Non-violent Coordinating Committee and the Voter Education Project, as discursive points of departure to challenge the politics of gender in civil rights discourse that circumscribes women's roles in the movement and curtails the movement's ability to envision a space for empowered black women. Walker, then, like Gaines, defamiliarizes normative definitions of civil rights and expectations for civil rights leadership and demonstrates how they restrict an expansive vision of the movement's strategies and goals.

Several scholars, including Susan Danielson, Roberta Hendrickson, Melissa Walker, Karen Stein, Seongho Yoon, and Madhu Dubey, have rightfully maintained that in *Meridian* Walker analyzes sexism within the civil rights movement, and, for Dubey in particular, the Black Power movement, to challenge the viability of a racial liberation movement that ignores cross-cutting gender and sexual disenfranchisements.[8] My argument, however, supplements these arguments by positing that *Meridian* does not merely castigate the civil rights movement for its sexism. Rather, it uses the examples of sexism as discursive points of departure to trouble the distinctions drawn between activism and leadership and the separations made between women's rights, sexual rights, and civil rights. *Meridian* addresses three of the four questions I ask in the Introduction: (2) *Who* will lead the movement, and how can leadership be redefined to include the work both men and women do to mobilize participants? (3) *What* paradigms of leadership—communal or individual—are African Americans employing to direct their efforts? and (4) *How* will society measure material and symbolic gains of the civil rights movement when the changing political landscape has made the remnants of Jim and Jane Crow practices more complicated to identify?

Laying the Foundation: Phase One of the Civil Rights Movement

Meridian, like *The Autobiography of Miss Jane Pittman*, chronicles the protagonist's development of a political consciousness, which, emerging with the nation's increasing concern about African Americans' quest for civil rights, shapes her leadership roles. Learning from a television newscast that a house that was the site of a black voter registration drive has been bombed and that "the bombs, exploding, set fire to—not just the house—the whole cluster of houses on that street" and have injured small children and killed adults, Meridian becomes drawn to the movement (70). Although she does not sign up to volunteer until a month later, the narrator reveals that "one day in the middle of April in 1960 Meridian Hill became aware of the past and present" (70). By connecting Meridian's raised consciousness to an awareness of the "past and present," Walker situates Meridian's realization of "forms of protests available to civil rights activists" within a trajectory of black freedom struggles,[9] suggesting that activists' future gains depend on the redressing of earlier instances of discrimination. If as Alan Nadel has contended, *Meridian* "conducts an historical search in that it tries to recontextualize the past," it does so to defamiliarize the tropes of the civil rights movement that have fixed on patriarchal leadership as necessary for black political organization and have asserted the eradication of Jim and Jane Crow segregation as the movement's primary/only goal.[10]

Walker binds the beginning of Meridian's rise to political consciousness and civil rights leadership to a news broadcast in order to demonstrate how the mass media, by making the movement visible to ordinary individuals like Meridian, awakened them to become involved. The 1950s and 1960s saw the establishment of media that targeted black audiences specifically, and the increase in black news venues allowed African Americans who otherwise might have been disconnected from the civil rights movement to be "a part" of it. Mamie Till Mobley, Emmett Till's mother, would capitalize on this cultural moment, not only holding a public viewing of her son's mutilated body but allowing *Jet* magazine to publish a photograph of his corpse.[11]

Till's bloated corpse and disfigured face, which reflected the cost of defying Jim and Jane Crow racism, also catalyzed African American involvement, directly and indirectly, in the movement. To this day Till "remains one of the seminal icons of the civil rights movement,"[12] and the mass media's ability to distribute the written and visual narratives helped give him his iconic stature. Deborah Barker has chronicled the mass media's complicity in the oppression of African Americans, and although she persuasively contends that Walker also criticizes this history, *Meridian* emphasizes the mass media's positive influence, showing how the media engendered interest in the civil rights movement and attracted popular support in ways that were impossible in the time of *Miss Pittman*, when the media were almost absent.[13]

Whereas Meridian was one of a group of civil rights leaders during the 1960s, when the novel opens in the 1970s she is the only one left who has not become disillusioned with the movement. For her former lover Truman, a fellow activist from that period, the deaths of King and Malcolm X mean that the movement has ended and further political activity is pointless. For Meridian, however, the deaths of these icons are not a final crushing blow. She never views men's formal leadership as necessary for black people's political enfranchisement, and she understands that no one man has the power to secure these rights, so the deaths of Dr. King and Malcolm X, instead of ending her involvement in the movement, show her the inadequacy of exodus politics as a strategy for securing civil rights over the long term.

Meridian, in the 1970s, decides to "go back to the people, live among them, like Civil Rights workers used to do" (19). She recognizes that neither the civil rights movement's legislative gains nor Black Power's espousal of violent revolution have resulted in the economic, employment, or educational gains that would render her bridge leadership unnecessary. She believes that the civil rights movement bears the responsibility of making its goals understandable and meaningful to people, and she thinks critically about the new role she must play in light of how the movement has changed the contemporary moment. Truman, in contrast, maintains the civil rights movement was a fad that has died: "Meridian, do you realize no one is thinking about these things any more? Revolution was the theme of the sixties: Medgar, Malcolm, Martin, George, Angela Davis, the Panthers, people blowing up buildings, and each other. But all that is gone now. . . . The leaders were killed, the restless young were bought off with anti-poverty jobs, and the clothing styles of the poor were copied by Seventh Avenue" (206). Thus for Truman Meridian's notion that the movement still matters is delusional, and her related idea that she can effectively lead whatever that movement may be by living among the people and engaging in bridging activities is foolish and politically ineffectual. Stripped of his onetime belief that formal leaders can enact immediate systemic changes, Truman has become passive and cynical. Meridian, however, emphasizes the important role that she, as bridge leader, plays in advancing the black freedom struggles—especially insofar as she foregrounds the role bridge leaders play in raising consciousness through prefigurative strategies.

The differing perspectives of Meridian and Truman that Walker portrays in the novel emblematize a larger, continuing dispute among African Americans about the movement's significance and its future that arises from a tension between bridge and formal leadership philosophies. On the one hand, for many the deaths of the movement's iconic leaders solidify both a loss of faith in politics and a paradoxical yearning for a new class of black leaders; on the other, they illuminate the pitfalls of an exodus politics that defines a social movement's longevity in terms of male formal leaders' leadership tenure; conceptualizes the civil rights movement as a bounded fifteen-year historical phenomenon separated from preceding and subsequent historical periods; and privileges formal leadership over bridge leadership and ordinary activism. Unsettling the embeddedness of black men's patriarchal authority in civil rights discourses, Walker champions Meridian's bridge leadership to further undercut the saliency of exodus politics in the black political imagination. Walker dramatizes Truman's and Meridian's differing perspectives to contest prevalent notions in social movement theory that primarily credit formal leadership for organizing, mobilizing, and sustaining black freedom struggles.

As Truman notes, the 1970s marked a significant change in black political energies. The Black Power movement waned, and the entry of more black people into political office and the middle class, coupled with white backlash against civil rights advances, dulled the spirit of revolution that had animated political movements of the 1960s. As Manning Marable explains:

> By the mid-1970s, the black nationalist impulse had been effec-
> tively splintered, repressed and removed from political discourse.
> The black elite was retrieved from its marginal and defensive stance
> within the black community and, with the election of Carter, had
> unprecedented access to middle-to-upper levels of political bureau-
> cracy.... Radicalism and militancy were defeated.... Urban riots
> had been quelled, and ghetto blacks seemingly succumbed to the
> quiescence of the dominant society. The general interpretation of

the period was, at least for the black elite, one of tremendous optimism. There was no longer a need to march in the streets. . . . Black freedom would become a reality through gradual yet meaningful reforms within the existing system.[14]

The gains of the civil rights movement widened the gulf between the black middle and poor classes, and between the advocates of revolution and the advocates of gradual reform. Newly elected officials had to consider how, if at all, they would challenge the status quo to upset public policies and laws that harmed their constituencies.

The limitations of black electoral politics, however, became increasingly clearer as black elected officials were, as political scientists Ronald Walters and Robert Smith put it, "incorporated" into mainstream political structures. If, as these researchers contend, there is "meager evidence that such persons' tenure has much impact on the quality of life in any measurable sector of the Black community," their roles appear to be more symbolic than substantive, and their election will not necessarily produce better material conditions for black people.[15] According to Walters and Smith, once black formal leaders have benefited from the power structure they become more interested in maintaining their position than in dismantling the status quo. Because incorporated leaders cannot *both* maintain and unsettle, they shift from "protest" politics to "accommodation" politics with the aim of reforming the system from within. The government aims to maintain the status quo, so the reforms are typically minor, cosmetic changes, and black politicians' entrance into electoral politics cannot produce the "equality—in terms of group results" that Moynihan deemed necessary. Such progress would require a fundamental shift in government practices and policies regarding civil rights. Truman's disillusionment shows the cost of an overreliance on legal redress and formal leaders in the quest for equality. Moreover, he ignores the role of everyday people in holding black officials accountable for empowering black communities.

For Meridian, the civil rights movement is in a new phase and black people are still struggling to make meaning of the movement, as well as to understand their roles within it. Bewildered by Truman's sense that the civil rights movement no longer has any use, Meridian asks him: "But don't you think the basic questions raised by King and Malcolm and the rest still exist? Don't you think people, somewhere deep inside, are still attempting to deal with them?" (206). Although Truman responds with a deafening "No," Meridian's questions raise several issues that the text has foregrounded. Earlier in the conversation Meridian has claimed that teaching, which lies at the heart of bridge leadership strategies, ultimately starts "revolution." Much like Ned in *Miss Pittman,* Meridian believes that at their core people want (and need) to be taught how to live, and not simply to be told what to do. In her roles as bridge leader and activist, this particular notion means educating people so that they will understand not only the choices available to them (rights) but also the consequences of exercising them (responsibilities).

Meridian's contrasting perspective forces Truman and the reader to think about how to raise consciousness and develop skills so that individuals and communities play active roles in black freedom struggles. Walker's interrogation of the limitations of exodus politics demonstrates her awareness that it obscures the roles of bridge leaders and everyday citizens in sustaining and extending the civil rights movement through phase two. Yet Walker also underscores that the responsibility for ensuring long-term change should not reside solely within the communities that have been disenfranchised or otherwise neglected; the government, too, must shoulder this responsibility.

As Meridian's return to grassroots activism illustrates, post–phase one civil rights workers are still needed to translate equality of opportunity into equality of outcome. It is therefore telling that the opening scene reflects how in some southern towns equality of opportunity actually does not yet exist because discriminatory practices and policies remain uncontested. As the narrative opens, Truman returns from New York to find Meridian literally facing a tank—a metonymic representation of local and national obstructions to civil rights justice and of the backlash against civil rights that is developing across the nation. This tank was acquired, as the narrator explains, to defend white supremacy against those attempting to unsettle the racial status quo: "The town of Chicokema did indeed own a tank: it had been bought during the sixties when the townspeople who were white felt under attack from 'outside agitators'—those members of the black community who thought equal rights for blacks should extend to all" (2). Walker highlights the irony of the white townspeople's concern that black people thought that "equal rights for blacks should extend to all." The white population of Chicokema is upset because they perceive that an "underserving" black population is encroaching upon rights that whites have supposedly earned. Yet as critical race theorists have clarified—especially George Lipsitz, through his notion of a possessive investment in whiteness—white privilege is unearned, unmerited, and built upon the disadvantages of nonwhite people.[16]

Whereas the town had bought this tank in the 1960s to stake its claim against the civil rights movement, its continued presence in the 1970s evidences segregation's persistence in the body politic and whites' enduring resistance to African Americans' obtaining and enjoying their civil rights. King's prophetic declaration rings true in both the fictional setting of *Meridian* and the community more broadly: "In the event that strong civil-rights legislation is written into the books in the session of Congress now sitting, and that a Bill of Rights for the Disadvantaged might follow, enforcement will still meet with massive resistance in many parts of the country."[17] Although Congress never instituted a Bill of Rights for the Disadvantaged that laid out specific corrective measures in the areas of housing, employment, and education, even the mere promise of equality engendered hostility against African Americans.

Meridian returns to challenge white obstructions to civil rights justice by empowering the communities to be, as Ella Baker would have it, their own leaders and activists against violence and injustice. She is there not to save black people from white racism but rather to teach people how to live and lead themselves. She wants them to reject the faith in a political messiah and move beyond the frustration that the deferral of equality has produced so that they continue to demand tangible changes. By having the text open with a scene that shows the continued practice of segregation despite its legal end, Walker signals the contradiction between the theoretical promise of equality that the law bestowed and the failure to achieve that equality in material ways.

When Truman asks a resident of the town what is happening, the old man tells him that some of the black children wanted to see the exhibit in the circus wagon but that "their day" for seeing it wasn't until Thursday. Truman's stunned reply, "*Your* day? . . . But the Civil Rights Movement changed all that!" reveals an expectation that contradicts the disillusionment he expresses about the movement's efficacy in the aforementioned conversation. In actuality, however, the persistence of segregation in this fictional town, even in the post–civil rights era, that the circus incident demonstrates reflects a larger pattern of continuing segregation across the United States following the Civil Rights Act of 1964, the Voting Rights Act of 1965, and even the Fair Housing Act of 1968. With the passage of these acts, de jure segregation gave way to de facto segregation, but pervasive and long-standing residential, educational, social, cultural, and economic segregation continued. The civil rights movement did bring African Americans, particularly the working class, specific gains in income and employment. As Manning Marable reports, "From

1964 to 1969, the median black family income in the U.S. increased from $5,921 to $8,074," and "unemployment rates for non-white married males with families dropped from 7.2 percent in 1962 to a low of 2.5 percent in 1969."[18] *Meridian*, however, discourages readers from interpreting these gains as evidence of a larger pattern of social improvement. As Marable continues, "Non-white youth unemployment actually increased in these years, from 24.4 percent in 1960 to 29.1 percent in 1970. The quality of black urban life—poor housing, rat infestation, crime, high infant mortality rates, disease, poor public education—continued to deteriorate."[19] Without systemic infrastructural changes, equality of outcome remained elusive.

The deteriorating quality of black life that Marable describes for the United States as a whole was characteristic of the rural South as well, but the rural South was actually even worse off. These conditions do not lead Marable to question the efficacy of the movement as Truman does in Walker's novel; instead they lead him to reassert Rustin's notion that black political agendas must shift their focus from the single issue of ending segregation to a "package deal" that concurrently addresses the aggregate effects of inequality. Truman's despair reflects bridge leaders' increasing frustration as they witnessed state and federal institutions failing to fulfill their obligations and thus eroding the gains that they and their communities had achieved. SNCC activist Jean Smith lamented: "It is a subtle problem to acknowledge that there was some value in having achieved these rights and yet to understand that there was no basic gain. . . . The value was in the solidification of the Negro community, in our recognition of the possibility that we could work together to build decent lives. But you must see that there was no basic change. . . . I had invested so much of myself in the fight that I didn't want to admit that it came to so little."[20] It was this kind of dismay, this doubt over whether the lives sacrificed (literally and figuratively) had been worth the costs, that caused some bridge and formal leaders to raise fundamental questions among African Americans about the long-term potential of the civil rights movement and about the need to reevaluate the movement's leadership strategies and political philosophies.

In "The Civil Rights Movement: What Good Was It?" Walker cautions readers against dismissing the importance of the civil rights movement simply because it has provided African Americans only limited material gains. She accentuates the importance of psychosocial dimensions of the movement that helped to develop a black political consciousness that was justice-seeking. Although the civil rights movement has provided some African Americans with material comforts, and, more importantly, has laid a foundation upon which further progress might be built, it has also fundamentally altered how black people see themselves and their potential in relation to white America. Walker argues that one of the movement's most enduring contributions to black politics is that it has awakened the political consciousness of the black masses. Thus the bridge leadership strategy of consciousness-raising that she describes in *Meridian* is for her a metonym for what the movement does for African Americans more generally. She argues that the movement has shown black people that they have a right to become whatever they want to become, to have the opportunity to choose.

Much as Miss Jane's name change from "Ticey" to "Jane" shifts Miss Jane's apprehension of the world in *Miss Pittman*, the civil rights movement, for Walker, "awakens people to the possibilities of life" and this knowledge "is better than unawareness, forgottenness, and hopelessness."[21] With the publication of *Meridian*, which grounds the protagonist in Walker's perception of how the movement affected her own life, Walker further developed the plan for a continuation of the civil rights cause that she first began to sketch in "The Civil Rights Movement: What Good Was It?" She uses *Meridian* to unsettle popular and scholarly accounts of the movement's short-term and long-term goals and to readdress Martin Luther King Jr.'s question, "Where do we go from here?" Resisting the notion that the movement is dead or irrelevant, Walker's 1967 essay marks the beginning of a process of thinking about how the movement's leadership strategies would need to change in the wake of the legal accomplishments gained and the continued deferral of equality.[22]

Critics have dismissed Walker's portrayal of the mutually constitutive relationship between "personal" and "political" transformations. According to Bernard Bell, for example, the book "resounds with personal self-indulgence," and "Walker does not describe the revolutionary role of the working class in contemporary society."[23] Walker, however, shows bridge leadership as raising people's awareness of both the personal and the political stakes of the civil rights movement, and Meridian's personal and political awareness as developing in tandem with the movement. Bell's conclusion that the novel's explorations of personal life somehow detract or are unrelated to its political concerns disregards the feminist concept that the personal is political and vice versa. As feminist historiographers of the civil rights movement have explained, the movement challenged societal expectations and norms for black women.

In "The Civil Rights Movement: What Good Was It?" Walker thus describes how the movement transformed her own consciousness, acknowledging that "because of the Movement, because of an awakened faith in the newness and imagination of the human spirit . . . because of the beatings, the arrests, the hell of battle during the past years, I have fought harder for my life and for a chance to be myself, to be something more than a shadow or a number, than I had ever done in my life."[24] Walker's autobiographical revelation contextualizes her choice to situate Meridian's rise to consciousness at a juncture when her early marriage is dissolving, she cannot bond with the child whose arrival forced her to marry and drop out of school, and she sees that white racists have bombed the site of the voter registration drive. At that critical moment, she realizes that, like Walker, she does not want to be "a shadow or a number," that she will not let social norms limit the contributions she can make. Bell's conclusion that "the civil rights movement . . . provided a means of spiritual and moral redemption from a guilty past for individuals like Meridian, not a radical new social order in which all could realize their potential," seems to ignore the many ways that *Meridian*, like Walker's essay "The Civil Rights Movement," challenges this reading by weaving personal and political concerns together and by suggesting that a new social order must complicate the very concepts of "revolutionary politics" and "radicalism" in light of the movement's decline in the late 1960s and early 1970s.[25]

If Meridian's bridge activities of canvassing neighborhoods to assess people's needs, registering them to vote, and promoting literacy do not exemplify a form of leadership that compels African Americans to "realize their potential," it is unclear what would. Madhu Dubey's conclusion that "the novel envisions political change as a continuous process" better apprehends not only what occurs in Meridian herself but also what occurs as other black people, who are initially sometimes reluctant, become committed to the struggle for political rights—a struggle that requires the ongoing involvement of the entire community, not just formal leaders.[26]

Shifting the Foundation: Bridge Leadership and Phase Two of the Civil Rights Movement

While Walker epigraphically inscribes the names of thirteen civil rights activists and leaders at the beginning of chapter 2 to remember and honor well-known and less well-known civil rights icons, her engagement with historical civil rights activists, organizations, and philosophies remains largely allusive. The book's title and the protagonist's name, for example, are that of the town in Mississippi where Student Non-Violent Coordinating Committee (SNCC) workers James Chaney, Michael Schwerner, and Andrew Goodman disappeared in 1964. A sense of loss permeates *Meridian*, as Melissa Walker has noted: "Knowing that *Meridian* is about civil rights activists, readers might expect it to be about their contributions to the movement, but in fact this novel is more about what was lost than what was gained."[27] While Walker wants to pay homage to these slain civil rights activists, she also wants readers to think critically and energetically about how focusing on the losses reshapes conceptualizations of the gains. Rather than engaging these people, and other events, places, and organizations, merely to record history, Walker follows Gaines's lead in *Miss Pittman*, using the referents as discursive points of departure to defamiliarize normative understandings of civil rights, civil rights leadership, and civil rights historiography.

Walker's indirect allusion to SNCC rather than the Southern Christian Leadership Council (SCLC) is in keeping with her exploration of the strategies of community organizing and participatory democracy that SNCC introduced, strategies that challenged the notion of the sole leader that pervaded so much of African American politics. Consequently, I focus here more on SNCC's approach to activism and leadership as it reveals Walker's engagement with the civil rights movement than on the interracial conflict between Lynne and Meridian, or Truman and Lynne, as they work together in the text's SNCC.[28] While both SNCC and the SCLC had hierarchies that contributed to the suppression of women, SNCC's basic philosophy of leadership and empowerment reflects the type of community activism that Walker suggests is necessary to sustain civil rights gains.

In a provocative analysis of Walker's deployment of SNCC as a trope in *Meridian*, Roberta Hendrickson argues that Walker models Meridian on activist Ruby Doris Smith, who "was the only woman to hold one of the two top leadership positions in SNCC, and [is] remembered by women who were in SNCC as one of the first to raise the issue of women's equality within the organization."[29] Although Elliott Butler Evans has suggested that Meridian's feminist consciousness and her commitment to the black freedom struggle are mutually exclusive, Meridian, like Smith, combines the two in her desire to improve black lives.[30] Like Smith, Meridian also willingly calls into question how the movement intentionally and unintentionally ignores cross-cutting issues and sub-ordinates black women's political concerns.

Thus Lauren Berlant seems unpersuasive in suggesting that while *Meridian* "is critical of the sexism within the civil rights movement" it "subordinates the struggle within gender to the larger questions raised by the imminent exhaustion or depletion of the movement itself."[31] The exhaustion or depletion of the movement does play a significant role in the novel, but Walker actually connects it to gender politics. *Meridian* foregrounds gender by focusing on how bridge leadership exhausts black *women*. Recall that Ruby Smith died at age twenty-five and that her death is often attributed to the exacting work she did while she was in SNCC.

Susan Danielson has suggested that *Meridian* shows how sexism, by circumscribing women's participation, made the movement's vision of civil rights less expansive than it could have been: "By reflecting the personal core of the Movement away from public view of demonstrations, sit-ins, and marches, onto the personal lives of its participants, Walker deepens our comprehension of what the Movement actually was and broadens women's discontentment into a feminist interpretation of social events. Sexism, Alice Walker implies, permeated the already complex issues of race and class."[32] Danielson presents Meridian as representative of women's "grass-roots activist" and "nurturer" roles in SNCC and reflects a critical tendency to link the two roles, but Walker makes this link a problematic one.

Meridian notably rejects motherhood, giving her child away to relatives and choosing to get an abortion when she becomes pregnant again. Her perception is that it consigns women's concerns and influence to the private sphere and implicitly leaves the public sphere and politics to men. For Barbara Christian, however, "within the Civil Rights Movement, she [Meridian] is able to probe the meaning of motherhood, not solely in a biological context, but in terms of justice and love";[33] Meridian's work within communities, which includes actions that ultimately save the lives of children, shows that black women's contributions to social justice can extend beyond what are ordinarily considered the activities of nurturing to achieve the ends of nurturing on a larger scale.

Walker invokes SNCC's leadership strategies and civil rights philosophy because the organization's less hierarchical structure and desire to empower individuals challenged the hierarchical leadership models that were characteristic of the SCLC. Civil rights movement historians have illuminated women's successes as activists and leaders in the movement and specific organizations, despite infrastructures that tried to suppress their voices or to call their work something other than leadership. Yet some organizations were more invested in notions of patriarchal leadership than others. As the historians Anne Standley and Belinda Robnett have revealed, the SCLC was predicated on a gender hierarchy that affirmed the notion that men were the best and ideal (formal) leaders.[34]

Although this notion persisted throughout the movement, activist and leader Ella Baker challenged it on several occasions, most vocally when the SCLC wanted to become the governing body of SNCC. She believed that her gender should not circumscribe the roles she occupied and that organizations focused on the leadership of one man failed to equip constituents with the skills they needed to become empowered. In the early 1970s, reflecting on her career, she remarked, "My basic sense of it has always been to get people to understand that in the long run they themselves are the only protection they have against violence or injustice"—a view very similar to the one that fuels Meridian's activism.[35] Accordingly, Baker spent much of her time working to empower individuals who could then carry on the work that she had started. Not only did she reject the SCLC's model of hierarchical leadership, but she refused be a leader of SNCC once the SCLC had taken control of it. Baker writes, "I had no ambition to be in leadership. I was only interested in seeing that a leadership had a chance to develop. . . . My theory is strong people don't need strong leaders."[36] Civil rights, then, for Baker, were not something that only the government held the responsibility of conferring, and black people were not passive recipients awaiting the gains that formal leaders demanded.

Baker's desire to keep SNCC from replicating the hierarchy that existed in organizations such as the SCLC might more generally be read as a call to destabilize the hierarchy that the formal leadership of exodus politics creates and reinforces. This type of leadership gives formal leaders too much power and fosters a sense of political impotence among constituents. In contrast, organizations that stress more egalitarian forms of leadership, such as participatory democracy, refuse to confer too much power on any one person and instead work to form communities that can function in the absence of a specific formal leader. SNCC's eventual expulsion of white people from its organization troubles its status as an exemplary organization for civil rights leadership or for a more expansive notion of civil rights and antiracist politics, but its emphasis on participatory democracy provides an alternative to exodus politics that remains important today even though the organization itself has splintered and disintegrated.[37]

As sociologist Carol Mueller theorizes, participatory democracy consists of three elements, each of which helps to undermine the paradoxes of exodus politics. She writes that "in the 1960s, a complex set of ideas coalesced under the label 'participatory democracy,' bringing together in a new formulation the traditional appeal of democracy with an innovative tie to broader participation. The emphasis on participation had many implications, but three have been primary: (1) an appeal for grassroots involvement of people throughout society in the decisions that control their lives; (2) the minimization of hierarchy and the associated emphasis on expertise and professionalism as a basis for leadership; and (3) a call for direct action as an answer to fear, alienation, and intellectual detachment."[38] By involving would-be movement participants in decisions that directly affect their lives, leaders in the tradition of participatory democracy not only compel constituents to claim ownership of the movement but also foster an environment in which several people have the knowledge and skills to effectively organize and lead a movement. Further, participatory democracy's "emphasis on expertise" as a basis for leadership diminishes the tendency, which *Miss Pittman* chronicles, to treat men as a priori leaders by virtue of their gender and to select only men to groom for formal leadership positions.

Walker not only foregrounds the centrality of SNCC's civil rights leadership and influence in southern rural towns but also frames participatory democracy as indispensable to Meridian's bridge leadership once she returns to Chicokema. This emphasis provides an effective contrast to the exodus politics that has contributed to the movement's decline by not only ignoring the important role of black women in leading and sustaining these struggles but also failing to empower their constituents in ways that would make them less dependent on leaders. Exodus politics, as *Meridian* characterizes it, cannot provide a long-term vision for maintaining the gains achieved.

Strategies of community empowerment were especially important for SNCC because it targeted areas in the Deep South that other organizations, including the National Association for the Advancement of Colored People (NAACP), effectively ignored. Even with the mass media, these regions were disconnected from the rest of the movement in cities such as Birmingham, Selma, and Atlanta. Consequently, bridge leaders in these locations were not just liaisons between formal leaders and the masses: they were the movement itself. The SNCC model of civil rights activism that *Meridian* portrays positions leadership primarily in the framework of bridge leaders' responsibilities for closing the gap between local communities and the broader movement. The text models how bridge leadership functions by emphasizing the processes bridge leaders use to raise consciousness: discuss with people the benefits and disadvantages of getting involved in the movement, demonstrate how communal involvement would improve their lives, and ensure that community members remain involved and connected.

Walker's larger concern is that communities continue the civil rights movement's transition into phase two rather than focus on phase one as the movement's be-all and end-all. As Walker emphasizes, if African Americans frame the movement's goal solely in terms of securing legal rights, they will ignore its related goal of ensuring that legal changes produce substantive material gains. Although Walker values the contributions that activists made to the movement, she remains concerned about the movement's longevity; for her, the legislative achievements of the 1960s must be seen as the *beginning* and not the *fulfillment* of the quest for civil rights.

Voting Rights and Civil Rights

Walker grounds Meridian's bridge leadership in the context of registering people to vote in order to argue for the necessity of voting, expose its limitations as a tool for civil rights attainment, and illuminate how the issue of voting bridges the different phases of the movement. Meridian's voter registration efforts in the 1970s are an extension of the Voter Education Project of the 1960s. In *Meridian*, however, voting, though necessary for political empowerment, is not sufficient: securing the vote is an important step in attaining civil rights (the right to vote is a civil right), but the possession of this right does not in and of itself suddenly guarantee increased access to economic and political institutions. Voting does allow for the possibility of enacting changes within the political system that can increase access to economic and political opportunities. Walker disrupts the notion that the legislative achievements of the 1960s were the essence of the civil rights movement, while simultaneously capturing how those achievements have helped bridge leaders encourage voter education and mobilization as important tools for continued civil rights agitation.

The Voting Rights Act of 1965 allowed the number of African Americans registered to vote to skyrocket. Increases in voter registration from 19.3 percent to 61.3 percent in Alabama, 6.7 percent to 66.5 percent in Mississippi, and 27.4 percent to 60.4 percent in Georgia did significantly alter black politics and black people's ability to shape American politics and public policy.[39] Voting rights could not, however, immediately give African Americans equal access to America's institutions or correct the effects that a long-standing history of discrimination had produced. The deep roots of inequality required more than the right to vote to achieve systemic transformation. The increased black participation in elections did, however, create an influx of local, state, and federal black legislators. Black communities believed that these politicians would be instrumental in ensuring an equality of outcome—an expectation that sometimes problematically transferred political power from the electorate to the elected and from bridge leaders and activists to formal leaders.

The disagreement that emerges between Meridian and Truman on the subject of voting echoes, in some respects, the disagreements among civil rights leaders during the Voter Education Project about the efficacy of voting as a tool for obtaining civil rights. The Voter Education Project began as an attempt by Attorney General Robert Kennedy to shift civil rights activists' focus away from nonviolent direct actions like the Freedom Rides, which had publicized the white racism and violence in southern towns and forced the federal government to display its authority by protecting participants, and to direct it instead toward the less controversial project of voter registration. Kennedy secured funding for the project from several nonprofit foundations so that SNCC, the SCLC, CORE (Congress of Racial Equality), and other civil rights organizations could register voters in rural southern counties. He thought that the project would increase black voters' knowledge about the political process, ensure that the Democratic Party received the "black vote," and allow the administration to safely affirm its commitment to civil rights while not aggravating segregationists. By framing support of the project as a "strategy of appeasement"—as one that would not fundamentally alter the status quo and would in fact aggravate segregationists—Kennedy suggested that voting, in and of itself, would not necessarily overturn institutional discrimination. Although civil rights leaders understood Kennedy's support as "lukewarm" and viewed him as intending to "forestall just the sort of intensified activism that Freedom Rider veterans intended to maintain," the money did provide activists with the financial resources they needed to fund long-standing initiatives that otherwise would have languished.[40] More to the point, the critics of the project underestimated, as did Kennedy, just how the right to vote could empower African American communities. White communities that obstructed African Americans from registering to vote, or evicted African Americans from their lands for doing so, understood the potential for African American votes to upset the hierarchy on which whites' arbitrary power depended. For example, civil rights activist Fannie Lou Hamer recalled being evicted from the plantation where she had lived for eighteen years simply because she had registered to vote.[41] The fictional Miss Jane faces a similar threat from Robert Samson for participating in a demonstration. Such historical and fictive incidents exemplify why leaders such as Forman embraced the opportunity to expand voter registration.

Recognizing that voting as a tool for political change was both powerful, materially and symbolically, and insufficient to achieve radical transformation, SNCC treated voter registration much as Meridian does later in the novel, as a crucial opportunity to teach African Americans about the larger political system. In educating people about the right to vote and registering them to vote, SNCC voter registrars used their bridge leadership skills not only to connect adherents to the larger movement for civil rights but also to perform needs assessments and develop community-specific initiatives. Of the methods they used, Steigerwald reports: "They considered themselves guerillas whose job was to move into a community, learn its particular needs, and teach people how to stand up for themselves. To fit into the communities they served demanded sensitivity to local customs and conditions. Knowing that good guerillas always identify with the people, they adopted the traditional dress of sharecroppers, bib overalls and t-shirts. Theoretically, when SNCC members moved on, they would leave behind viable, self-governing organizations of people who could work for their own interests in their own way."[42] Their leadership in the Voter Education Project frustrated the paradoxes of exodus politics by building self-sufficient communities that had indigenous leaders who could sustain their own freedom struggles following SNCC's departure. In underscoring the idea that neither one moment nor one person could obtain civil rights, SNCC emphasized the need to establish a network of leadership: if the initial accomplishments of the movement's earlier phases were to be sustained, communities, led by "ordinary" people, would hold the responsibility for pressuring the power structures to confer their rights. In the stead of Ella Baker, Meridian returns to Chicokema to develop these types of politically conscious, self-empowered communities.

Walker's engagement with the Voter Education Project not only reflects an ongoing dispute among African Americans about the efficacy of voting rights campaigns but also questions, more fundamentally, what "revolutionary" politics are. What is at stake for Walker is not whether voting will change the status quo—Meridian's insistence on registering people to vote seems to suggest that it will. Rather, what is at stake is that black people can exercise this political right to shape their future. Through its invocation of the Voter Education Project, *Meridian* not only asks what—in addition to voting rights—might secure civil rights equality for African Americans but also imagines how voting rights specifically could contribute to that end. Both of these issues haunt Truman and Meridian as they attempt to register voters or persuade registrants to vote.

Walker juxtaposes Meridian's clear sense of the potential of voting for achieving institutional changes against some registrants' skepticism to demonstrate how bridge leaders must raise basic levels of political consciousness to tie would-be participants to the movement's goals. During one of their voter registration initiatives, Meridian and Truman visit a family where a woman identified only as Johnny's wife and Johnny Junior's mother is dying. After engaging in casual conversation, Meridian says, "We just came by to ask if you all want to register to vote" (224). Before Meridian and Truman leave, the elder Johnny asks, "What good is the vote, if we don't own nothing?" (224).

Like Booker T. Washington, the husband places the acquisition of property before the acquisition of voting rights; he questions whether voting can better his life in a tangible way and get him anything more than "a lot of trouble." When Meridian suggests voting could bring access to better medical care, jobs, and schools, Truman interjects, "Voting probably won't get it, not in your lifetime," a cynical comment that may reflect his understanding of how slow the movement's progress toward equality is or perhaps the broader idea that voting will not transform black people's material realities (225).

Meridian disagrees with Truman's cynicism, arguing that if black people do not stake their political claims by using the right to vote, any potential for transformation vanishes altogether: "I don't know. It may be useless. Or maybe it can be the beginning of the use of your voice. You have to get used to using your voice, you know. You start on simple things and move on" (225). Although voting may not be sufficient, it certainly is necessary. Yet Johnny initially counters this reasoning, asserting, "No. I don't have time for foolishness. My wife is dying. My boy don't have shoes. Go somewhere else and find somebody that ain't got to work all the time for pennies, like I do" (226).

The grim circumstances of Johnny's life render him unable to imagine how voting might improve his and his family's life chances and opportunities. Yet his ultimate decision, following his wife's death, is to indicate that he "WILL BE BRAVE ENOUGH TO VOTE" (226). This declaration suggests that Meridian (and Truman?) have raised Johnny's consciousness and that he is at least willing to test the political process. Meridian's bridge leadership—her willingness to "teach people"—has helped transform him into an active participant in the long civil rights movement, willingly fighting to secure his rights.

Johnny represents many African Americans in the wake of the Voting Rights Act who were too ground down by poverty to believe in the promises about what political activism could achieve. Walker also portrays another group who are reluctant to exercise their right to vote: those who do not believe the political act of voting is radical enough. She tells the story of one community that has suffered from their city's refusal to integrate public facilities. Rather than integrate a public swimming pool, the city shuts it down, so that the black neighborhood's children have no place to cool off in the hot weather except for a long ditch that fills when it rains, "which the residents of the area called, with impotent bitterness, 'the pool'" (208). The community warns children not to play there because "the water in the pool could rise silently as a thief and cover the head of a three-year-old" and because few children have ever had the opportunity to learn to swim (208). The neighborhood that Meridian visits is prone to flooding (rather like pre-Katrina New Orleans), which is "especially bad in the spring and fall because the heaviest rains came then," and when the city builds "a huge reservoir very near the lower-lying black neighborhood," the flooding only gets worse: "When the reservoir rose from the incessant rains, the excess was allowed to drain off in any direction it would. Since this was done without warning, the disobedient children caught wading in the pool were knocked off their feet and drowned" (208). The same racism that closed the public swimming pool also sites the reservoir that protects white neighborhoods but harms black ones.

This flooding has happened every year, but although the neighborhood's men typically "[stand] about in groups, cursing the mayor and the city commissioner and the board of aldermen" (208), it is not until Meridian, "bearing in her arms the bloated figure of a five-year-old boy who had been stuck in the sewer for two days before he was raked out with a grappling hook," leads the community to the mayor's office that the city hears the community's grievances (209). By "plac[ing] the child,

whose body was beginning to decompose, beside his [the mayor's] gavel,"
Meridian sends a clear message to the mayor: he, too, has a responsibility to this black community (209). Meridian thus models behaviors this
community must enact.

As she tells Johnny, they must use their voices (and votes) so that their
elected officials will hear them. She reiterates this point when the community attempts to thank her with a variety of gifts: "She made them
promise they would learn, as their smallest resistance to the murder of
their children, to use their vote" (209). The narrator uses the term *learn*
to underscore that voter education can be a process, one in which voters
gradually come to understand the significance of voting. Moreover, her
characterization of voting as the "smallest resistance" does not detract
from the effectiveness of voting as a political empowerment strategy;
instead, it emphasizes her larger claim that voting is only a part of what
they will need to do in order to become fully enfranchised. Meridian suggests that holding the officials whom they elect accountable for ensuring
that their community is not neglected is as important as participating in
the electoral process.

When Meridian instructs the members of the community to vote,
the text relates, "At first the people laughed nervously. 'But that's nothing,' these people said, who had done nothing before beyond complain-
ing among themselves and continually weeping. 'People will laugh at
us because that's not radical,' they said, choosing to believe radicalism would grow over their souls, like a bright armor, overnight" (209).
Ironically, their objection actually confirms her point: voting, in and of
itself, is not "radical." At the same time, by mocking their notion that
radicalism "would grow over their souls . . . overnight," the text suggests that through voting one begins to acquire the potential to change
whatever shortcomings a system has. Later, readers learn that "Meridian
sat, watching the workmen from the city begin to clear debris from the
ditch, preparatory to filling it in (yes, the voters had won this small, vital
service)" (235): a testimony to the potential political power of exercising
the right to vote responsibly.

For Keith Byerman, Walker's novel, despite its affirmation of the continuing significance of voting in black freedom struggles, reveals that
for people like Johnny, "civil rights as an ideology and a movement is
largely irrelevant. As Truman and Meridian admit in their recruiting
visits, voting will have little immediate impact or direct impact on individual lives. The people who sign up do so largely out of gratitude for the
kindness and attention of the civil rights workers rather than because

they have any belief in the efficacy of the political system."[43] Byerman's conclusion here, much like his conclusion that the narrative of *Miss Pittman* does not adequately prepare the reader for Miss Jane's final (and, for him, only) act of leadership, draws upon normative conceptualizations of the civil rights movement that limit its scope to phase one's goal.

Meridian's and Truman's acts of kindness while canvassing may indeed make the potential voters more amenable to registering, but Walker also suggests that voter education, while perhaps not providing immediate results, teaches community members that voting can effect positive change. *Meridian* thus demythologizes the civil rights movement, while showing how the movement's role can change in light of legislative gains. While the book reveals "anxieties for the future in the mid-1970s, when the spirit of the movement seems to have visibly eroded and most activists and many ordinary folk are floundering," it simultaneously offers models for communities to move forward, having generated and sustained their own leaders.[44] Walker compels readers to think more robustly about definitions of civil rights and expectations for civil rights leaders in order to better understand the complexity of the civil rights movement.

Meridian undermines exodus politics both by foregrounding women's bridge leadership during the civil rights movement and by showing its necessary role in effecting the movement's transition from phase one to phase two. Yet Walker warns that bridge leaders, too, must reject the messianic complex and recognize their finite abilities as human beings. Resisting notions of what Michele Wallace would call the myth of the superwoman, Meridian balances the demands of bridge leadership and her commitment to eradicating injustice against the physical toll that this type of work exacts on her body and mind.[45] Her attitude toward civil rights work transforms as she moves from "volunteering to suffer" (at her return) to believing that "all saints should walk away" (when she exits). No one person—man or woman—can bear the responsibility for empowering a community.

Walker thus posits that Meridian's epiphany about her relationship to the movement rests not only on her understanding of how exodus politics has affected African American communities' understanding of politics but also on her understanding of how exodus politics has harmed her as an individual. Her mysterious illness that causes her to lose her hair and have bouts of paralysis allow the reader, as Susan Willis argues, "to experience the absolute energy-draining work of political praxis, as with each demonstration Meridian must struggle to regain her vanquished strength, patiently forcing her paralyzed limbs to work again."[46] Only by renouncing the messiah complex can Meridian overcome the paralysis that would otherwise portend her death.

Meridian's final assertion is that both men and women must avoid the messiah complex by resisting the temptation to overextend themselves in black freedom struggles. She argues that the messiah complex, which reflects gender norms and expectations, differs for male formal leaders and female bridge leaders. Nonetheless, in both cases, it demands the leaders' deaths: whereas men's martyrdom results from murder or assassination, women's martyrdom results from "working to death." Neither is viable for African American leadership, as Meridian herself reflects: "'The only new thing now,' she said to herself, mumbling aloud so that people turned to stare at her, 'would be the refusal of Christ to accept crucifixion. King,' she said, turning down a muddy lane, 'should have refused. Malcolm, too, should have refused. All those characters in those novels that require death to end the book should refuse. All saints should walk away. Do their bit, then—just walk away. See Europe, visit Hawaii, become agronomists or raise Dalmatians.' She didn't care what they did, but they should do it" (162). In a moment of clarity, Meridian realizes that although civil rights work is important, it cannot become so encumbering that one suffers and dies for it. For this reason she walks away at the end of the narrative, returning to Truman a task that remains unfinished both for the community and for him. By rejecting martyrdom and asserting that all saints should walk away, Meridian reinforces the notion that communities should not rely on one leader. Since civil rights struggles often exceed the longevity of one leader's life span, communities that rely on one leader run the risk of "stalling" any progress made as they await another leader to fill this vacant role.

The refusal to accept the "crucifixion," to position oneself as the sacrificial leader, reinforces the idea that communities need indigenous bridge and formal leaders who can sustain the movement in the absence of any one leader. This blatant rejection of exodus politics reinforces the critique that runs throughout the text, thus threading together a broader engagement with civil rights issues. As Walker herself suggested in an interview, Meridian's observation also elucidates the shortcomings of ideas of martyrdom in Christianity more broadly:

> It's just that in addition to all of her other struggles, her struggle is not to die. That's what she means when she's talking about martyrs

not permitting themselves to be martyrs, but at some point just
before martyrdom they should just go away and do something else.
    She talks about Malcolm and King going off to farm or raise
Dalmations or doing something else other than permitting martyrdom. This impulse to flee represents her struggle to break with
Christianity because Christianity really insists on martyrdom. She
can see that the life of Christ is exemplary. It truly is. It's a fine life.
But just before the crucifixion, according to Meridian, Jesus should
have just left town.[47]

Just before what might have become her own "crucifixion," when Meridian might have succumbed to physical exhaustion, the toll that bridge
leadership had taken on her body, she walks away.
    Meridian's decision to walk away, to reject exodus politics' champion-
ing of self-sacrifice, anticipates Kate Ruskin's "Bridge Poem" (1981). The
poem's speaker recounts the stresses of being the "bridge"—the connecting point for the various people who place demands on her personhood.
The persona's opening declaration,

> I've had enough
> I'm sick of seeing and touching
> Both sides of things
> Sick of being the damn bridge for everybody[48]

echoes Meridian's breakdown, her bodily response to the difficulties of
being a sole bridge leader. Not only does she lack support from other
bridge leaders, but she has yet to develop a critical mass of potential
bridge leaders within the community she tries to build. While Meridian
understands the importance of her task, what the poem calls "mediating
with your worst self / On behalf of your better selves" to raise consciousness about the importance of civil rights and to cultivate indigenous
communal leadership, she simultaneously realizes that this task will
ultimately exact the price of her life.[49] Her departure then, acknowledges
a recognition like that of the speaker in the poem:

> The bridge I must be
> Is the bridge to my own power
> I must translate
> My own fears
> Mediate
> My own weaknesses
> I must be the bridge to nowhere

But my true self
and then
I will be useful.[50]

Neither Meridian nor the poem's speaker expresses resignation or withdrawal from the community. Neither suggests that the individual is more important than her community. Rather, both proffer the idea that the self is as important as the community, that there are limitations to being a "bridge," and that the recognition of these limitations proves useful in terms of sustaining both healthy individuals and vibrant communities. If Meridian's body initially served as a bridge, her refusal to stay locked in that position—to have her back be a bridge—underscores the evolution in consciousness that civil rights leaders themselves experience.

Meridian suggests that the civil rights leader must refuse to accept "crucifixion," while the community simultaneously must refuse to "crucify" the leader. That Truman moves into her physical space when Meridian leaves suggests he will assume the role Meridian has held. The ending implies that Truman's transformation has just begun, that he has finally grasped how the movement matters and will assume his role as a bridge leader. Truman, who during the 1960s seemed just as uninterested with actually doing the work of registering voters as he is when he and Meridian first reunite, no longer seems disillusioned by a narrow vision of the civil rights movement's goals and leadership strategies.

At the end of the book, readers are left to imagine how Truman will lead now that he is no longer invested in exodus politics. Meridian's exemplary leadership has helped him to establish "contact with [potential registrants] . . . on their own terms" and has helped him to see participatory democracy as an important process in phase two of the civil rights movement.[51] Having done her part, Meridian walks away, thereby allowing Truman to do his.

Truman's transformation challenges the gender norms and expectations that surround male leadership and activism in the movement. But if *Meridian* provides an optimistic view of black men and women working together as bridge leaders to increase African Americans' civil rights, *Corregidora* suggests, as I argue in chapter 3, that the ubiquity of black male privilege in civil rights and leadership discourses makes such a cooperative relationship difficult. *Corregidora* places black women's rights at the center of black civil rights discussions to contest the heteronormative and masculinist tropes that permeate civil rights and leadership discourses. This decentering of the normative black subject in civil rights discourses does not always sit well with black communities that are deeply invested in black heteropatriarchy. *Corregidora* further demonstrates how such a shift in perspective might benefit black political organization and activity.

3 / "The Important Thing Is Making Generations": Reproduction and Blues Performance as Forms of Civil Rights Leadership in Gayl Jones's *Corregidora*

People pay for what they do, and, still more, for what they have allowed
themselves to become. And they pay for it very simply: by the lives they
lead.

—JAMES BALDWIN, *NO NAME IN THE STREET*

Gayl Jones's first novel *Corregidora* (1975), like Gaines's *Miss Pittman* and Walker's *Meridian*, provides a fruitful discursive space to call into question the tendency of exodus politics to idealize black male formal leadership and conceptualize civil rights as separate from black women's gender and sexual rights. Whereas *Miss Pittman* and *Meridian* complicate how the politics of gender and sexuality masculinize civil rights leadership, *Corregidora* emphasizes how they reproduce discourses that privilege the enfranchisement of normative black subjects, and shows that the suppression of black women's sexuality and the violation and exploitation of their bodies are civil rights issues that, when not conceptualized as such, undermine the civil rights and Black Power movements' goals of empowering all black people. While *Miss Pittman* and *Meridian* foreground racial struggles that typically are thought of as "civil rights," this historical referent is primarily implicit in *Corregidora*. Yet the long civil rights movement remains integral to Jones's examination of black people's enfranchisement in relation to black women's gender and sexual rights.

Corregidora, like many works that black women writers produced during the early 1970s, elucidates the paradoxical nature of civil rights and black power struggles that, while purporting to liberate all black people, do not champion the empowerment of black women and black gays and lesbians and ignore the cross-cutting political issues of black communities.[1] As the civil rights historian Jacquelyn Dowd Hall has suggested in her examination of black women's prominent roles in the 1963 March on Washington for "jobs and freedom," black women's participation not only asserted their equality to men but, by also "helping to link race, class, gender, thus foreshadow[ed] both black feminism and the expansive movements that civil rights struggles set in motion."[2] Although Hall rightfully points out that the civil rights movement energized other freedom movements, the civil rights struggle itself foregrounded gender and sexuality alongside race. It did so, however, to restore the black heterosexual middle-class man, the normative black subject, to his putatively rightful position in the body politic and the black family. *Corregidora*, according to Toni Morrison, who at that time was the book's editor at Random House, "changed the terms, the definitions of the whole enterprise" by weaving together women's rights, civil rights, and Black Power discourses in unprecedented ways.[3]

While *Miss Pittman* and *Meridian* elucidate how women and men might work as bridge leaders to empower black communities, *Corregidora* takes a decidedly different approach, emphasizing the need for black women themselves to collaborate as bridge leaders to resist patriarchal oppression. Jones's historical framing, extending from the late 1800s under Brazilian slavery to the late 1960s in civil rights / Black Power Kentucky, situates *Corregidora*'s discussion of civil rights within a long civil rights history. Jones thereby interrogates not only what Calvin Hernton refers to as the "sexualization of racism," which began under slavery, but also the "racialization of sexism" that subtends the contemporary moment.[4] Analogizing the white slave owner and breeder, Old Man Corregidora, to the contemporary black men in the text, Jones characterizes patriarchy as a persistent threat to women, debunking any notion that black men's political agendas necessarily benefit or consider the interests of black women. As *Corregidora*'s plot develops against the backdrop of the long civil rights and Black Power movements, it invokes ideologies central to each movement to call into question the masculinist and heteronormative logics that exodus politics perpetuates by excluding or otherwise disconnecting feminist concerns, problems, and issues from black people's struggles for civil rights. It simultaneously troubles the related tendency to foreground patriarchal formal leadership as necessary for civil rights attainment.

Corregidora further engages the politics of race, gender, and sexuality by examining the implications of black women's exclusion from the women's rights movement that is also expanding under second-wave feminism. Black women's omission from much of second-wave feminist theory led black women to articulate how their intersecting experiences of race, gender, class, and sexuality complicated the monolithic category of "woman" that second-wave white feminist theory was deploying. As Elizabeth Spelman adeptly demonstrates in *Inessential Women: Problems of Exclusion in Feminist Thought* (1988), second-wave feminist theory, while purporting to articulate the interests of a universal woman, articulated concerns that were specific to white middle-class women. This triple exclusion of black women from the theorizations of three of the major "liberation" movements of the 1960s—the civil rights movement, the Black Power movement, and the white women's rights movement—compelled black women to theorize an emancipatory politic that included their political concerns and interests.

Corregidora uses the discursive category of black women's rights to show that exodus politics' emphasis on male formal leadership and failure to conceptualize civil rights intersectionally undercut its power as a useful strategy for political enfranchisement because exodus politics does not adequately foreground cross-cutting issues or consider the political interests of non-normative black subjects. Jones uses the tropes of reproduction and black women's blues to make a related argument about leadership and civil rights. First, Great Gram's command to "make generations" in order to pass down testimony of her rape and enforced prostitution on a Brazilian coffee plantation during the time of legal slavery functions as a form of bridge leadership that makes black women's ability to control their reproductive rights central to their historical and contemporary quests for civil rights. While critics including Katherine Boutry and Stephanie Athey argue that the command to make generations replicates the oppressive structures that the Corregidora women seek to escape, Madhu Dubey's point that mere replication is not the final product compels further thinking on this matter.[5]

Second, the protagonist's physical inability to make generations after her emergency hysterectomy, but her ability to substitute black women's blues to pass on the testimony and hold the Brazilian government accountable for its crimes against humanity, makes black women's blues a kind of bridge leadership and positions it in a broader history, one in which black blues women have functioned as civil rights leaders for black women's rights specifically and black people's rights more generally. An examination of Ursa's blues performances as instances of bridge leadership not only disrupts the primacy of black men as the ideal civil rights leaders but also troubles definitions of civil rights that disconnect racial rights from gender and sexual rights. My exploration of exodus politics in this chapter consequently addresses the following questions: (1) *What* liberties are to be included in the term *civil rights* when racial discourses implicitly and explicitly invoke the constructs of gender and sexuality to conceptualize "race," or, to put it another way, how can the inclusion of gender, sexual, and economic rights in the term *civil rights* reshape an understanding of its meaning? (2) *Who* will lead the movement, and how can leadership be redefined to include the work both men and women do to mobilize participants? (3) *What* paradigms of leadership—communal or individual—are African Americans employing to direct their efforts?

Reproductive Politics

While the contemporary setting of *Corregidora* is post–World War II Kentucky, the narrative arc covers ninety years of history, beginning in pre-Emancipation Brazil and culminating in the (allegedly) post–civil rights era of the United States in 1969. Ursa Corregidora, the text's protagonist, is the most contemporary witness to the transnational and transgenerational traumas that her foremothers experienced and bears the responsibility of synthesizing these nine decades of politicized familial history. This history has overdetermined the life chances of her foremothers, Gram and Great Gram, and Ursa resists succumbing to their fate. Raped by Old Man Corregidora, a Portuguese slave owner and breeder, both Gram and Great Gram survive Brazilian slavery only to discover that the government has destroyed all "official histories" documenting Brazil's participation in the slave trade. To "record" the past and thereby establish evidence that someday will hold the Brazilian government accountable for its crimes against humanity and violation of black women's civil rights, Great Gram instructs her descendants "to make generations": that is, to have children (daughters) who will bear witness, who will, in effect, become the historical record of and witness to this erased history.

The women of each successive generation not only testify to the Brazilian government's violation of black women's civil rights but, just as important, acknowledge their foremothers' survival through those experiences; Great Gram demands that her descendants (re)produce in order to produce a counternarrative to official Brazilian history. Her directive aims to reclaim the black female body, elevating it from a locus of physical abuse and debasement to a site of sociohistorical memory and personal-political triumph; her very survival and production of offspring testify to Corregidora's inability to obliterate her subjectivity and agency. However, the command ignores the possibility that the body can be destroyed just as easily as the papers were. The very fact that Great Gram herself needs to tell this story ironically demonstrates the vulnerability of black bodies in this system of slavery. As the text emphasizes in its parallels to the modern period, black bodies in the contemporary moment also find themselves susceptible to erasure and censure.

Great Gram never uses the terms *leadership* or *activism* to describe the mission she lays out for her descendants, yet both words aptly characterize the roles she sees the Corregidora women undertaking: as they seek reparations to raise consciousness and empower black women to resist the oppression that they experience in racist patriarchal societies, they are functioning as bridge leaders. While the chances of Ursa becoming enslaved as Great Gram remain slim, contemporary debates about abortion, sterilization, and birth control reveal that black women's sexual autonomy remains embattled. Just as Brazil's Free Womb Law of 1871, and related lawsuits against masters and mistresses, did not entirely emancipate black women from the shackles of enslavement, the civil rights, Black Power, and white women's rights movements did not significantly diminish black women's experiences of oppression in the 1970s.[6] This oppression persisted not only in terms of reproductive choices, which the intersecting discourses on race, class, gender, and sexuality constricted, but also in terms of economic and social options. Gender politics consigned black women to a domestic sphere, thus ignoring, constricting, or otherwise devaluing their contributions to society and politics.

The mission of the Corregidora women, which is predicated on their right to control their bodies and reproductive capabilities, converges with civil rights struggles, which demand equal rights and opportunities *for all*. By emphasizing the mutually constitutive aspects of these two movements, Jones shows that black women must have control over their bodily rights if they also are to be politically empowered. Yet by elucidating precisely how all do not obtain their rights—that is, by clarifying how black women in particular have not controlled their reproductive and bodily rights and the economic values that derive from them—Jones emphasizes the necessity of the imperative to make generations. "Leadership" in *Corregidora* has much to do with the ability to tell stories and speak to larger communities, and not only through words. The ability to speak what lies beneath words is important, and black women's blues underscores this point by speaking the unspeakable. Just as voting in *Meridian* is significant because it provides individuals and communities a way to "speak" to governments and leaders, reproduction and blues performance in *Corregidora* provide ways to speak in a context where the suppression of black women's rights is predicated on silencing black women. Remaining silent only helps maintain oppression.

Although popular opinion and scholarly perspectives have sometimes disconnected reproductive issues from black civil rights issues, law professor Dorothy Roberts has compellingly argued that black women's reproductive rights are central to their civil rights. In her groundbreaking *Killing the Black Body: Race, Reproduction, and the Meaning of Liberty* (1999), she asserts that because public policy and laws that curtail black women's rights are often rooted in intersecting racial, gender, sexual, and class discourses, the entanglement of gender, sexuality, and race makes it impossible to conceptualize black women's civil rights apart from their gender and sexual rights. She makes three points that help clarify the reparative project that Great Gram undertakes in her mission to make generations: first, that "regulating Black women's reproductive decisions has been a central aspect of racial oppression in America"; second, that "the control of Black women's reproduction has shaped the meaning of reproductive liberty in America"; and third, that "we need to consider the meaning of reproductive liberty to take into account its relationship to racial oppression."[7] Roberts traces a long historical trajectory, from slavery's exploitation to 1990s birth control coercion, to demonstrate the interconnectedness of these discourses. Her analysis explores the political repercussions of affirming this relationship as well as the costs of denying it.

Great Gram's notion of reproduction could be seen as problematic in that, as Ursa's second husband Tadpole suggests, slave breeders forced black women to procreate. At the same time, however, black women's control over their own reproductive capacities remains at the heart of Great Gram's imperative, which thus actually constitutes a form of resistance to the forced reproduction that restricts black women's autonomy. While the feminist critic Luce Irigaray's examination of reproductive politics compellingly foregrounds how divisions of labor that exclude women from many economic activities on the grounds of their special reproductive responsibilities contribute to women's oppression, the institution of slavery complicates this matter for black women by collapsing the distinctions between human and capital, private and public spheres, and men and women.[8] As feminist critic and activist Angela Davis clarifies in "Women and Capitalism: Dialectics of Oppression and Liberation," black women's enslaved status made them instrumental both in and as "the production of commodities."[9] This dual status intertwined reproduction with their commodification and helped build a nation that excluded them from citizenship.

Hortense Spillers, concurring with Davis's analysis, further argues that forced labor commodified black women's bodies in terms that valued them *only* as units of exchange. Spillers explains: "Since, in the United States, the market of slavery identified the chief institutional means for maintaining a class of enforced servile labor, it seems sufficient that the biological captive female body locates precisely a moment of converging political and social vectors that mark the flesh as a prime commodity of exchange."[10] Slavery, then, inextricably tied reproductive rights to civil rights, and black women's disenfranchisement, as black queer studies scholars demonstrate, has continued to be predicated on intersecting forces of racial, class, gender, and sexual oppression. This history contextualizes why Great Gram wants to invert the perverse ends to which slavery has used reproduction and instead to deploy it as a means to assert black women's civil rights.

The mission of the Corregidora women "to make generations," to have female children who will attest to the atrocities slave owners committed with the Brazilian government's complicity, diverges from masculinist formulations of reproductive politics in which men dictate the conditions under which black women reproduce. *Corregidora*'s engagement with male-defined reproductive discourses illuminates the more pervasive context in which patriarchy exerts power over black women and robs them of their most "personal" rights. Jones characterizes Ursa in particular, and Great Gram's imperative to make generations more generally, as examples of bridge leadership that use the politics of reproduction to raise a black feminist consciousness. She emphasizes that black women's ability to control their reproductive rights is central to their political enfranchisement and thus complicates the nationalistic desire to consign black women's leadership to reproduction. Rather than reaffirm a long-standing tradition of racial uplift ideology that considered, in the words of historian Kevin Gaines, "the only legitimate realm for black women's activity [to be] their reproductive capacity within patriarchal black families," Jones explores what reproductive politics could mean for black women's civil rights in a historical-political context where reproduction always bears the burden of politics and produces political burdens.[11]

The feminist Adrienne Rich, like Jones, argues that reproduction and women's empowerment are not mutually exclusive, despite patriarchy's attempt, through reproductive politics, to subjugate women. For Rich, reproductive control is only one aspect of a more ubiquitous propensity to discipline women's bodies: it "enables the perpetuation of patriarchal principles which dictate to women when to eat, sleep, exercise, have sex, breast feed, feel pleasure and endure pain."[12] Yet reproduction and motherhood are not disenfranchising in and of themselves; they can take on new forms when women gain control over their bodies and reproduction and experience both without the controlling interference of men. Here Rich is articulating a notion of reproductive agency, control, and assertiveness that situates women as the *primary* decision makers on reproduction and related issues. Walker expresses a similar viewpoint in *Meridian* when she separates the social value ascribed to reproduction and motherhood from the experiences themselves. Jones, like Rich, and like her black contemporaries Alice Walker, Toni Cade Bambara, and political activist Shirley Chisholm, does not see reproduction in and of itself as disempowering for women, but she reveals how the conditions of black disenfranchisement complicate the generic category of "woman" (read as white) that Rich theorizes.

Because of reproduction's vexed politicized history, conceptualizing it as a politically empowering act, as a form of bridge leadership, presents complications. In fact, several critics of *Corregidora* deny the potential of reproduction to be transformative or oppositional; to elucidate the pitfalls of Great Gram's reparative mission, they compare Great Gram's imperative to make generations to black nationalists' call for women to produce male revolutionaries. For example, in "Poisonous Roots and the New World Blues: Rereading Seventies Narration and Nation in Alex Haley and Gayl Jones," Stephanie Athey proposes that Great Gram's mission to make generations mirrors the practices of Corregidora's brothel: "Corregidora used Ursa's ancestors for prostitution and breeding, and Corregidora's women, in turn, use black men for breeding purposes so that they have children to pass on their personal history to."[13] Even if Athey rightly contends that Great Gram has internalized some of Corregidora's values, her characterization of Great Gram as a breeder misses important nuances that distinguish the two. Corregidora is a pimp who prostitutes women and compels them to engage in sexual acts for *his* profit. That their consent is irrelevant and unnecessary underscores the magnitude of the power he exerts over their sexuality; Great Gram has not willingly become "his gold piece," earning money herself from the sex work in which she engages. And although Great Gram exerts her will by encouraging her descendants to make generations, none of these women forces men to have sex with her, and there is no systematic, government-sanctioned practice that makes these women profit economically from their sexual encounters. Were the situations as similar as Athey suggests, the Corregidora women would not need to make generations: the system of inequality that necessitates the oppositional strategy would not exist, and the women would not need to demand their rights.

The Politics of Reproduction

In *Wayward Reproductions: Genealogies of Race and Nation in Transatlantic Modern Thought* (2004), feminist critic Alys Weinbaum offers a compelling genealogy of reproduction's deployment as a metaphor and tactic for nation building that illuminates Jones's discourse on reproduction and black female leadership in *Corregidora*. Although philosophers have tried to disentangle reproduction and race, Weinbaum argues that these concepts are bound together. Because racial, imperialist, and nationalist agendas have used reproduction as a tool for subjugation, political thinkers find themselves in a bind when they try to disentangle these concepts or ignore reproduction's politicized uses. She thus offers a "defamiliarized account of how race and reproduction are bound together within transatlantic modernity's central intellectual and political formations" to suggest that the relationship between reproduction and nation building does not always have to be antagonistic, even though historically reproduction has been used to further oppressive ideologies or subjugate women.[14]

Acknowledging reproduction's nonexploitative uses, Weinbaum recuperates the potential for reproduction to function as an empowering, antiracist discourse. She contends that one question her book seeks to explore is "how have thinkers who comprehend the incompatibility of racism and human liberation sought to transcend the race/reproduction bind altogether by rethinking or reappropriating the concept of human reproduction to antiracist ends."[15] Because reproduction always has political implications, even if it is not necessarily used for explicitly political purposes, Weinbaum attempts to uncover how reproductive politics might be used in ways that do not further systems of domination. *Corregidora* offers an example of how reproduction can be conceptualized outside the patriarchal ideas that have circumscribed it as "oppressive." It also explores the complications that arise from such a conceptualization and clarifies the ends to which that notion of reproduction might be used. In other words, Weinbaum underscores the historicity of reproductive politics and thus cautions readers not to collapse Great Gram's and Corregidora's reproductive imperatives.

In *Private Bodies, Public Texts: Race, Gender, and a Cultural Bioethics* (2011), law professor and cultural critic Karla Holloway argues that contemporary debates about women's reproductive rights continue to illuminate how women's rights remain at the center of public, legal, and ethical discourses and thus have political implications. One central question is: "If women's bodies can be associated with rights in which others might have (or claim) legal, if not ethical, interests[,] [i]s a woman's womb a private space? If so, whose?"[16] Holloway's question helpfully brings into focus the legal, ethical, and political dimensions of reproductive discourses, and each of these contexts seems necessary for a full apprehension of reproduction's cultural implications. Holloway's question echoes a question that lies at the heart of Jones's imperative to make generations: For black women to have their civil rights, in what ways must they control their reproductive rights? Weinbaum's and Holloway's studies suggest that reproduction always—however problematically—has political consequences and is entangled in some type of political discourse. Moreover, both studies help break down the division between the public and private spheres that historically has been so central to women's oppression. Their work then raises other important questions, which Jones explores: Where racial oppression coerces reproduction, as is the case under American and Brazilian slaveries, are the consequences of reproduction different from those of uncoerced, chosen reproduction? Under what circumstances can reproduction be a politically empowering act? And what factors cut off that potential?

Madhu Dubey's contention that Jones engages black nationalist ideology to achieve a "complex transformation of these discourses" best approximates Jones's interrogation of reproductive politics in *Corregidora* because Jones does reject black nationalist ideologies that limited black women's contribution to the devalued role of breeder.[17] Like many roles black women held in the civil rights and Black Power movements, this role was not viewed as "leadership" in any way that I am using the term here. Unlike the black female imperative to make generations in *Corregidora*, a masculinist one calls for the production of male offspring who will continue a public revolution and act as the movement's formal leaders. The black women's imperative to make generations, by contrast, engages a dilemma: as feminist critic Shane Verge contends, "one means of strengthening the community and asserting racial pride [two goals of the Black Power movement] entailed racial perpetuation, which was alternatively viewed as the production of new soldiers for the revolution,"[18] but the emphasis on this role can make black women, in the most literal sense, merely conduits for nation building. *Corregidora* questions how, if at all, these at times conflicting ideas can be reconciled.

While black nationalist ideology may have tried to limit black women's roles to reproduction, the necessity of reproduction for nation building means it is integral to this liberation movement. Like Rich's *Of Woman Born*, Great Gram's imperative to make generations demands an examination of how reproduction, without the controlling interference of men, might actually propel the movement forward. Jones portrays a kind of generation making that makes black women's rights central to civil rights and thereby displaces the normative black subject in civil rights discourses. The idea that the womb can function as a site of resistance is not problematic in and of itself. Rather, it becomes problematic when the Corregidora women define their value and worth *solely* in terms of their ability to reproduce.

Madhu Dubey underscores the potential for reproduction to be an oppositional strategy when she explains why the Corregidora women need to control this aspect of their lives: "As a means of making generations, the womb becomes the site of these women's political resistance, and of their definition of themselves and their value. Clearly, for the Corrregidora women to claim the power of their wombs is an important oppositional strategy, for it is precisely this power that Corregidora's peculiar sexual exploitation of them had denied."[19] By repossessing their sexuality, the Corregidora women resist objectification within a sexual economy that values them only as units of production and not as human beings who participate actively in a nation's formation and development. By attributing this desire to the black women, Jones plays with the idea of how a revolutionary movement led by black women and rooted in reproductive politics might differ from movements where men use reproductive politics to control black women's sexuality. She suggests the paradoxes that such a movement might encounter but she brings out the significant ideological differences between Great Gram's reparative and generative project, black nationalist ideology on reproduction, and Corregidora's breeding and sexual exploitation.

Debates surrounding black women's, black men's, and nonblack women's civil rights in the United States during the 1970s clarify Jones's notion that black women's attainment of their civil rights is predicated on their ability to control their bodily and reproductive rights. Although the majority of the plot develops prior to the 1970s, this historical period not only figures significantly in Jones's novel but also facilitates understanding of the many discourses that *Corregidora* engages. In "Reproductive Health, Race, and Technology: Political Fictions and Black Feminist Critiques, 1970s–1990s," Stephanie Athey articulates how *Corregidora* "place[s] issues of sexual and racial politics, including issues of reproductive health, in the historical context of enslavement and its legacy in the twentieth century."[20] By framing these issues in a long historical trajectory, a long civil rights movement, that extends back to chattel slavery, Athey highlights the contradictions developing in the 1970s. Increased access to reproductive *choice* does not necessarily translate into increased access to reproductive *control*.

Although twentieth-century black women had greater reproductive choice and control than their enslaved nineteenth-century foremothers did, they were far from being autonomous. While the landmark *Roe v. Wade* decision gave women the right to have an abortion, that specific right should not be confused with "the ability to regulate one's own reproductive capacity"[21] or thought to apply to nonwhite women in ways that were particularly liberating. This difference between "right" and "ability" is not merely semantic: *Roe v. Wade* theoretically gave all women safer options if they decided to terminate a pregnancy, but the stipulations attached to the abortion rights legislation certainly restricted those choices. Even in the twenty-first century, women's rights to control their own sexuality and reproduction remain central to women's rights and civil rights discourses.[22]

Even after *Roe v. Wade*, class and racial biases ensured that many women, particularly black and poor women, who exercised the newly granted reproductive rights that *Roe v. Wade* afforded found themselves conceding other rights. Athey cites the case of Dr. Clovis Pierce, a South Carolina gynecologist who, in the 1970s, under the excuse of protecting taxpayers' dollars, refused to give welfare recipients abortions unless they agreed to be sterilized. In making this stipulation, Pierce conjured up the stereotype of the sexually irresponsible and otherwise promiscuous black woman, an image that in the 1980s would become the welfare queen, as the *ur*-example of black female sexuality. The result of Dr. Pierce's policy, and many others like it around the country, was that black women had higher rates of sterilization during the 1970s, as indeed they had in previous decades from the Progressive Era onwards. Coerced and forced sterilizations illuminate how far black women were from obtaining their reproductive rights despite the achievement of *Roe v. Wade*.

To some degree, *Roe v. Wade* highlighted the limitations of the legal victory as the state, explicitly and implicitly, continued to exert control over black women's reproductive capacities. In the wider historical framing of *Corregidora*, the case of Dr. Clovis recalls other instances of the historical exploitation of black women's bodies, some of them even in the name of medical advancement. Recall, for example, that it was through Dr. Sims's medical experimental operations on black women without anesthetic that he earned the title "father of gynecology," and that it was the institution of chattel slavery that made these bodies readily available. Because black women were enslaved and the law did not recognize their rights—reproductive or otherwise—Sims did not have to treat black women as "human" subjects. Therefore, he was able to push the limits of modern medicine while ignoring the harm he was inflicting on black women's bodies.[23] Thus black women's sexual exploitation historically has been tied to their reproductive rights.

According to Athey, the opening scene in *Corregidora*, where Ursa reveals that she must have a hysterectomy as a result of her falling/being pushed down the stairs, thrusts Jones into a conversation about black women's history of involuntary sterilization. The text's ambiguity as to whether doctors performed Ursa's emergency hysterectomy unnecessarily opens up "many possible medical, social, and racial lines of interpretation,"[24] and Athey's focus on the historical context of forced sterilization of black women complicates Jones's examination of black women's rights and reproductive politics.

Great Gram's desire to make generations serves a purpose beyond black nationalism's goal of racial perpetuation; it forces readers to reconsider how reproductive rights and gender rights more generally remain integral to civil rights and interrogates the leadership roles these women are expected to and can have in this context. Her imperative is an instance of bridge leadership that raises people's consciousness about the specific ways that black women's rights have been violated, while calling for an end to parallel exploitation in the present. The examination of Great Gram's imperative in this framework makes three important interventions; first, it contests exodus politics' tendency to separate civil rights from gender rights; second, it foregrounds civil rights discourses as always simultaneously articulating and negotiating the intersections of racial, gender, sexual, and class ideologies and conflicts; third, it interrogates the strategies black women have used to lead campaigns that treat civil and women's rights as inseparable.

Raising black women's consciousness—that is, making them aware of their choices and the consequences of enacting them, is central to black feminist discourses on reproduction, as Toni Cade (Bambara) suggests in "The Pill: Genocide or Liberation?" Her essay provides another framework for understanding the bridge leadership of women such as Ursa, Irene, and Great Gram in *Corregidora*. Echoing Rich, Cade argues that "the pill gives control and control is the way to raise revolutionaries, not chance fertilization, chance support, chance tomorrow."[25] Understanding how reproduction and poverty can be related, Cade's admonition to black men against encouraging black women "to fight the Man with the womb" also dissuades black women from producing children for the revolution out of "inbred Messianic impulses."[26] She cautions women against believing that their role in black liberation struggles lies solely in their reproductive capacities—that to save the race they must uncritically and sacrificially assume the role of revolutionary breeder. Cade takes issue with the limiting of black women's roles to reproduction and the notion that black women should have little say (through access to birth control) about the conditions under which they reproduce. She maintains that black women who reproduce children who are impoverished undermine the development of an economically viable and politically empowered community.

Rather than altogether castigate the nationalist impulse to reproduce, both Cade and Jones, however differently, consider the circumstances under which reproduction might indeed be used as a form of civil rights activism. They join the related issues of civil rights, women's rights, and Black Power to challenge the politics of black reproduction in the historical and contemporary contexts in which reproduction remains a racialized politic. The imperative to make generations ultimately calls attention to black women's inability to control their bodies, their reproductive decisions, and the economic values that derive from them, while simultaneously demanding that they be afforded these rights. The institution of chattel slavery, both in the United States and in Brazil, was based on denying black women these two prerogatives, and it capitalized on the profits obtained by violating and controlling their bodies. From American slave owners raping black women and producing children who ultimately were increased units of production, to Brazilian slave owners prostituting black women's sexuality, black women's bodies bear the markers of exploitation and devaluation.

Great Gram's imperative to make generations also turns attention to how, as in *Miss Pittman* and *Meridian*, ordinary people engage in acts of resistance that help gain their civil rights. As I have argued, communities that rely on male formal leadership assume that only the formal leader has the ability and resources to secure their civil rights and thus inhibit community members from acting on their own behalf. While Brazilian slavery ended peacefully, in neither Brazil nor the United States did its end immediately result in the rise of male formal leaders who began to mobilize communities to participate in a developing national movement. Moreover, these movements, even once under way, did not foreground black women's rights of control over their bodies and reproductive capacities as central to black people's civil rights (though some leaders, like Frederick Douglass, did argue for women's rights generally and connect them to civil rights).[27] Therefore, Great Gram is asserting leadership and orchestrating a call to action for black women in a context where their political interests and concerns would not otherwise be recognized. Her imperative is what womanist theologians would call a survival strategy: one of the tactics disenfranchised black women in particular have employed to resist being completely without rights in systems that abrogate their civil rights. Womanist theologians argue that the biblical character Hagar exemplifies a sexually exploited black woman who overcomes her experience of dispossession in the wilderness through her own volitional acts and without the help of men. Delores Williams, for instance, describes how, "like Hagar in her wilderness experiences, black women [have] used resistance strategies to counteract the persecution aimed at them" and points out that "today many black women like Hagar, raising families alone, demonstrate courage and personal ingenuity as they struggle to find resources for survival. . . . These women find ways to augment their income, but they do not depend upon men for this."[28] This narrative undermines the messiah complex that is central to exodus politics, for God does not send a messianic figure to lead the captive out of bondage; rather, the captive herself acts. Survivalist strategies like Great Gram's are acts of the bridge leadership that are essential to empower self-sustaining communities. Although the imperative to make generations has limited reach in that it is restricted to a family of women, its implications extend beyond the familial group, and even within a limited context its purpose remains significant and instructive.

Whatever the limitations of Great Gram's attempt to preserve testimony to slavery's crimes through living beings, the Brazilian government's attempt to erase its complicity in slavery from the historical record feeds her desire to leave physical evidence to correct this willful denial of historical exploitation. She refers to an actual directive that the Brazilian government's minister of finance, Rui Barbosa, gave in 1891 to burn all slave trade documents so that, according to Great Gram, "there wouldn't be no evidence to hold up against them" (14). Brazil had been one of the biggest importers of Africans in the transatlantic slave trade and was the last to abolish slavery (in 1888).

Given Brazil's deep roots in chattel slavery, the decision to write this sordid affair out of its past was an act of malfeasance as reprehensible as the country's centuries of involvement. For Great Gram, making generations, or, as Christina Sharpe and Stelmaris Coser would have it, using the womb as an archive, recuperates the cultural amnesia that the Brazilian government has orchestrated and holds the country account-able.[29] Great Gram's idea that the Brazilian government needs to "pay" for its crimes thus has a double signification: the word encapsulates a moral judgment on the dehumanization of an entire class of human beings and perhaps even an idea that those responsible should answer and suffer consequences for their crimes; it also refers to compensating black women, and, metonymically speaking, other enslaved members of the African diaspora, for their uncompensated (sexual) labor. Consid-ered together, these meanings reaffirm the historical and contemporary urgency for the Corregidora women to make generations as a political and sociocultural corrective.

While in *Miss Pittman* the fictional history teacher notes the absence of women like Miss Jane from the historical record of the civil rights movement, *Corregidora* recounts an even larger-scale erasure of his-tory. In the last decades of the twentieth century and the first decade of the twenty-first century, apologies and reparations for slavery, intern-ment, and genocide abound. Moreover, public discourse continues to debate the legacies of these atrocities for the affected groups' civil rights. In this context, the fictional and actual Brazilian government's action has especially devastating implications, since the historical grand narrative, as the urtext of a nation's events, shapes the histori-cal memory and becomes the record to which the government must answer. By writing slavery out of history, the government effectually renders itself not culpable for the crimes against humanity that it sanc-tioned and not responsible for paying for the civil rights it denied. Nei-ther black women nor any other survivors of slavery would be able to redress their grievances against the Brazilian government because the very crime for which they might sue or seek reparations would not have even "happened."

On June 18, 2009, the U.S. Congress passed a resolution that apologized for and condemned American chattel slavery—something that could never happen in Jones's Brazil because slavery never "occurred." Underscoring the symbolic and material benefits of such an acknowledgment, the resolution stated:

> Whereas millions of Africans and their descendants were enslaved; . . .
> Whereas Africans forced into slavery were brutalized, humiliated, dehumanized, and subjected to the indignity of being stripped of their names and heritage; . . .
> Whereas after emancipation from 246 years of slavery, African Americans soon saw the fleeting political, social, and economic gains they made during Reconstruction eviscerated by virulent racism, lynchings, disenfranchisement, Black Codes, and racial segregation laws that imposed a rigid system of officially sanctioned racial segregation in virtually all areas of life; . . .
> Whereas an apology for centuries of brutal dehumanization and injustices cannot *erase* the past, but confession of the wrongs committed and a formal apology to African Americans will help bind the wounds of the nation that are rooted in slavery and can speed racial healing and reconciliation and help the people of the United States understand the past and honor the history of all people of the United States; . . .
> . . . the Congress— . . .
> . . . apologizes to African Americans on behalf of the people of the United States, for the wrongs committed against them and their ancestors who suffered under slavery and Jim Crow laws.[30]

The use of the term *erasure* here has particularly important implications for *Corregidora*, where the erasure of the historical record of Brazilian slavery compounds the political, epistemological, and physical violence that slavery has already enacted upon black women. Although the U.S. resolution recognizes the limitations of an apology, it argues that the very acknowledgment of America's history of enslavement might begin to "bind the wounds of the nation" and "speed racial healing." The U.S. resolution rules out any potential for monetary compensation by appending a statement that absolves the government from having to address these legacies in a substantive, nonsymbolic way and includes the disclaimer, "Nothing in this resolution authorizes or suggests any *claim* against the United States; or serves as a statement of any claim against the United States."[31]

By appending this disclaimer, the government accepts (and denies?) responsibility for its actions while simultaneously shielding itself from any financial sanctions. Such a context clarifies Great Gram's urgency to ensure that each successive generation will supply a counternarrative in the physical form of a female descendant who will provide the requisite evidence to hold the Brazilian government accountable whenever the judgment comes. The name Corregidora itself, which is the feminine form of the Portuguese *corregidore*, or "judicial magistrate," and comes from the Portuguese verb to "correct," further suggests that these women have the mission, in the words of Melvin Dixon, to "'correct' . . . the historical invisibility they have suffered, 'to give evidence' of their abuse, and 'to make generations' as a defense against their further annihilation."[32] The mission is thus a civil rights mission—one that is both reparative and generative.

Black Women's Blues as Bridge Leadership

After Ursa is forced to undergo a hysterectomy, she experiences the crisis of being no longer able to carry out the mission of "making generations" with which she has been charged, and she turns to her music as a different way of giving evidence. Here Jones not only admits the limitations of reproductive politics but draws attention to another group of leaders—black women blues performers—who specifically conceptualized black women's gender and sexual rights as "civil rights" issues. *Corregidora* thus figures black women's blues as a disruptive force that queers exodus politics' championing of male formal leadership by foregrounding how black women's non-normative bridge leadership advances civil rights struggles. Even as it does so, it raises questions regarding licit and illicit, recuperable and nonrecuperable forms of sexuality in the text. Yet the blues, because of its willingness to deploy sexual tropes unabashedly, becomes an important vehicle through which to examine how racial discourses articulate gender and sexual ideologies. Therefore, when Ursa posits that she will "sing" the way her foremothers have "told" the history of Corregidora, Jones suggests that the blues politic will function as a replacement for reproductive politics.

In this formulation, black women's blues becomes a tool through which black women blues performers, in the capacity of bridge leadership, raise consciousness about black women's gender and sexual rights as these intersect with civil rights. As Cheryl Wall persuasively contends, Ursa's blues performance "inscribes the connection between Ursa's maternal legacy and her own experience. It enacts her determination to make that legacy the subject of her art and to make her art the legacy she will leave instead of the children her ancestors commanded her to bear."[33] By allowing Ursa to make generations through the blues, Jones contextualizes the more general role music had in advancing the civil rights movement and situates Ursa's performances within a broader history of black women's blues performances. She thus illuminates how blues performers and performances function as instances of bridge leadership and activism that emphasize individuals' roles in securing civil rights. Finally, she foregrounds the inextricable relationship between race, class, gender, and sexuality in civil rights struggles that exodus politics ignores. Although several critics have theorized the literary, formal, and social functions that the blues performs in *Corregidora*, few have explicitly considered the roles that black women's blues has played in their struggles for civil rights.[34]

Black blues women have been influential in raising consciousness about the issues this chapter has analyzed, yet civil rights discourses have not conceptualized them as civil rights leaders, and this omission has as much to do with the subjects they interrogate as it does with their subject positions as black women. The exodus politics model of leadership would not consider black blues women to be "civil rights leaders" because their leadership opposes what exodus politics, intentionally and unintentionally, signifies and champions: they resist the patriarchal bias embedded in formal leadership in that much of their songs' content challenges male domination (both personally and politically). These women's propensity to contest normative constructs of gender and sexuality undermines the hierarchies of oppression that appropriations of exodus politics reaffirm.

Civil rights discourses do not consider a figure like Billie Holiday, whose song "Strange Fruit" illuminated the horrors of lynching, to be an activist or leader. Yet because lynching is predicated on the confluence of racial, gender, and sexual discourses, and because lynching sometimes relied on ideas that black people's putatively non-normative gender and sexualities justified the need to control them through this brutal practice, "Strange Fruit" can be read as an antilynching protest song that weds gender and sexual rights to racial civil rights. For this reason, it is a cultural production that can take a place in Erin Chapman's list of "the production of films, the recording of music, the publication of scholarship, the consumption of these and other products, and the formulation of mass politics" as a way that "African Americans themselves participated in racial and sexual discourses forming their world" and "consciously re-created themselves and the racial discourses that shaped their society."[35] While some biographers argue that Holiday was not conscious of the political statement this song was making, it has been consistently invoked as a civil rights call to action.[36] Holiday's performances not only (re)shaped the discourses of race, gender, and sexuality but also expanded the role of music in black freedom struggles.

Ursa's performances build on this tradition of refusing to accept black people's alleged gender and sexual non-normativity as the basis for their disenfranchisement, while reminding readers of the role of music in shaping formal and informal politics. They undermine the tendency to privilege normative black subjects in civil rights discourses and challenge popular and scholarly conceptions of civil rights and civil rights leadership. Linking Brazilian slavery to contemporary experiences of black female oppression, Ursa's songs situate the oppression that her foremothers experienced within a broader discursive call for black women's rights to suggest that black people's enfranchisement is predicated on black women obtaining their civil rights too. As a blues performer, Ursa not only reaches an audience that was uncaptured when the imperative was confined to a reproductive politic but also helps ensure that neither political institutions (government) nor personal ones (within intimate relationships) will replicate Corregidora's legacy.

Whereas the telling that was central to Great Gram's imperative to "make generations" demonstrates the metonymic power of voice in the campaign for black women's rights, the blues emphasizes the voice's connection to a broader chorus of voices that are not necessarily tied to a body politic. Moreover, Jones makes speaking interchangeable with singing and humming in order to demonstrate how singing substitutes for telling. She constructs a polyphonic understanding of voice to "asser[t] that a polymorphous orality is more emancipatory than the restrictive biology could allow [and] instead argues that women's real labor lies not in producing matter with voice, but voices that matter."[37] This shift, from a politic rooted in reproduction to a politic rooted in the voice, clarifies Jones's notion that producing voices that matter is integral to any campaign for civil rights.

While Ursa wants to construct "a new world song," "a song that would touch me, touch my life and theirs," she meets resistance not only from her ex-husband, Mutt, but also from her mother, Irene, because neither can conceptualize Ursa's performances as consciousness-raising political statements that use specific examples of sexual exploitation to address a more pervasive historical and cultural phenomenon of black women's oppression (59). In the opening pages of *Corregidora*, Jones demonstrates how the blues threatens several patriarchal principles, foreshadowing how black women's blues will ultimately function to argue for black women's civil rights. As Ursa explains, Mutt resents her performing the blues because he sees her performances as undermining the authority he believes he should exercise over her. From his perspective, the blues emasculate him:

> It was 1947 when Mutt and I was married. I was singing in Happy's Café on Delaware Street. He didn't like for me to sing after we were married because he said that's why he married me so he could support me. I said I didn't just sing to be supported. I said I sang because it was something I had to do, but he never would understand that. We were married in December of 1947 and it was April 1948 that Mutt came to Happy's drunk and said if I didn't get off the stage he was going to take me off. I didn't move and some men put Mutt out. (3)

The interrelated concerns that this passage articulates operate within the ideological matrix that animates my discussion of exodus politics and its paradoxes in this chapter; they also preface the discussion below of Angela Davis's notion that the blues combats patriarchal authority by defying the expectation that women submit to men.

Juxtaposing Ursa's *need* to sing with Mutt's desire to support her, Ursa foregrounds their main source of disagreement: Mutt wants to control Ursa sexually and financially, while Ursa wants to maintain her sexual and financial independence. Mutt warns Ursa that either she will submit willingly to his authority or he will compel her to do so: "That's what I'm gon do [offer Ursa as a prostitute]. One a y'all wont bid for her? Piece a ass for sale. I got me a piece a ass for sale. That's what ya'll wont, ain't it? Piece a ass. I said I got a piece a ass for sale, anybody wont to bid on it?" (159). By acting like Corregidora, who prostituted Ursa's foremothers as "his gold piece," Mutt demonstrates that he is more concerned with the possibility that her performances will threaten his patriarchal authority than he is with Ursa's general well-being. Ursa's singing doubly affronts him in that it gives other men access to what should be his (sexually) and portrays him as inadequate (financially). If as Stelmaris Coser contends, Mutt "has inherited the sexist morality established in the Americas by the colonial system," Ursa has inherited her foremothers' will to resist multiple objectifications.[38] The imperative to make generations shapes Ursa's resistance toward Mutt's authority.

Jones establishes the historical parallel between Mutt and Corregidora, "linking Mutt's physical brutality to Corregidora's depravity," to reinforce the urgency of the struggle for black women's rights that pervades the narrative; the impulse to control black women's sexuality undergirds both Corregidora's treatment of Great Gram and Mutt's possessive attitude toward Ursa and thus "exposes power's undue concentration in the male figurehead in all intra-familial matters."[39] If, as Ann DuCille cogently argues, "*Corregidora* is literally and figuratively a blues novel; more specifically, in its treatment of erotic coupling and marriage, *Corregidora* is a particular variety of art that focuses (often as a lament) on the problems of married life and romantic relations," Ursa as blues singer remains engaged in the project of making generations, of leading this movement for black women's civil rights, that is central to the Corregidora women's legacy.[40]

Ursa's new appreciation for the blues' potential to make generations is significant because after her hysterectomy she was "feeling as if something more than the womb had been taken out" (12). Because reproduction has defined her subjectivity and her role as a bridge leader, the hysterectomy shatters Ursa's concept of who she is in relation to her family and society, both of which, ironically, have also defined black women's roles in reproductive terms. As Ursa laments during her recovery: "I'd always thought I was different. *Their* daughter, but somehow different. Maybe less Corregidora. I don't know. . . . But I am different now. I have everything they had, except generations. I can't make generations. And even if I still had my womb, even if the first baby had come—what would I have done then? Would I have kept it up? Would I have been like *her*, or *them*?" (60). Even before Ursa finds an alternative way to make generations, she doubts whether she wants, or indeed ever wanted, to continue this legacy because she understands how making generations, while important, has been detrimental to her foremothers.

Ursa's foremothers were not only preserving and transmitting history but also, as scholars who have examined this text through trauma theory have argued, intergenerationally transferring the trauma associated with that history.[41] But when her mother shares her "private memory," Ursa discovers yet another example of physical violence her foremothers have endured and understands that her own experiences with Mutt fit within a wider range of black women's historical experiences with oppression.[42] Accordingly, Ursa's contempt for Mutt's desire to regulate her sexuality, to "sell his piece of ass," fits into a broader scheme of sexual control that extends from Corregidora prostituting his enslaved black women, to his wife trying to mutilate Great Gram's genitals, to her father abusing her mother, to Mutt trying to control her. This continuum engenders Ursa's internal struggle and shapes her ultimate decision to make generations by singing black women's blues.

After struggling to process the historical, familial, and personal losses that the hysterectomy signifies, Ursa realizes that black women's blues will serve as a viable substitute for her absent womb; the blues gives her the opportunity to become a bridge leader who raises consciousness about the intersection of black women's rights and civil rights in black freedom struggles. As Ursa thinks: "I'll sing as you talked it, your voice humming, sing about the Portuguese who fingered your genitals. His pussy. 'The Portuguese who bought slaves paid attention only to the genitals.' Slapped you across the cunt till it was bluer than black. Concubine daughter" (52). To Ursa's mind, the blues provides a medium through which she can translate the sexual trauma that Corregidora inflicted upon "his pussy," while also addressing a more generalized "Portuguese" phenomenon of sexual exploitation that violated black women's human and civil rights. The placement of the remark "The Portuguese who bought slaves paid attention only to the genitals" in quotation marks is significant because the quotation marks reflect Ursa's desire to integrate Great Gram's corrective narrative of Brazilian exploitation into her articulation of her story, to keep the history alive. Ursa's blues performances therefore are not, as Mutt imagines them to be, lewd expressions of sexuality that are disconnected from a broader history or tradition.

In *Blues Legacies and Black Feminism: Gertrude "Ma" Rainey, Bessie Smith, and Billie Holiday* (1998), the feminist activist Angela Davis argues that black women's blues songs foreground their gendered and sexualized experiences in America: black women blues performers used the blues to raise social awareness/consciousness and transform politics to include black women's rights. Building upon the insightful formulations of Hazel Carby about black blues women, Davis describes black women's blues songs as forms of cultural criticism that reflect, contest, and shape gender, racial, sexual, and class discourses. As Davis states, "The blues women openly challenged the gender politics implicit in traditional cultural representations of marriage and heterosexual love relationships. Refusing, in the blues tradition of raw realism, to romanticize romantic relationships, they instead exposed the stereotypes and explored the contradictions of those relationships. . . . They forged and memorialized images of tough, resilient, and independent women who were afraid neither of their own vulnerability nor of defending their right to be respected as autonomous human beings."[43] Accordingly, black blues women defied a more general control over women that extended beyond intimate relationships to constrict black women's political and economic opportunities on the basis of the principle that men had the right to control all women's sexuality. Through her blues performances, Ursa publicizes the familial tale that for too long has been concealed within her familial circle, thereby reaffirming the dialogic ways that the personal remains political and vice versa.

Social historians' work on the roles of music in shaping black freedom struggles has increased awareness of the larger scope of black women's blues in raising consciousness about civil rights struggles during the twentieth century by articulating the political work that music performs. Brian Ward's *Just My Soul Responding: Rhythm and Blues, Black Consciousness, and Race Relations* (1998) is one of the most comprehensive analyses of black music's evolving perspective on political and social issues relevant to the civil rights movement. It explains how black music, across genres, became increasingly politically explicit as black cultural producers became increasingly frustrated with the slow pace of civil rights transformations. Although originally rhythm and blues "largely skirted political issues," by the late 1960s and early 1970s it was "full of songs explicitly about the struggle, about the social, political and economic plight of black Americans, and about the state of American race relations."[44] As chapter 2 discussed, the frustration that Ward argues rhythm and blues artists capture has much to do with the broader failure of phase one's legislative accomplishments to improve black life materially. More importantly, as Supreme Court cases challenged the constitutionality of affirmative action programs, the movement to translate equality of opportunity into equality of outcome slackened.

Ward cautions against assuming that black musicians constituted some sort of political vanguard; although "by the late 1960s it was more than any self-respecting soul sister or brother could afford in terms of conscience, credibility or commerce not to be pledging very public allegiance to the struggle . . . and often very boldly speaking or singing out against racism," in the early to mid-1960s black musicians tended to avoid such roles: "The claims that Rhythm and Blues provided some sort of explicit running commentary on the Movement, with the men and women of soul emerging as notable participants, even leaders, tacticians and philosophers of the black struggle, have usually depended more on partisan assertion than hard evidence."[45] Even so, black music often expressed the frustrations of the black predicament, and whether it was intentionally influential or not, it altered the discursive terrain just by entering it.

Nina Simone, as Ward notes, was unusual in that she was a musician who took an active role in the black freedom struggle early in the 1960s, before the politicization of soul later in the decade.[46] Her role, more strikingly than Billie Holiday's, underscores the tradition of fighting for black women's rights that black women's blues built upon as the blues staked its claims in civil rights agitation. Simone explicitly declared her desire to be an activist and centered her activism on civil rights obstructions that black women in particular faced.[47] Yet despite her stated objections to gradualism and her articulation of racism as a nationwide problem that extended beyond the South, Simone has been absent from most scholarly treatments of music's relation to the civil rights movement. One reason for this absence, as Ruth Feldstein astutely observes, is that "certain kinds of cultural productions and particular expressions of female sexuality have often been placed beyond the parameters of African American political history."[48] By demonstrating the interconnections of black women's rights, Black Power, and second-wave feminism, and by positioning Nina Simone as a point of entry into that early genealogy, Feldstein constructs a revisionist civil historiography that articulates a discernible pattern of women's explicit and implicit leadership and activism in civil rights struggles.

Feldstein's history of this activism through musically informed bridge leadership further informs *Corregidora*'s engagement with the black women's blues tradition. Simone was not a background organizer who happened to contribute to the civil rights movement; rather, she specifically conceptualized her music and her performances as "political work." She satirized and called into question the civil rights movement's notion of nonviolent resistance, as "Mississippi Goddam" and "Go Limp" evidence. Her music thus unsettled the roles black women were thought to occupy; by espousing armed resistance, for example, she challenged the politics of respectability that had circumscribed black women's roles in African American culture and called for black women to be more explicitly involved in securing black freedom. Her national and international influence emerged from a context in which black cultural performances had worked to shake the status quo, while specifically building upon black women's cultural performances.

For Jones, history figures significantly into Ursa's perception of her role as a blues performer and the continuing potential of black women's blues for black freedom struggles. As she explains in an interview,

> History affects Ursa's personality—the history of the women before her—their conflicts, frustrations, etc. She wants to make sense of that history in terms of her own life. She doesn't want to be "bound" by that history, but she recognizes it as important: and she accepts it as an aspect of her own character, identity and present history. However, she doesn't want to be told by those women and their Corregidora stories how she must feel about that past. Her story is connected to theirs but she also wants her own choices and acts of imagination and will—most of which come through singing her own songs.[49]

Ursa, then, is not disconnected from the leadership role; rather, she transforms the terms under which she leads. As Ashraf Rushdy notes, "What Ursa has inherited from Great Gram is a formula she rehearses without a requisite amount of revisionist energy, without a sufficient investment of herself and her personal identity, to give that formulaic story a renewed and animated circulation.[50] Rather than continue to reiterate that formula, Ursa redefines her role in terms that extend beyond Great Gram's command and respond to Ursa's changed personal circumstances and political context.

Just as Meridian struggles to find ways to remain true to the black freedom struggle without "volunteering to suffer," Ursa finds a way to lead without "volunteering to be retraumatized." As Madhu Dubey argues, "Ursa's blues voice allows her to express a feminine sensibility that is at least partially free of the oppressed and repressive collective tradition represented by the Corregidora women's narrative."[51] Though this "feminine sensibility" is partially free, her desire to resist black male objectification informs it; many of Ursa's blues performances refer to the Corregidora women's history as a way to remember, raise consciousness, and continue the fight for black women's civil rights. Ursa metonymically demonstrates how blues performers function as bridge leaders: raising consciousness about gender and sexual violence within black intimate relationships, then connecting those issues to a broader struggle for black women's civil rights that cannot deny the inextricability of racial, gender, sexual, and class relationships in black freedom struggles.

Bridge Leadership through Black Women's Blues: Ursa Enters the Tradition

Even though Ursa's mother, Irene, refuses to recognize the blues' ability to "make generations," Jones's textual parallels between Great Gram's stories and Ursa's blues renditions make it difficult not to consider Ursa's blues performances as examples of generation making because of the care they take to render the Corregidora history legible. For example, Great Gram recounts the story of a woman, who, like several enslaved women of the African diaspora, resisted how slavery obliterated their agency and compelled unchecked submission. Of this woman, Great Gram recalls, "The master shipped her husband out of bed and got in the bed with her and just as he was getting ready to go in her she cut off his thing with a razor she had hid under the pillow and he bled to death. They cut off her husband's penis and stuffed it in her mouth, and then they hanged her. . . . They made her watch and then they hanged her" (67). Now, consider what Ursa inwardly describes to her mother as "trying to explain it, in blues, without words, the explanation somewhere behind the words": "*O Mister who come to my house You do not come to visit You do not come to see me to visit You come to hear me sing with my thighs You come to see me open my door and sing with my thighs Perhaps you watch me when I am sleeping I don't know if you watch me when I am sleeping I don't know if you watch me when I am sleeping who are you*" (66–67). Or, in one of her songs:

> While mama be sleeping, the ole man he crawl into bed
> While mama be sleeping, the ole man he crawl into bed
> When mama have wake up, he shaking his nasty ole head
>
> . . . .
>
> Don't come here to my house, don't come here to my house I said
> Don't come here to my house, don't come here to my house I said
> Fore you get any of this booty, you gon have to lay down dead
>
> (67)

Not only does Great Gram's story testify to black women claiming possession over their bodily rights and the economic rights that derive from them, it also foregrounds the consequence of that resistance: lynching. This reference to lynching is significant given the role of blues woman Billie Holiday's song "Strange Fruit" in antilynching campaigns (civil rights). It is no small point that Great Gram shows this black woman witnessing a lynching spectacle and then being lynched herself. The scene, which illustrates both the sexualization of racism and the racialization of sexism, warns black women that they are protected by neither law, custom, nor individual will. Ursa approximates this history with two songs, both of which grasp the historical context and serve as a call to action.

Irene, Gram, and Great Gram could object to Ursa's blues performances on the grounds that they obscure the historicity of the Corregidora women's specific exploitation. The songs, however, do mirror Great Gram's stories, and the performances still serve the broader goal of obtaining black women's rights. Irene apparently shuns Ursa's blues performances because she sees the blues as apolitical expressions of black women's sexuality—the same viewpoint that has ignored black blues women's role as civil rights leaders. It is not simply the explicit expression of sexuality that perturbs Irene, for Great Gram's stories are certainly sexually explicit. Rather, it is the perception that the blues performances, unlike Great Gram's stories, serve no purpose beyond lewd entertainment. Ursa's investigation of sexual pleasure in her blues songs significantly distinguishes her songs from her foremother's stories and explores the tension that exists between women's experiences of exploitation and their desire to assert agency.[52] Yet Jones characterizes Irene's attitude as disdainful to emphasize society's generalized anxiety about musical expressions of black female sexuality that, in defying patriarchal norms to assert black women's rights, rely on explicit and latent sexual codes to buttress their claims.

Irene's response to Ursa's decision to sing the blues reveals not only her failure to see what Bakhtin would call the polyphonic or collective quality of voice but also the Afro-Protestant mores that helped to marginalize black blues women.[53] Ursa recalls a conversation with her mother:

> "Songs are devils. It's your own destruction you're singing. The voice is a devil."
> "Naw, Mama. You don't understand. Where did you get that?"
> "Unless your voice is raised up to the glory of God."
> "I don't know where you got that."
> "Where did you get those songs? That's devil's music."
> "I got them from you."
> "I didn't hear the words." (53–54)

Recollecting the disagreement she and Irene have about the blues' ability to communicate the narrative that her foremothers have commanded

her to pass on, Ursa probes her mother's notion that the blues are neither generative nor reparative by demanding, "Where did you get that?"
Irene's contention that the blues is "the devil's music" and contrary to
"the glory of God" confirms popular perceptions of blues performances
as sites "where the Devil's music was performed by irresponsible and
sexually fearless women."[54] This demonization of the blues and black
blues women's performances in Afro-Protestant Christian discourse
provides another reason why civil rights historiography has excluded
black women's blues leadership and activism.

Given the biblical roots of the Exodus story, the related divine ordination of the formal leader that follows from it, and the patriarchal
interests that exodus politics propagates, it is not surprising that civil
rights paradigms that champion exodus politics would consider black
blues women as threatening. By refusing to privilege male dominance
and formal leadership, by reasserting the inextricability of racial, gender, and sexual politics in civil rights campaigns, and by foregrounding
raised consciousness among the masses as central to civil rights campaigns' success, black blues women and blues music expose the paradoxes of exodus politics. The blues thus "helped produce new feeling
of community, one in which black culture was affirmed and the male
dominance of the black church powerfully contested."[55] Through this
contestation, the black blues engages in a broader repudiation of the
discourses of exodus politics by demonstrating their insufficiency in
engaging cross-cutting issues or the political concerns of non-normative
black subjects; it also challenges a judgmental strain that Davis argues is
endemic to Christianity.[56] The blues explicitly describes black women's
gender and sexuality, as well as black men's gender and sexuality, in
such a way as to illuminate the respective political disadvantages and
privileges associated with each. By elucidating these power dynamics,
black blues women contribute to developing a liberatory politics that is
truly liberating.

Whereas black blues women's performances must be conceptualized
in the context of civil rights leadership that prioritizes black women's
rights and interests in black freedom struggles, Ursa's method of making
generations encounters problems because her blues performances are
not disembodied; even as a consciousness-raising blues performer, she
finds that patriarchal culture objectifies her body and commodifies her
performance in ways akin to her foremothers' experiences of bodily dispossession. For this reason it is necessary to heed Hazel Carby's admonition not to overemphasize black blues women's agency and resistance. In

"It Jus Be's Dat Way Sometime: The Sexual Politics of Women's Blues," Carby examines how female blues singers during the 1920s articulated gendered patterns of sexual behavior among African Americans. She argues that although fictional representations of the black woman blues singer mythologized the potential of black women's sexuality to subvert their objectification, the commercialization of the blues through race records helped undermine that power. Yet in her reading of *Corregidora* she does assert that Ursa emblematizes a figure who resists letting static notions of sexuality circumscribe her choices.

Women announcing sexual desire while resisting sexual commodification figure centrally in *Corregidora*, where Ursa learns that while black blues women's assertion of the sexual self may explore new possibilities for black women's advancement, it cannot be undertaken without impunity. When an audience member, for example, tells Ursa that "the next best thang to the blues is a good screw," she "started singing a song, hoping that would make him quiet" and "it did" (168). As Katherine Boutry argues, by "consciously inserting her song for her body, she quiets him while choosing to give him what he wants [sexually?] musically."[57] If music exemplifies another instance of the polymorphic figuration of voice in *Corregidora*, the music's ability to satisfy his physical desire returns readers to the notion that the blues functions as an effective alternative to Great Gram's original imperative to make generations; blues politics and reproductive politics are interchangeable. Ursa's performance, beyond reflecting how black women continually face and resist commodification, demonstrates the interplay between the two ways of making generations that is central to the text's unfolding.

The Blues and Non-normative Black Subjects Revisited

Although black women's blues offers Ursa the opportunity to think about sexuality in ways that go beyond the confines of her foremothers' thinking, it is impossible to ignore the heteronormative perspective that governs the blues' figuration in the text. This heterosexual focus in *Corregidora* reflects the pattern that Barbara Smith rebukes in "Toward a Black Feminist Criticism." Moreover, Jones's representation of lesbian characters not only relies on stereotypes but insufficiently conceptualizes the possibilities available to queer, non-normative black female sexuality. One way to engage this tension is to examine the text's treatment of Ursa's former best friend, Cat Lawson, whom Ursa retreats from when she realizes Cat is a lesbian, and who is outside Ursa's understanding of black womanhood and black women's sexual rights. When telling Ursa that she is a lesbian, Cat juxtaposes the oppression she feels as a domestic working for a white family with the lack of desire, and thus the awkwardness, that she feels in sexual relations with her male partner. Here the issues of racial, gender, and sexual rights all intersect. An incident of sexual harassment by her employer that makes Cat feel "foolish" at work reminds her of how she has also felt "foolish" at home in her "own bed" with her male partner, in ways she never explicitly clarifies. This conversation compels readers to consider why this hypersexualization in the kitchen calls to mind Cat's desexualization in the bedroom.

Whereas the kitchen incident illuminates the sexualization of racism and the racialization of heteronormativity, the bedroom scene recalls the normativization of black heteropatriarchy. Taken together, these scenes situate Cat's status as a marginalized black woman subject within a history that makes the silence surrounding black women's expression of sexual desire outside heteronormative parameters contiguous with the sexual and gender disenfranchisements that the Corregidora women face. Ursa, however, remains unwilling to listen to Cat's testimony about her sexual harassment and feelings of foolishness, and her unwillingness undermines the expansiveness of her vision for black women's civil rights. Cat, then, is positioned as an important commentator: she draws attention to how black women's sexual rights need to incorporate a kind of non-normative sexuality that remains illicit for Ursa even in the context of women's blues.

Although Jones depicts the expression of heterosexual desire as problematic at best, and perhaps even warns against overinvesting in black heteropatriarchy, *Corregidora* never wholly renounces the economy of heterosexual desire; in fact, as Richard Hardack and Sally Robinson have pressed in their readings of the text, Jones actually reinforces heteronormativity within black culture.[58] Not only does she reunite Ursa with her estranged and previously abusive husband Mutt, but she also punishes Cat with gratuitous physical violence by the narrative's end. Cat's loss of hair further marks her as "unfeminine," and this characterization, coupled with her lesbian relationship, reinforces, as Dubey has argued, the notion that society punishes black women who express their sexual desire outside the parameters of black heteropatriarchy. While I do not intend to justify this narrative violence that Jones inflicts upon Cat, it is important to understand the threat Cat poses to Ursa's sense of self and psychic well-being in order to see why Jones subordinates Cat's narrative to Ursa's. It is not Cat's being a lesbian per se that unsettles Ursa; rather, it is the way that Cat's testimony undoes Ursa's sense of who she is, as a black woman who is unable to reproduce; because reproductive politics damages Ursa's identity immediately following her hysterectomy, Cat's testimony reminds Ursa of how she herself now exists on the outskirts of sanctioned black female sexuality.

On the one hand, Ursa's initial resistance to supporting Cat's lesbianism might be understood as a defense against her own insecurity about her inability to fulfill the imperative to "make generations." On the other hand, when she later thinks about how singing the blues is for her a way of expressing the sense of sexual disconnection that she has not shared with Cat, her failure to include Cat's narrative in that context demonstrates how even black women's blues in the text does not transgress sexual boundaries in the ways that Davis says it does in society. In an intense exchange between Cat and Ursa, Cat begins: "You don't know what it's like to feel foolish in a white woman's kitchen and then have to come home and feel foolish all night in the bed at night with your man. I wouldn't a mind the other so much if I didn't have to feel like a fool in the bed with my man. You don't know what that means, do you?" (64). When Cat ends her confession by inviting Ursa to relate to, or at least validate, her feelings of inadequacy, her vulnerability in speaking strikingly contrasts against Ursa's silence.[59] This moment is pivotal for several reasons: Ursa's response not only might have forestalled Cat's revelation but also might have begun an intersubjective exchange in which Cat and Ursa shared their different approaches for grappling with the crisis of heteronormativity in black heteropatriarchal contexts. Had Ursa, for example, responded that she did not know what it was like to feel foolish in the white woman's kitchen but that she had in fact felt foolish in her bedroom, she would have opened up the opportunity to think about her own and Cat's rights, reproduction, and economic autonomy within a broader discursive field of black women's rights.

However problematic Ursa's silence is for Cat's need to have an engaged listener, Ursa does relate to Cat. She thinks of the precise ways that she has felt foolish in her own bed, elucidating a parallel moment in her and Cat's lives:

> She was looking at me, expecting something. She wanted me to tell her that I knew what it feels like, but I wouldn't tell her. I remembered that night I was exhausted with waiting and I waited but he didn't turn toward me and I kept waiting and wanting him and I got close to him up against his back but he still wouldn't turn to me

and then I lay on my back and tried hard to sleep and I finally slept and in the morning I waited and still he didn't and I thought in the morning he would but he didn't. (64)

Ursa's internal monologue demonstrates the sexual power play she and Mutt engage in, and how, in the context of their heterosexual relationship, Mutt determines the when, where, and how of the sexual encounter. Considered within the overall discursive field, this specific conflict between Ursa and Mutt highlights the more pervasive battle they engage in as Mutt attempts to control Ursa's sexuality. These parallels between the present and the past, between Cat's foolishness and Ursa's, share the thread of black women having to negotiate how to express desire and pleasure within a heterosexual economy that considers their sexual pleasure secondary or otherwise irrelevant. For example, although Ursa cannot "feel pleasure" during sex immediately following her hysterectomy, it is perhaps even more disturbing to her that it has never really mattered to Mutt how "she felt." The crisis of heteronormativity for Ursa requires her to balance the demands of heterosexual expression of desire against the knowledge that her desire does not matter.

While the historical context of Ursa's crisis of heteronormativity is described more explicitly than Cat's, Cat's story situates her feelings of foolishness within a historical context in which the sexualization of racism and the racialization of sexism challenged black women's sexual autonomy. Jones emphasizes how Cat's feelings of foolishness in the kitchen are part of a historical continuity in which white men exploit black women's sexuality and white women co-sign, even if unwittingly, on this behavior. As Cat relates, the white husband, Mr. Hirshorn, tells her, "You pretty, Catherine. A lot of you nigger women is pretty." He elaborates, "You ought to let me watch you straighten your hair sometime. Beatrice [his wife] said you were in there straightening your hair" (65). As the narrator shares, Cat "was saying nothing and then when she'd got the can of coffee grounds down and was opening it to pour it in the pot, he was behind her touching her arm, and she dropped the can" (65).

The scene is significant because it depicts white patriarchy as an ongoing threat to black women. The comparison of Cat's beauty to that of other women and the positioning of Mr. Hirshorn behind Cat underscore black women's presumed hypersexuality as the impetus that allows (white) men to make sexual advances toward them with impunity. This scene calls to mind a parallel one in Harriet Jacobs's *Incidents in the Life*

of a Slave Girl, Written by Herself (1861), in which the young protagonist depicts enslaved black women as having to fend off their licentious
and lascivious masters, without garnering sympathy from their (jealous)
mistresses. Cat, Ursa, and Great Gram all share the historical experience
of having their sexuality commodified to satisfy the sexual and economic
interests of both white and black heteropatriarchies.

Although Cat's lesbianism, as Madhu Dubey has suggested, may be
presented more as an "evasion of heterosexuality" than as an affirmation
of sexual desire, and although Jones's depiction of lesbianism conforms
to what Gloria Wade-Gayles maintains are "silences and denials," my
examination of this scene invites a consideration of the stakes of com-
pulsory heterosexuality as it informs Ursa's decision to reunite with
Mutt and Cat's separation from her partner (and loss of hair).[60] Might
the narrative end of both women's lives suggest that sexuality, as African American culture and American culture construct and police it, is
always embedded within civil rights discourses? Moreover, *Corregidora*
allows past, present, and future contexts to shape the reader's understanding of how these women exercise their sexuality.

I juxtapose Cat's and Ursa's ways of responding to the crisis of heteronormativity in the context of black women's rights to underscore the
urgency of conceptualizing race, gender, and sexuality in civil rights
discourses as always intersecting. Jones's treatment of Cat, as Sharon
Holland's theory of "dead subjects" in African American literature
considers, situates Cat in the "afterlife" beyond the limits of black life
precisely because of her queerness. Rather than "bring [her] back from
the place of silence," Jones "places queer subjects in the space of the
unnamed" because "black queer sexuality is the body that no one wants
to be beholden to."[61] That Jones does not reconsider Cat's non-normative
sexuality in the context of black women's blues is significant in that the
blues gives black women a voice to challenge their limited opportunities
and freedoms; by keeping silent on Cat, the blues undermines its trans-
gressive potential and reaffirms normativity.

As a blues performer, Ursa bears witness to the atrocities that Old Man
Corregidora inflicted upon her foremothers and testifies to her foremothers' wills to resist dehumanization. Ursa also situates her family's
personal struggles for sexual autonomy within a broader discursive context of black women's rights and reminds readers that black blues women
functioned as bridge leaders who raised consciousness about black wom-
en's rights. For Ursa, achieving Great Gram's mission is no small feat, not

only because she undergoes a hysterectomy that unsettles the foundation upon which she defines her womanhood, but also because she must balance the desire to affirm history with a need to not be bound by it. In this way, her struggle as a civil rights leader recalls the internal gendered conflicts observable in Jimmy, Ned, and Miss Jane in *The Autobiography of Miss Jane Pittman*, and Meridian and Truman in *Meridian*. As a blues performer, Ursa finds herself able to share the intimate tale of personal and public violence with a larger group of people than just the Corregidora women and the men with whom they are intimately connected. She can raise consciousness in ways that her foremothers have been unable to do.

At the same time, Jones interjects issues of agency and desire that shake the oppression/victim binary that informs much of Great Gram's recollection of her experiences with Corregidora.[62] While there are theoretical problems that arise from a sexually commodified blues performance, public blues performances engage in social critique and transformation and create voices that matter. Providing a voice that "matters," of course, lies at the heart of consciousness-raising bridge leadership activities and is indeed what black blues women have attempted to achieve through their music. By constructing a black female subject who exerts agency, despite institutional and personal attempts to objectify her, black blues women decenter male formal leaders and displace the normative black subject's political interests from the center of black political agendas, while foregrounding cross-cutting issues.

Whereas *Corregidora*'s analysis has specifically focused on civil rights campaigns that foreground black women's civil rights as central to black people's liberation ethic more generally, *Dreamer*'s analysis of civil rights issues in the 1990s (though the text is set in the 1960s) reaffirms exodus politics' tendency to champion male leadership and exclude women's rights from black freedom struggles. *Dreamer* reveals how these tendencies ultimately undermine the goal of liberation that drives black freedom struggles. In this way, *Dreamer* reaffirms *Corregidora*'s skepticism toward collaborative leadership efforts in civil rights struggles where black male formal leadership remains privileged as necessary for black empowerment; such formulations can only oppress black women, who in turn, to resist this oppression, must form their own coalitions.

4 / "We All Killed Him": The Limits of Formal Leadership and Civil Rights Legislation in Charles Johnson's *Dreamer*

We are coming to demand that the government address itself to the problem of poverty. We read one day, "We hold these truths to be self-evident, that all men are created equal, that they are endowed by their Creator with certain inalienable Rights, that among these are Life, Liberty, and the pursuit of Happiness." But if a man does not have a job or income, he has neither life nor liberty nor the possibility of the pursuit of happiness. He merely exists. . . .

. . . It is our experience that the nation doesn't move around questions of genuine equality for the poor and for black people until it is confronted massively, dramatically in terms of direct action.

—MARTIN LUTHER KING JR., "REMAINING AWAKE DURING
A GREAT REVOLUTION"

Published at the end of the twentieth century, Charles Johnson's *Dreamer* (1998) engaged debates about civil rights, black leadership, and black politics that had persisted throughout the twentieth century. In 1903, for example, W. E. B. DuBois famously prophesied that "the problem of the twentieth century is the problem of the color line,—the relation of the darker to the lighter races of men in Asia and Africa, in America and the islands of the sea."[1] DuBois suggested that unless white and nonwhite people could live together in a society without racial hierarchies, race relations would remain antagonistic. Despite the legislative changes that the civil rights movement achieved during phase one, white backlash against the movement, black incorporation into mainstream politics, and a move away from the "politics of protest" have left racial hierarchies, and the problem of the color line, intact. During phase two it became clearer that corrective measures, such as affirmative action, would prove necessary to address the aggregate effects of slavery and Jim and Jane Crow segregation if black people were to obtain their civil rights.

Conceptualizations of civil rights enfranchisement that foreground the importance of affirmative action programs also acknowledge the limitations of legal and legislative redress for ensuring that the goals of phase one of the civil rights movement are actualized during phase two. Because, as Ian Lopez has claimed, the law "is one of the most powerful mechanisms by which any society creates, defines, and regulates itself," phase one of the civil rights movement necessarily emphasized legal change as a central component of civil rights attainment.[2] Yet because "the operation of law does far more than merely legalize race; it defines as well the spectrum of domination and subordination that constitutes race relations," phase two recognized that the law might not readily diminish "the spectrum of domination and subordination that constitutes race relations."[3] In the phase two shift from agitation to implementation, legal redress was recognized to be necessary but insufficient for solving civil rights crises.

Throughout the long civil rights movement, bridge and formal leaders continually have requested that black political agendas demand a civil rights "package deal" rather than just an end to Jim and Jane Crow segregation. Such a deal, as chapter 2 explains, would implement specific measures to eradicate inequities in housing, employment, and education and thus would help materialize the equality that civil rights legislation alone could not achieve. While the beginning of the twentieth-century struggles for civil rights focused on transforming laws that structured inequality, in phase two leaders and everyday citizens recognized that such a focus was too narrow and would subordinate the related goals of black freedom struggles—to institutionalize legal gains and ensure that black communities achieved equality. *Dreamer* considers how, if at all, material equality can be achieved in light of the backlash against civil rights movements that has emerged in the "post"–civil rights era.

Dreamer's examination of civil rights and black leadership foregrounds competing theories of black political activity to demonstrate the challenges black leaders experience during phase two when they attempt to materialize equality. According to political scientist Fredrick Harris, black leaders have often found themselves trying to strike a balance between building alliances—through "coalition politics"—and encouraging black communities to be "self-reliant"—through "independent black politics"—as they seek equality. As Harris explains, coalition politics "calls on voters to build coalitions with whites and other racial and ethnic groups to develop support for issues and policies that help everyone."[4] By contrast, independent black politics "presses blacks to work independently of other groups to push for community interests with the aim toward building support with other groups around both universal policies and community-specific issues."[5]

Although Harris's discussion reveals the sometimes competing political strategies black leaders have employed throughout the long civil rights movement, the independent-black-politics model appeals because it champions affirmative action measures. It posits that the history of discrimination against black people has necessitated policies that are "racially" marked and specifically geared toward helping black individuals and communities. Anti–affirmative action movements challenge this notion of addressing "community-specific issues," maintaining that such corrective initiatives practice reverse discrimination. *Dreamer's* engagement with phase two of the civil rights movement calls into question the logic of reverse discrimination and presents independent black politics and coalition politics as *equally* necessary for black political advancement.

Dreamer connects "post–civil rights" instances of African Americans' disenfranchisement to the broader history of civil rights infringements. It challenges the idea that phase one of the civil rights movement removed structural inequalities, eliminated political, economic, and social disparities, and created a society in which African Americans have equal access and opportunity. Further, it shows how the backlash against affirmative action programs instituted "to monitor inequality, to reduce poverty, and to redress the centuries-long exploitation and social degradation of African Americans" has blocked civil rights progress and eroded civil rights gains.[6] The undercutting of affirmative action policies has not only limited black people's access to civil rights equity but also shifted the responsibility of civil rights attainment to black people. Those opposing affirmative action policies have therefore reinforced the notion that civil rights movement's only goal was to achieve equality under the law.

Whereas a text such as *Meridian* examines the challenges civil rights leaders faced during the first decade of phase two of the civil rights movement, *Dreamer*, though set in the years between 1965 and 1968, draws on a broader historical scope encompassing three decades of the long-term consequences of anti–civil rights backlash. Johnson uses his witnessing of this history as a point of departure to argue that ongoing direct action remains necessary to ensure that the theoretical promise for equality materializes in the everyday lives of African Americans. He also suggests that phase two of the civil rights movement faltered between the late 1960s and the late 1990s partly because of the paradoxes that exodus politics produced. Johnson engages exodus politics, especially as the twentieth century draws to a close and the backlash against affirmative action programs and civil rights gains becomes increasingly clear, to show that neither civil rights legislation, formal leadership (or even bridge leadership), nor middle-class civil rights ideology without affirmative action measures can achieve civil rights equality.

While *Dreamer* echoes the concerns that *Miss Pittman, Meridian,* and *Corregidora* express about the tendency of the messiah complex to kill formal leaders and inhibit the development of indigenous leaders within communities, it diverges in how it conceptualizes the class ideologies that civil rights discourses propose. More specifically, *Dreamer* elucidates how middle-class ideology undermines the civil rights movement's goal of eradicating class stratification because this ideology depends upon the exploitation of the labor of non-normative groups. Like the other authors *Exodus Politics* examines, Johnson deploys iconic figures, events, and tropes of the civil rights movement in order to defamiliarize them. As he reimagines Dr. King's involvement in the Chicago Freedom Movement, the establishment of the Poor People's Campaign, and the organization of the Memphis sanitation workers' march, Johnson writes *Dreamer,* as Gaines writes *The Autobiography of Miss Jane Pittman,* in the tradition of the historical novel. Yet neither author engages in mimetic history, and Johnson in particular wants to imagine the psychological dimensions of civil rights history that have eluded historical studies of King.

In this chapter, I posit that *Dreamer* vacillates between rejecting the paradoxes of exodus politics and championing exodus politics' political efficacy to show how difficult it is to unsettle the exodus politics paradigm in African American politics and culture. My analysis juxtaposes Johnson's expressed wish to be "historically accurate," specifically as it relates to illuminating the drawbacks of middle-class ideology in civil rights discourses, against the book's omission of women bridge and formal leaders during the 1965–68 period in which the book is set, in order to question what it means to be "historically accurate." That is, I examine the implications of Johnson rewriting a more inclusive "historiography of the civil rights movement" without engaging women's leadership and specific civil rights concerns. While *Dreamer* repositions the centrality of social class in civil rights discourses and questions the long-term consequences of privileging male formal leadership, it ignores black women's civil rights leadership, oppression, and specific political concerns altogether. Whether Johnson needed to engage these subjects is less significant than the fact that his failure to do so provides an occasion to further consider how these omissions exacerbate the paradoxes of exodus politics in *Dreamer*. By not engaging "King's sexism and homophobia" as well as "the relatively undemocratic character of his organization [SCLC]," Johnson leaves readers to wonder where women fit into contemporary discussions of leadership and civil rights, as well as whether there is a space for non-normative gender and sexualities.[7]

My examination of exodus politics here weaves together the arguments I have been advancing throughout this book and thus considers each of the questions that guides this study: (1) *What* liberties are to be included in the term *civil rights* when racial discourses implicitly and explicitly invoke the constructs of gender and sexuality to conceptualize "race," or, to put it another way, how does the inclusion of gender, sexual, and economic rights in the term *civil rights* reshape an understanding of its meaning? (2) *Who* will lead the movement, and how can leadership be redefined to include the work both men and women do to mobilize participants? (3) *What* paradigms of leadership—communal or individual—are African Americans employing to direct their efforts? and (4) *How* will society measure material and symbolic gains of the civil rights movement when the changing political landscape has made the remnants of Jim and Jane Crow practices more complicated to identify?

Phase Two of the Civil Rights Movement: Dreams Deferred and Other Contradictions

Dreamer opens in the mid-1960s and takes as its point of departure the historical Dr. King's shift of civil rights campaigning from the South to the North, and specifically his Chicago Freedom Movement. It ends with Dr. King's funeral in 1968, a week after he marched with the sanitation workers in Memphis, Tennessee. The majority of the narrative directly and indirectly alludes to King's leadership and civil rights philosophies, with the fictive closely paralleling the historical. Building upon the historical King's decision to move his family into a substandard housing tenement on the south side of Chicago, *Dreamer* charts King's collaborations with local leaders, authorities, and communities to address the injustices that rendered black life in northern urban areas separate and unequal. By setting *Dreamer* in Chicago, Johnson disrupts the problematic tendency to draw rigid dichotomies between the racial politics of the South and those of the North. The mid-twentieth-century Great Migration from the South to northern and midwestern cities reflects the historical reality that African Americans had more opportunities in cities like Chicago than in places like Birmingham. Discrimination, however, extended beyond the Mason-Dixon line. As Richard Wright illuminates in *Native Son* (1941), northern cities were not bias-free havens where African Americans enjoyed equality or even significantly improved material conditions.[8]

The famed opening scene of *Native Son* where Bigger Thomas, the protagonist, attempts to kill a rat that has invaded his home illustrates the blighted economic conditions African Americans faced in the North. Johnson, like Wright, demonstrates that de facto segregation in housing and education proved to be just as deleterious for African Americans as de jure segregation had been. This representation of black life in the North not only counteracts the propensity for African Americans to idealize the North's commitment to equality but also suggests that what Wright called an "ethics of Jim Crow," based on denying African Americans rights to which they are entitled, pervades the entire American body politic;[9] recall from Lorraine Hansberry's famous *A Raisin in the Sun* (1959), also set in Chicago, the ubiquity of real estate agencies and mortgage brokers conspiring to exclude African Americans from white neighborhoods and/or to encourage white flight. Situating *Dreamer* in this larger national context, Johnson aids the historiographical project of challenging normative representations of the civil rights movement. Like the historical King, Johnson underscores the insufficiency of the law alone to achieve civil rights equality. In northern urban areas that did not have Jim and Jane Crow laws, leaders nevertheless had to transform the de facto institutions that caused inequality.

Dreamer's story line unfolds through the perspective of Matthew Bishop, King's aide, who, along with his coworker Amy, is on the Chicago SCLC staff that coordinate King's speaking and rallying engagements and who works as a bridge leader for the Chicago Freedom Movement. Whereas Bishop recounts the events surrounding King's leadership, the meanings of those events and prior ones grow out of the chapters in which Johnson situates the reader within King's psyche. Johnson weaves together Bishop's account and analysis of these events with King's own self-reflective chapter vignettes. In providing both perspectives, Johnson constructs Bishop as a historiographer of the movement, while affording the reader what historiographers typically do not have—access to King's thoughts, feelings, fears, and inner struggles about the vicissitudes of leadership and the attainment of civil rights throughout the Chicago

Freedom Movement and the longer civil rights movement. Through these chapters, Johnson helps the reader to find the man whom "we think we know" but who is "strangely absent."[10]

Dreamer thus gives a multidimensional image of the historical King and his role in the civil rights movement to challenge popular and scholarly conceptualizations of the man, the movement, and black leadership.[11] It overturns popular images of King by reimagining his views on the civil rights movement's goals and philosophies through representations of King's inner struggles and by focusing on how King's philosophies about civil rights changed in the wake of the civil rights movement's gains. As the historian Jacquelyn Dowd Hall has argued, the public imagination has frozen King in 1963, at the March on Washington.[12] Thus his "I Have A Dream" speech, which the nation replays as sound bites to identify King's desires for integration and equality, becomes King's only, final, and exemplary statement on civil rights and the civil rights movement. *Dreamer* and King studies, however, show that this speech should not be read as emblematic of King's views on civil rights: King would come to embrace much broader goals, championing economic justice and reparations and demanding measurable time lines for civil rights implementation.

Further, by exploring the "representations of the tensions between the private man and public figure," *Dreamer* reveals the underexamined psychic burdens that exodus politics places on leaders and communities. Johnson examines the "essence," or, as Toni Morrison would have it, "the interiority," of King, presenting him as a man who self-consciously reflects on his leadership, life, and family.[13] In these moments of self-reflection, King privately resists reproducing the paradoxes of exodus politics, not only questioning the efficacy of formal leadership as the movement's primary leadership strategy but also recognizing how middle-class ideology keeps the poorest of black people from obtaining their civil rights.

In these chapters, King also ponders his failure to meet the expectations of his family, especially lamenting his shortcomings as a husband and a father. Public discourse, as the Moynihan Report exemplifies, argued that the absence of black men from their families (particularly lower-class families) contributed to black people's lack of economic standing and access to the opportunities that economic privilege provided. Yet King's formal leadership role demanded and excused his absence from his family on account of his contributions to the black nation conceived as an extension of the family. In the book, this conundrum, as the fictional King envisions it, contributes to the physical and mental anguish that leading the movement causes him.

Yet even as *Dreamer* calls into question paradoxical aspects of exodus politics, it remains deeply invested in that politics. Although Johnson urges African American communities to avoid an overreliance on male formal leadership to secure civil rights, he never wholly rejects the need for such leadership, just as Jones never challenges the normativity of heterosexuality in *Corregidora*. Even as Johnson brings out the central role of social class in the fictional King's conceptualization of civil rights, he does not trouble the notion that the black heterosexual male subject is the normative black subject, or consider how gender and sexuality intersect with social class.

Dreamer looks back from the 1990s at a critical juncture in the civil rights movement, in light of the developments with regard to civil rights that have occurred between the two time periods. Thus it is important first to provide a historical context showing how a rejection of King's vision for economic justice and reparations led to a dismantling of affirmative action initiatives that had been put in place to ensure that African Americans could enjoy their civil rights.

Anti–Affirmative Action: Unmaking the Dream

Like postracialists in the twenty-first century, the New Right of the 1970s through the 1990s frequently invoked King's "I Have a Dream" speech to claim that integration was the civil rights movement's primary goal, that integration had been achieved, that because of integration black people were now equal, and that consequently black people did not need any "special privileges" such as affirmative action. Such programs, they maintained, presumed black inferiority and undermined the notion of equality for which the civil rights movement had fought.[14] King's speech was thus perverted and "manipulated to justify the demise of affirmative action programs, civil rights enforcement, and other social reforms designed to provide compensatory justice to the disadvantaged."[15] By arresting King's vision of civil rights at the historical moment of the speech, conservatives have misread his statement on color blindness and have used that misreading to undermine the civil rights for which he fought. They have also ignored King's more complicated vision of economic reparations, which—like Rustin's call for a package deal—addressed the concurrent forces that were diminishing African Americans' life chances.

The historical King's demand for a "radical redistribution of economic resources" in 1965 makes it difficult to see King's notion of color blindness as intended to perpetuate disenfranchisement. Whereas the 1963 speech allows for an affirmation of the "theoretical" claim that black and white people deserve the same opportunities, the 1965 speech requires America to devise a plan to achieve equality in fact—to implement community-specific policies that independent black politics demand. King's vision for civil rights did not stop at integration, for black exploitation and disenfranchisement persisted throughout the nation even after "integration" was enacted into law.

Celebration of phase one of the civil rights movement as a "triumphal moment in a large American progress narrative" overlooks the significance of the civil rights movement after 1965/8, during phase two.[16] It also underestimates the structural embeddedness of Jim and Jane Crow and their effects throughout the nation (not just "the South") and shifts the responsibility for civil rights implementation from national institutions to black individuals personally. A focus on phase two, however, reminds readers of the expansive scope of the civil rights movement, connects phase one's goals to those of phase two, and discourages the use of a short historical framework when analyzing the civil rights movement. *Dreamer*, like the other texts *Exodus Politics* examines, frustrates the tendency to truncate the political goals and vision of the movement by situating civil rights leadership and attainment in a long civil rights movement historical framework. Like the new civil rights studies and King studies, *Dreamer*, in its continuing emphasis on the necessity of phase two, highlights "the radical King" who has been banished for so long from the cultural psyche and challenges the notion that ending de jure segregation was the be-all and end-all of the movement.

In the 1990s, the most contemporary decade informing *Dreamer*'s historical context, civil rights issues became more and more contested, and different populations within American society increasingly viewed civil rights problems as "solved" or "irrelevant." A decade of conservatism had already begun to erode the progress that (middle-class) African Americans had made by dismantling the "corrective" initiatives that federal and state governments had implemented to address the interrelated education, housing, and employment crises that structural discrimination had institutionalized. Yet even in the late 1960s, public support for civil rights had begun to wane, and "further attempts to expand access to better housing and education, and employment were fiercely resisted in the North."[17] Moreover, the belief that "the government should do less, not more, and that strong civil rights enforcement threatened white liberty" began to alter the nation's attitude toward civil rights, thus revealing the obstacles that black people would face in phase two as they sought to actualize phase one's goals.[18]

During Ronald Reagan's term as president in the 1980s, states turned away from egalitarianism, which, as historian Manning Marable explains, "implies that a fairer and more democratic society can only be achieved through the deliberate intervention of the state, promoting more equal distribution of income, wealth, and ownership of productive resources."[19] Reagan's championing of trickle-down economics also widened the gap between the nation's poorest and wealthiest classes. Given the interrelationships of race, class, and gender, black men and black women emerged disproportionately among the poor. The deliberate intervention of the state that the historical King had demanded seemed especially important because it was the state (both the federal government and individual states) that had sanctioned the legal enslavement of people of African descent and later Jim and Jane Crow segregation. Recall that Great Gram's imperative to make generations in *Corregidora* is predicated on the notion that the state needs to "pay" for its "wrongdoing." Changes in the law, says Marable, prove insufficient to correct a history of disenfranchisement, and the historical and fictive Kings agree: the government has a responsibility to enforce those legal changes and make opportunities available. As the government fails or otherwise shirks its responsibilities, black communities, through bridge leaders, must continue to rally in order to achieve equality.

If during the 1970s and 1980s there was diminishing enthusiasm for implementing the long-term goals of phase one of the civil rights movement, the 1990s introduced an outright assault on affirmative action initiatives. More narrow interpretations of laws, for example, curtailed policies that were designed to give African Americans and other historically underrepresented groups, including white women, opportunities that would improve their material conditions. Although the executive branch of government has limited powers to enforce policy, the president's attitude toward equality, democracy, and civil rights can set the tone for the legislative and judicial branches. Whereas the former has an active role in constructing and implementing laws and public policy, the latter interprets public policies and laws. Because the president appoints justices to the Supreme Court, it is worth noting that "the appointment of conservative Supreme Court justices during the era of Ronald Reagan and George Bush led to the recession of key affirmative action laws that had been designed to protect African Americans from discrimination in housing, education, labor, and health care."[20]

Under both these presidents, the nation moved away from redressing the racial disparities that persisted; by explicitly defunding housing, education, and other social welfare initiatives, these executives failed to acknowledge how formerly legally disenfranchised groups remained at a disadvantage, and they did not uphold the government's obligation to diminish this inequality. Much of Johnson's examination of civil rights and leadership in *Dreamer* seems influenced by these trends, and the context of the decades between the book's and the author's present becomes important not only for his engagement with history but also for his more general philosophical outlook that underwrites the text's perspective on social and racial (in)justices.

Rethinking the Paradoxes:
Formal Leadership, Black Men, and Social Class

While the complex relationship between the fictive King and the Chicago Freedom Movement that he historically led anchors many of the concerns of *Dreamer*, some critics have examined religion as a topic that pervades Johnson's wider oeuvre, and most especially his engagement with Buddhism.[21] For Marc Conner, Johnson shifts from Buddhism to Christianity in *Dreamer* because Buddhism's desire to understand the self irrespective of politics proves insufficient to conceptualize the racial strife that is central to Johnson's examination of the long civil rights movement. As Conner elaborates, "The primary importance lies in the novel's depiction of a world in strife, a world in which blood-hatred dominates. On the novel's opening page, the narrator Matthew says of King that 'violence followed him like a biblical curse,' that the world King is attempting to heal consists of 'families divided, fathers at the throats of their sons, brothers spilling each other's blood.'"[22] Conner particularly notes Johnson's invocation of the biblical story of Cain and Abel, as well as that of Joseph and his brothers, to examine America's racial climate during the 1960s. The explicit references to the Cain and Abel narrative and *Dreamer*'s typological identifications of King with Abel and of Chaym Smith—the poor man who looks just like King and offers to serve as his double—with Cain buttress Conner's contention that this narrative allegorically admonishes America to achieve the beloved community that the historical King desired.

Conner's treatment of the role of Christianity in *Dreamer* has significant implications of Johnson's representation of exodus politics, formal leadership, and the civil rights movement. Conner emphasizes the persistence of Afro-Protestant biblical appropriation traditions in African American political thought and draws attention to the authority of patriarchal strife in biblical narratives, demonstrating how those ideas continue to shape understandings of black leadership during the 1960s and beyond. The exodus narrative, as an urtext of masculine authority and leadership in the Bible, becomes an antecedent text to the Cain and Abel story and frames the significance of that story in *Dreamer*. The opening description of a world of "fathers at the throats of sons" illuminates how societies problematically pose political conflict as what Eve Sedgwick would call an "affair between men."[23] Johnson further implies that men need to solve this crisis.

Using the negotiation between God and Moses, the original "affair between men," as the foundation upon which to build models for civil rights leadership, black civil rights struggles have replicated this tendency to imagine black men as the *only* black people waging the battles for black people's civil rights. If readers (re)position this "affair" within the context of the "originating" tale on civil rights, they can see the significant role of gender in shaping political discourses that privilege the normative black subject's political concerns and interests as representative of all constituencies within those communities. The exclusion of black women and their leadership from contemporary appropriations of the Exodus narrative further reveals the material implications of not calling into question the politics of gender that exodus politics reinscribes: these politics undermine the achievement of equality for all black people by diminishing the significance of cross-cutting issues.

While scholarly treatments of the historical King have called into question the usefulness of the trope of the black messiah in understanding King's career, *Dreamer* goes further to combat the paradoxes of exodus politics that this trope (re)produces. With regard to the historical King, Linda Selzer echoes the arguments of Conner, Nash, and Byrd that "[King's] elevation to the status of Black Messiah was already being undermined by several factors, including failures in Albany, Chicago, and Memphis that suggested he was no longer the unifying leader he had once been."[24] While Selzer rightfully observes that King's "Black Messiah" status was losing its cultural currency, she frames the civil rights movement's inability to unify as a result of the decline in messianism. The larger question is whether unification is possible or even desired, given the diversity of political concerns and interests that African Americans possess.

Perhaps the inability to unify should not be interpreted simply as a symptom of messianism's decline. *Dreamer* suggests the impossibility of unification under any political philosophy, such as exodus politics, that suppresses difference—that is, cross-cutting issues. Even the southern constituency of the civil rights movement, which had been able to organize around eradicating Jim and Jane Crow segregation and securing voting rights, faced challenges in "unification": the common grounds of racial oppression under which exodus politics organized could not suppress the paradoxes that exodus politics reinforced. As *The Autobiography of Miss Jane Pittman* and *Meridian* clarify, the entrenchment of exodus politics in male formal leadership, and the refusal of exodus politics to conceptualize civil rights outside paradigms that privileged racial rights over gender equity, contributed to the breakdown of exodus politics' viability. *Dreamer*, too, emphasizes how exodus politics insufficiently theorizes the diversity of black politics and concerns, and the book invites readers to consider how, if at all, exodus politics can offer an emancipatory vision that acknowledges and engages difference.

In *Dreamer*, the ubiquity of the interlocking forces that defeat the campaign for African Americans' civil rights and liberties in historical Chicago further impedes exodus politics' ability to achieve long-term transformations and causes the historical King to question the black messiah role. Even though his rhetoric and metaphors often appropriated messianic discourses, King did not want to take on this role. In *Why We Can't Wait* King articulates his own shortcomings as the movement's *sole* leader and expresses his wish not to be a martyr.[25] Although he seems to understand the need to build self-sustaining communities that are effective in the absence of formal leaders, it is less clear whether he believes that women should be bridge leaders. This ambiguity reflects again a tension between his resistance to the exodus politics paradigm and his emphasis on black male leadership as necessary for black freedom struggles to succeed. Johnson capitalizes on both of these revelations in *Dreamer*, particularly through King's decision to allow Chaym Smith to be his double. While the fictive King, in agreeing to employ Smith, admits the impossibility of formal leaders fulfilling all the roles thrust upon them, he simultaneously realizes that American capitalism circumscribes the civil rights movement's potential to achieve equality.

This second epiphany further bridges the mid-1960s setting of the novel with the 1990s era in which Johnson lives.

The demands of phase two of the movement propel King's entrance into the national body politic as the formal leader for *all* civil rights issues. *Dreamer* points out not only the unreasonableness of this expectation but also the stress that exodus politics imposes on leaders. As the historical King told his congregation when he resigned as pastor, a quote repeated in *Dreamer*: "I've been faced with the responsibility of trying to do as one man what five or six people ought to be doing. . . . What I have been doing is giving, giving, giving, and not stopping to retreat and meditate like I should—to come back. If the situation is not changed, I will be a physical and emotional wreck. I have to recognize my personality and reorient my life. I have been too long in the crowd, too long in the forest" (18–19). Sheer exhaustion pervades King's life in the final three years of his fictive leadership and life as he flies across the nation, leads demonstrations, and meets with community leaders. His frustration with "giving, giving, giving" reveals his desire not to let the movement deplete him, and he instead considers alternative ways to lead black freedom struggles.

Much like Meridian at the end of *Meridian*, King gives serious thought to refusing to accept his upcoming "crucifixion" by walking away from phase two of the movement. After the march in Memphis, for example, he agonizes: "His critics were right—sometimes he was a damned poor organizer. But how could he oversee everything? Be everywhere at once? He felt he was caught in a current sweeping him relentlessly forward" (218). His frustration indicates how the movement, as a "current sweeping him relentlessly forward," has overtaken all aspects of his life. Yet he recognizes that he cannot "oversee everything": the community must also facilitate its own empowerment. King therefore accepts Chaym Smith's offer to serve as his civil rights double in the Chicago Freedom Movement; if Smith appears in King's stead, King can be relieved from having to be everywhere at every moment.

The invention of Smith as King's literary doppelganger exposes the paradoxes of exodus politics by reinforcing the idea that it is impossible for any single male formal leader to "secure" black people's civil rights.[26] It also, however, draws attention to a significant yet understated ideology that shapes civil rights discourses: the black heterosexual male subject that civil rights discourses normalize is middle class. That civil rights discourses framed the increased opportunities legislation made possible as key to improving black people's upward mobility and life chances underscores the inextricable tie between social class and civil rights ideologies. Smith, however, contends that black poor people exist outside the system and will not have access to the opportunities that might improve their social condition. Further, he suggests that because capitalism operates through class stratification, middle-class civil rights discourses that are rooted in capitalistic ideas can never achieve equality. Given the overrepresentation of black people among the nation's poor, civil rights discourses that focus primarily on middle-class attainment and financial stability, without addressing how capitalism thrives on structural inequality, cannot ameliorate the class stratification Jim and Jane Crow segregation has produced.

Smith is antagonistic to the fictional King's emphasis on equality of opportunity because it champions a notion of upward mobility that seems available primarily to middle-class blacks, or poorer blacks who are close to middle-class status. He points out that for many blacks equality of opportunity is only theoretical: black people have never had or never will have access to equal opportunities and therefore will not achieve equal outcomes. Johnson's depiction of King and Smith as two men who have almost identical physical features but markedly different social class backgrounds and major ideological (social class and ensuing perspectival) differences undermines the notion that black people possess a unified set of black political interests and concerns, while simultaneously emphasizing cross-cutting social class issues.

The scene in which King and Smith first meet juxtaposes Smith's exact physical resemblance to King with his obviously different social class, not only to remind King of his middle-class privilege, but also to underscore the difficulty King has sharing that privilege with the black masses. Smith's hard-bitten look of poverty, which "makes him the kind of Negro the Movement had for years kept away from the world's cameras," contrasts with the polish of the historical King's middle-class upbringing on Auburn Avenue (31). For Smith this difference further evidences that all men are not created equal and that racism and classism deal hands unfairly to black people. More controversially, Smith argues that the government will not significantly diminish this inequality because it lacks the commitment to do so and is instead deeply invested in racism and capitalism. From Smith's perspective, the government never truly intended to ensure that equal opportunities would translate into equal outcomes. Smith's presence then raises fundamental questions about equality with which King must grapple: "The acuity, the clarity with which he'd dismissed 'equality' and all that hallowed word implied. There in the predawn shadows, in the unveiling parenthesis into which Smith's coming placed his most cherished beliefs, he wondered if perhaps it was no more than a word, an abstraction, empty sound signifying nothing. A chimera at the Movement's core, in fact, the very centerpiece of Jefferson's magnificent declaration" (44). The conversation with Smith haunts King by calling into question whether equality can be achieved and thus unsettles his "most cherished belief" and guiding philosophy. If not equality, what are they fighting for? Less inequality, accepting as fact that equality can never be achieved?

Not only the fictive but the historical King was increasingly challenged to examine more critically his conceptualization of equality. Johnson uses the fictive King to remind readers of how the historical King wanted to ensure that the rhetoric of equality materialized in African Americans' lives. As early as 1964, the historical King asked: "How can we make freedom real and substantial for our colored citizens? What just course will ensure the greatest speed and completeness? And how do we combat opposition and overcome obstacles arising from the defaults of the past?"[27] Both Kings emphasize direct action as a necessary communal strategy to press the government toward egalitarianism so that African Americans, especially poor people, will better their economic standing. King's language here is instructive: the term *default* suggests that the government "owes" African Americans for failing to have provided them fair access to the national economy. For King, affirmative action programs were not just economically necessary but morally responsible.

Congress never espoused King's Bill of Rights for the Disadvantaged, but the very proposition emphasized the role government should have in institutionalizing affirmative action programs to remedy inequality. While a principle of color-blind "fairness" and egalitarianism might seem to be a just response to economic disparities by race, it actually undermines the sociopolitical work of diminishing disparities. The failure to more explicitly foreground the dimension of social class in civil rights discourse reproduces the paradox of exodus politics that defines civil rights primarily in terms of "racial" rights. Civil rights discourses that emphasize middle-class attainment without explicitly analyzing how middle-class ideology undermines these efforts for most black people obscure the need for specific policies and programs aimed at helping the black poor.

In one of the most provocative analyses of African American literature's engagement with social class in the civil rights movement, Rolland

Murray argues that Johnson's representation of class stratification among African Americans in the civil rights movement foreshadows a trend of deepening class divisions in subsequent decades. Murray contends that the text's historical setting is brought into dialogue with Johnson's contemporary setting (the 1990s) as a way of exploring the future implications (in the twenty-first century) of not developing a civil rights platform, including leadership strategies, that would account for class differences among black people:

> In this case the class dynamic of civil rights activism surfaces in the figure of Smith to unnerve King. Though King often encounters members of the black underclass, he is rarely forced to consider their presence. The underclass that he and other black spokespersons presume to represent thus becomes the repressed other of the movement's bourgeois managerial class. At the same time the uncanny quality of Smith cannot be reduced to the oppressive ontology of King and his ilk. It must also be understood as an integral feature of Johnson's own mode of historicism. In fact, the narrative technique whereby King is construed as recognizing the movement's own repressive apparatus is somewhat misleading. King is not only spellbound by his recognition of something he has repressed; the uncanniness produced by Smith also facilitates Johnson's casting of a presentist concern with the intractability of class division as if it were the return of the repressed by making the past confront the full fruition of a class conflict that could never have been fully realized in the past. It is therefore not only King's encounter with the underclass that unsettles him but a meeting with the future of black class relations.[28]

Murray foregrounds the multidimensional role of social class in *Dreamer*, particularly in terms of the philosophical rift that social class engenders between King and Smith, and between middle-class and poor black communities. As the end of the narrative reveals, one of King's challenges in Chicago is that he cannot relate to community members who need to be bridged before he can successfully secure open housing. Murray distinguishes between "encountering" and "considering" the black underclass to demonstrate the chasm that exists between the visible formal leaders and the constituents whom they are thought to represent and/or whom they need to bridge. This argument reinforces how social class engenders the paradoxes of exodus politics in black leadership models and fractures black political interests along class lines. For Murray, *Dreamer* and black culture more generally have attempted to repress the concerns of the black poor because considering their plight and political concerns would necessarily contest some of the main ideologies and presumptions guiding middle-class ideology in civil rights discourses. Murray argues that Smith forces King to confront this excluded group. With their socio-economic concerns in mind, King must consider the potential long-term effects of not including black poor people in conversations about civil rights. *Inclusion* here refers not only to making poor black people part of the decision-making process but also to considering whether current conceptualizations of civil rights adequately grasp their socioeconomic needs.

Further, *Dreamer* presents the antagonism between the middle-class King and the poor black masses as parallel to the ideological differences between the civil rights movement and the Black Power movement. Bishop confirms this parallel, observing that while "the nonviolent Movement drew successfully from the ranks of the black middle class," it "stalled and sputtered in poor, grassroots communities" (60). Murray's earlier contention suggests that black formal leaders, who are middle class and promote middle-class civil rights ideologies, do not serve well the interests of all the constituents whom they presume to represent. The nonviolent movement stalls because the formal leadership tactics have failed to bridge—to raise consciousness within these communities. One might argue that these communities would altogether resist middle-class ideology and could never be bridged. Nevertheless, some black leaders and organizations were attentive to these potential class conflicts and differences.

SNCC, as chapter 2 discusses, made a conscious effort to work collaboratively with communities and not merely impose a vision on them. Recall that Meridian's bridge leadership involves canvassing communities and interacting with potential adherents to raise consciousness about the movement. For Meridian, the community's interests are important factors that (re)constitute the movement's goals and philosophies. By positioning themselves in a dialogic relationship with potential movement adherents, bridge leaders can disarm the resistance that emerges when formal leaders who are not members of the communities attempt to impose what communities perceive as an irrelevant or otherwise inchoate black political agenda.

The historical King's decision to engage in civil rights agitation in Chicago was multifaceted: he wanted not only to tackle the urban decay to which slum housing, inadequate education funding, and black underemployment contributed but also to revive and revolutionize the movement, which he saw splintering and losing pace. After visiting a variety of cities, including Philadelphia, King and the SCLC decided to work collaboratively with the Coordinated Council of Community Organizations (CCCO) in order to further dismantle patterns of segregation. Segregation and the resultant inequalities that it produced had become almost immovable under Mayor Richard Daley's leadership. Johnson portrays King's desire to revolutionize the movement as a simultaneous personal revolution that fundamentally alters King's concepts of civil rights and leadership.

King's new musings, which happen in the context of the violence that plagues the Chicago Freedom Movement, offer the most penetrating insights into how a critique against sole formal leaders arose. Because no one formal leader could take on full responsibility for the movement, it became clear that a long-term strategy was necessary that would train individuals within communities to share the responsibility for their own individual empowerment and that of the community. By exposing this particular paradox of exodus politics, Johnson illuminates the political costs of investing formal leaders with mythic powers. Yet his notion of shared governance still privileges male leadership.

While the historical King wanted to revive the movement, to correct what Rudolph Byrd describes as his failure "to devise a national strategy that would reach and inspire the young in the urban areas beyond the South," the fictional King encounters difficulty in meeting this goal in Chicago because of his continued investment in exodus politics.[29] Even as King develops more expansive notions of leadership, he excludes seemingly "unfit" leaders from leadership roles and thus limits the opportunities for potential leaders. As Belinda Robnett has argued, leaders needed a certain pedigree; even Bishop reinforces this point in *Dreamer* when he indicates that because Smith was poor he was kept away from the cameras—that is, from acting as the face of the movement. King understands that the movement must respond to the changed political opportunities that legislative accomplishments have made possible. He further grasps that middle-class ideology complicates civil rights missions and may inhibit the achievement of equality. He fails, however, to foreground the roles bridge leaders must play during phase two of the movement as it tries to develop a nationwide strategy for civil rights attainment.

Although white resistance, as manifested in the physical violence that the text portrays, exacerbates King's inability to develop a national strategy to address civil rights issues, his own vision of acceptable leadership styles, tactics, and philosophies is what most limits the scope of the movement. If, as Bishop relates, "King's efforts in Chicago had pried open a Pandora's box of racial paradoxes, not the least being that in the wake of Black Power's appeal in the northern ghettos his political approach was unraveling at the seams" (60), this unraveling results partially because there are no bridge leaders to engage in consciousness-raising strategies. Bridge leaders might not have made Black Power less appealing to young (and older) African Americans, but their "insider" status might, however temporarily, give them more communal influence than a formal leader would have.

Bishop later reveals that King "traveled by police escort to bars, churches, and meeting halls, begging angry black crowds to replace violence with mass action aimed at disruption" (61), and Johnson's portrayal of Zubena as a black nationalist whose plan for violence seems ill-conceptualized and misguided suggests that direct engagement with the constituents might have proved useful; as Meridian wants to ask questions that will engender conversations about civil rights, their importance, and their preservation, such dialogue in *Dreamer* might attract some would-be adherents to join. On this point, a return to *Meridian,* in which Meridian and Truman debate the merits of voting with skeptical potential black registrants who ultimately understand its potential to affect change and later register to vote, again proves instructive. Political consciousness develops in nonlinear ways, and bridge leaders undoubtedly shape this process through the prefigurative strategies they employ.

Rather than advocating that King, or any other formal leader, needed to relinquish nonviolent strategies and accept violence, I would argue that posing the question "What would violence achieve?" in a way that extended mutual dialogue would have helped bridge the class gap that *Dreamer* highlights. The historical King did meet with gang members, the black poor, and other especially marginalized segments of black communities, but it is unclear how much the meetings were marked by a dialogue in which ideas, concerns, and potential solutions were mutually considered. Whereas King encouraged black people to avoid violence, while warning white power structures that the conditions of the ghetto made violence inevitable, the perception that he ultimately compromised on an ineffectual housing deal reinforces the point Murray perceptively foregrounds about internal rifts.[30] The poor, black nationalists, and other black leaders believed that King had sold out the black poor to Mayor Daley by settling for a deal that they themselves would not have accepted.

The Absence of the Union to End Slums

The Union to End Slums played an active role in bridging communities to the larger civil rights movement and organizing direct action against Chicago's slumlords. Yet this organization is absent from *Dreamer*. While Johnson may not have deemed the Union to End Slums integral to the Chicago Freedom Movement, the omission effectually writes black women's leadership in the movement out of civil rights historiography. *Dreamer* may express skepticism about the effectiveness of leadership by a single man, but it still portrays men's leadership as necessary for black enfranchisement and fails to imagine a space for women in the movement that extends beyond secondary and supportive roles. Unlike Ernest Gaines, who tried to write a civil rights historiography that would correct the trend of black women's erasure from civil rights historiography, Johnson does not consider how women function in the movement.

This exclusion of women's leadership roles could stem more from King's opinion of women's subordinate status in the movement than from a failure of Johnson's imagination. Nevertheless, by not imagining a space for women's leadership in phase two, the book, in the words of Sharon Monteith, leaves "leadership as a masculine preserve."[31] Monteith has contended that "Johnson slips between the prevailing ideologies of civil rights history and historically skewed representations of black manhood to disentangle King and re-present him in interrogative and imaginative ways for contemporary readership, yet when he imagines an alter ego for Martin Luther King in *Dreamer*, he does not imagine women."[32] Johnson's portrait, then, does not challenge the historiographical tendency to define the movement's leadership in terms of men who, because of their access to state institutions, sat at the table of leadership in Chicago, even though women's bridge leadership forged communal involvement in the Chicago Movement. The Chicago Freedom Movement was organized hastily, was poorly focused, and had ill-defined objectives. The fictional King acknowledges each of these problems as a result of his inability to "oversee everything." Neither the fictional King nor the historical King had to oversee all aspects of the movement, given that female bridge leaders did in fact mobilize potential adherents. The micromobilization efforts of female bridge leaders to get communities to join the Unions to End Slums were central to the Chicago Movement but are underdeveloped in *Dreamer*.

Historians of the Chicago Freedom Movement note women's integral roles in Chicago's CCCO and the SCLC's coalition to address the problems of slum housing and to lobby for an open housing policy. These two goals were the main foci of the Chicago Freedom Movement. As David Garrow and Taylor Branch have elaborated, women, as bridge leaders, served as block captains, entering communities to canvass and organize blocks in order to prepare for the march scheduled for the summer of 1966.[33] Their planning and "behind the scenes" work, as well as their many admonitions about the movement's ill-preparedness and unwieldiness, do not emerge in *Dreamer*. Two challenges that the Chicago Freedom Movement faced beyond the magnitude of the problems it needed to address were defining clear goals for the movement (the province of male formal leaders) and organizing and mobilizing constituencies (the province of female bridge leaders). As my analyses of *Miss Pittman, Meridian*, and *Corregidora* insist, women's bridge leadership, and sometimes their formal leadership, were pivotal in raising consciousness and drawing potential constituents into the movement. As Septima Clark's and Ella Baker's leadership during the civil rights movement exemplifies, women also did hold titles, even though they did not receive the same public recognition that men did. Moreover, they set visions for the movement to advance, as did formal leaders, and implemented those visions through their own bridge leadership.

While violence and white resistance toward the marches hampered protesters' efforts, organizational challenges impeded progress as well. The inclusion of these issues, which are central to bridge leadership responsibilities, would better call attention to the insufficiency of exodus politics' tendency to privilege male leadership and reject shared governance. Positing the nation's conflict as an affair between brothers, an affair between men, Johnson, who himself has articulated the importance of preserving historical records "as much as possible, for delivering, say, aspects of the history of a marginalized people," actually renders women's rights, leadership, and activism invisible in the context of the Chicago Freedom Movement.[34] In effect, he keeps black women marginalized—when they are already some of the community's most marginalized people.

By not addressing women's roles in the Chicago Freedom Movement, Johnson in some ways preserves the popular static image of King as exemplary formal leader, despite King's desire to disperse his leadership responsibilities (perhaps only to other men). Some women, including Amy, her grandmother, and Mama Pearl, are indeed present in the text, and the novel mentions Bishop's deceased mother. They do not, however, have significant roles, thus recalling the flatly developed black women characters who populate Richard Wright's *Native Son* and Ralph Ellison's *Invisible Man*. In many respects, King's inability to fulfill his role as formal leader becomes part of Johnson's critique of exodus politics' tendency to champion male leadership, a practice that dissuades communities from becoming self-sufficient and self-empowered. As the forthcoming discussion of the open housing project reinforces, the desire to empower communities cannot be framed in a hierarchy—such as exodus politics—that positions the formal leader as the only person whose leadership and vision matter. Yet unlike *Miss Pittman*, *Meridian*, and *Corregidora*, in which the authors insist that redemptive male leadership fails partly because of its inability to consider seriously women's oppression, Johnson's text seems conspicuously silent on the issues of women's roles and women's rights. While *Dreamer*'s critique of exodus politics clearly repudiates the notion of a superordained male formal leader because of its deleterious effects on both leader and followers, it does not clearly stake out an argument against male formal leadership altogether or offer a position on women's leadership and activism.

King biographer David Levering Lewis contends that the three goals of the Chicago Freedom Movement were "to educate people about slum conditions, to organize slum-dwellers into a union to force landlords to meet their obligations, and to mobilize slum tenants into an army of nonviolent demonstrators."[35] The movement's organizers thus foregrounded "consciousness-raising" as their central prefigurative bridge leadership strategy to obtain communal buy-in and create self-sustaining communities. The Chicago Freedom Movement and the Union to End Slums shared the vision of creating, block by block, "[an] organization of people who *understood* the source of their problems and would be willing to work together on a number of issues."[36] Responsible for organizing the blocks and buildings, the SCLC staff functioned as bridge leaders who connected the prefigurative strategies aimed at individual transformation to the political strategies that situated their protests in a broader context of civil rights agitation.

Although absent from the text itself, the organizing and consciousness-raising work that the Union to End Slums performed was much like what *Meridian* describes regarding Meridian and Truman's house-to-house visits that attempt to capitalize on the legislative attainment of voting rights that the civil rights movement made possible. Both *Dreamer* and *Meridian* consider how the movement can be reinvigorated to respond to changing forms of discrimination. Although *Dreamer* does contest the paradoxes of exodus politics, particularly the limitations of male formal leadership, the absence of the Union to End Slums speaks to a more ubiquitous lack of engagement with bridge leadership and activism and calls into question whether Johnson proposes an alternative to exodus politics and the leadership and civil rights conundrums that it presents. Johnson's omission is both revealing and significant in that it illuminates one of the major organizational problems that plagued the summer march, in addition to violence and racism.

Although both the historical and the fictional King understood the importance of building coalitions and learning the particulars of Chicago before engaging in nonviolent protest, both underestimated the degree to which racism and violence, when coupled with insufficient preparation of constituents, would make Chicago an inhospitable place for civil rights improvements. Chicago's events foreshadowed the types of violence and resistance that would plague the nation long after King was assassinated. While the fictional Daley supports King's accomplishments in Selma, "he would not concede to the anticapitalist King of 1966 that his city was a bastion of bigotry based on economic exploitation," and therefore he blames the violence that erupts following the marches on King's presence (60). According to Bishop, black leaders sided with Daley and thought King's operations in Chicago were ill-conceived and ill-planned: "On local television Rev. Joseph H. Jackson pointed out to the minister that Chicago had problems but was not the Deep South. Furthermore, some said, the objectives of the Movement were hazy. Many blacks wondered if one of the fundamental goals of freedom should be the chance to live next door to white people in places like Cicero" (60). This last reflection incorrectly frames integration (living in Cicero) as the ultimate goal of the civil rights movement. While King did go to Chicago to fight against segregation, his dream for civil rights had long expanded beyond this goal.

The cancellation of the march in Cicero signaled a surrender to white authority, and the compromise that emerged from King's meeting with Mayor Daley was problematic for several reasons. One of the main objections to it was that the plan failed to institute specific time lines and measurable benchmarks by which to test whether "fair" housing practices were being "promoted" or "enforced." Whereas the historical King's summer march in Chicago garnered a few concessions from Mayor Daley, the black community viewed it as a failure, and Johnson's book portrays it as such. The agreement not only failed to meet all of the movement's initial demands but also granted "rights" that seemed more symbolic than substantive. As *Dreamer* describes it and the subsequent reactions:

> The Summit Agreement, though, not wholly satisfactory to King (it had no guarantees, no schedule, nothing but good intentions), was nonetheless broader in boons won for the black poor than anything he'd achieved in the South, and so he delayed the march into Cicero. Later, at a church on the West Side, he admitted, "Morally, we ought to have what we say in the slogan, Freedom Now. But it doesn't all come now. That's a sad fact of life you will have to live with." Some, like members of SNCC and Robert Lucas of Core, refused to live with that. They couldn't wait, they said. To their eyes, the Summit Agreement was a sellout, an emergency exit King used to parachute out of his promise to end slum dwelling in Chicago. Many proclaimed they were tired of being led by middle-class Negroes and rejected the Agreement terms. (152)

As Rudolph Byrd notes, "The Summit Agreement, the Chicago Movement's culminating document—drafted in collaboration by King, Daley, and the leadership of business and religious communities at Chicago's Palmer House—did not possess a timetable nor guarantees for the reformation of fair-housing practices and the abolition of the practice of red-lining that excluded African Americans from bank loans."[37] The agreement's shortcomings raise a question that persists after the rights that phase one of the movement fought for are consolidated in law: How do African Americans ensure that the theoretical promise of equality of opportunity translates into actual equality of outcome? If not freedom now, then when?

As David Garrow reports in his account of the historical meetings, these type of questions often frustrated Mayor Daley and members of the Chicago Real Estate Board, who thought that some of the black leaders were antagonistically questioning their commitment to addressing Chicago's housing slum crisis. Although Daley had promised to get the City Council to pass legislation requiring real estate brokers to post "antidiscrimination" policies in their windows, some leaders remained skeptical as to whether real estate agents would honor what they posted. Al Raby underscored this cynicism when he asked, "Is the Mayor going to ask for legislation to require brokers to post the ordinances in their windows; will he ask [the City Council] for that legislation next Tuesday and will he get it? Will that actually be implemented?"[38] Concerned that the mayor and the Real Estate Board were merely making promises to quell the ensuing unease among white Chicagoans about integrated neighborhoods, Raby, like other critics, saw the compromise as a symbolic gesture. Its purpose was to undermine African Americans' rights while maintaining segregated communities. If, as the fictional King elsewhere thinks, "integrated lunch counters cost the nation nothing" but "class struggle would indeed be costly," *Dreamer* shows Raby and the other activists at the meeting as understanding that Daley is taking such an ambiguous role in the proceedings because (like the Brazilian government in *Corregidora*) he does not want to pay (62).

The Chicago Freedom Movement, as *Dreamer* depicts it, metonymically encapsulates the problems that the movement and the nation have faced in the aftermath of phase one of the civil rights movement and in the wake of the backlash against affirmative action programs. The Chicago Freedom Movement's defeats reflect a broader problem: How can the nation address the long-term effects of civil disenfranchisement without policies and practices that account for the historical accumulation of inequality and yet ensure equality in the future? Bishop presciently ponders: "Mightn't whites come to perceive Negroes as no longer a victimized class but a privileged one, thus leading to a resentment and lack of respect and racial disdain greater than anything witnessed during the era of Jim Crow? Mightn't too much reliance on federal government, even in private affairs such as rearing a family, lead to the inability to do for oneself, unhampered by bad laws, that was the Movement's original purpose?" (62). As affirmative action policies came under attack in the 1990s in particular, and the rhetoric of "personal responsibility" dominated civil rights discourses, the notion that society should take into consideration the cumulative effects of segregation was opposed by a curious logic: affirmative action programs would lead to the "inability to do for oneself." Such arguments finally seemed to subvert the goals of the civil rights movement; rather than ensure that the theoretical equality of opportunity translated into the equality of outcome, the government left the attainment of this equality to chance and black people's own efforts.

In the context of housing, discourses of "color blindness," "fairness," and "qualifications" helped turn back civil rights progress, as the desire to ignore race only seemed to re-entrench inequity. Johnson's engagement with these issues in the context of the 1990s' assault on affirmative action raises related questions: How, for example, would a bank judge the qualification of an African American buyer who, because of having been excluded from credit markets or subjected to predatory lending practices, might score several percentage points lower in credit ratings? In an attempt to be color-blind and not make adverse judgments against an African American consumer, might a lending institution disadvantage a consumer by not considering how race had made the candidate "less worthy" of credit? Policies that aim to be "fair" by not accounting for race end up reproducing inequitable results because of race. Critical race theorists have especially made this case with regard to employment laws, since seemingly fair policies such as "last one hired, first one fired" disproportionately affect African American workers because of their history of having been excluded from workplaces.[39] *Dreamer*'s interrogation of civil rights demonstrates the dangers in succumbing to such ideologies of "fairness" that actually undermine the vision for empowerment that the civil rights movement proposed.

By the end of *Dreamer* the assassins have murdered King, as they murder Jimmy in *Miss Pittman*, and Smith has gone off with government authorities in an ambiguous disappearance that reinforces substantiated conjecture about the government's involvement in orchestrating the historical King's death. As the community experiences an overwhelming sense of despair following King's death, Bishop broods, "We all killed him" in that we failed to uphold our responsibilities as citizens and activists. Although the government official who solicits Smith's assistance in discrediting King suggests that "the sense that [King] had a racial mission—a destiny—to fulfill, that he was personally responsible for eliminating the world's suffering," was just King's "Messiah complex," the King whom Johnson portrays, at least in his thoughts, does not wholeheartedly embrace this complex (202); he merely recognizes that anyone taking up the cross of injustice will certainly be "crucified." Johnson's book contributes to the historiographical project to understand King's life and leadership, to contest the privileging of formal male leadership, to challenge middle-class discourses that undermine the goals of the civil rights movement, and to enlarge the scope of civil rights by considering how race intersects with class. By grappling with all these aspects of civil rights historiography, Johnson equally contributes to the literary project of calling into question the efficacy of exodus politics as a political strategy in wake of the modern civil rights movement.

Epilogue: Is There Life after Exodus Politics?

What had once been so easily defined as the ongoing black-against-white
conflict has metastasized into a polychromatic, polyglot, polyethnic stew of
a war. And within the black community, what once had been romanticized
as a monolithic voice from a mountaintop, a series of moral Elijahs and
Moses and Apostle Pauls condemning their pharaohs and Pilates, has
broken free of those old Biblical archetypes into a fractal world of politics
and economies, a chaos of cultures, a bouillabaisse of media, a shifting
tangle of strategies and agendas and ideologies. What once had been so
easily polarized by Huey Newton and Marcus Garvey is now not so easily
parsed.

—RANDALL KENAN, *THE FIRE THIS TIME*

Messianism, Charisma, Exodus Politics:
Black Leadership in Perspective

When Oprah Winfrey decided to endorse Barack Obama's presidential
bid, she carved out a new space for herself in American electoral politics.
Although Winfrey previously had not endorsed any presidential candidate, her use of messianic typology demonstrated her familiarity with
exodus politics' long-standing history. Winfrey emphasized Obama's
uniqueness as "the One" who could redeem America and deliver her into
a more democratic and equitable future. In an Iowa campaign speech in
December 2007, she invoked Gaines's *The Autobiography of Miss Jane
Pittman* to explain Obama's status as "the One" and thus situated him
within the exodus politics tradition. Winfrey recounted watching the
cinematic adaptation and seeing actress Cicely Tyson point her finger
and ask Jimmy, "Are you the One?" As Winfrey recalled, "I remember
her [Cicely Tyson as Miss Jane Pittman] standing in the doorway, body
bowed, frail, old, and holding the baby in her arms, and saying, 'Are you
the one, Jimmy: Are you the one?'"[1]

By framing Obama in this black messianic political tradition, Winfrey claimed that Obama would usher America into a new era of equality by disrupting political systems that produced inequality. As Winfrey
concluded, "I believe in '08 I have found the answer to Ms. Pittman's

question. It is the same question that our nation is asking. He [Barack Obama] is the One."[2] The audience thunderously applauded, thus showing the continued saliency of the male messianic figure as the desired political leader in (African) American political and cultural thought. Yet by isolating this particular moment in the film, and ignoring the fact that racists murder Jimmy, Winfrey celebrated black messianism and exodus politics. Her exaltation of redemptive patriarchal leadership was curious because both Gaines and Obama appeared skeptical of its potential to institute long-term change. Obama emphasized "we" in his inauguration speech and employed the slogan "Yes *we* can" throughout his campaign to deemphasize the singularity of "the One." Similarly, Gaines in his novel calls into question the political effectiveness of the black messianic figure by illuminating how an investment in male formal leadership undermines enfranchisement efforts. Although *Miss Pittman* contests the very premise that Winfrey champions, her invocation of an African American literary text to endorse a presidential candidate underscores the long-standing role African American literature has had in shaping political discourses.

In *Exodus Politics*, I have argued that contemporary writers of African American literature have challenged the dominance of exodus politics in black political thought and have called for increasingly complex notions of black politics, black leadership, and civil rights. Whereas earlier cultural forms, including spirituals, deployed exodus politics to argue for civil rights, more contemporary writers have contested the efficacy of exodus politics to achieve civil rights equality. They point to paradoxical logics inherent in exodus politics that prevent the development of political agendas that engage cross-cutting issues and consider the political interests of non-normative black subjects. When Winfrey framed Obama's leadership within this paradigm, she illuminated the tensions in black politics, leadership, and civil rights struggles that African American literature continues to engage. She also turned attention to the charismatic and messianic traditions that exodus politics has developed alongside.

In *Charisma and the Fictions of Black Leadership* (2012), Erica R. Edwards examines sociological and religious conceptualizations of charisma to challenge the valorization of charismatic authority in black leadership discourses. Edwards argues that charisma is "a political fiction or ideal, a set of assumptions about authority and identity that works to structure how political mobilization is conceived and enacted."[3] She maintains that political discourses have idealized black male leadership as "the necessary precondition for survival progress, political power, and social unity."[4] Contesting the authority of charisma in black political discourses, Edwards demonstrates how charismatic authority masculinizes black leadership. As I have argued in *Exodus Politics*, however, neither biological mandate nor divine ordination makes men a priori leaders. The idealization of a charismatic male leader is problematic in that it undermines the role of everyday activities and ordinary people in obtaining civil rights; ignores the roles women have had in orchestrating black freedom struggles; and privileges the normative black subject's political concerns and interests as the most important within communities. Each of these practices undercuts the development of self-empowered, self-sustaining enfranchised communities.

By conceptualizing charisma "as phenomenon, as formation of authority, and as the discursive material for the elaboration of black social and political identities, relationships, and movements," Edwards rightfully contests religious discourses that frame charisma as simply "gifts from God" (bestowed upon men).[5] She further upsets sociological theorizations of charisma that emphasize the authoritarian personality of the leader but do not historicize the contexts in which the charismatic leader emerges.[6] For instance, Max Weber suggests that revolutionary impulses create the conditions under which a charismatic leader arises, and he also argues that charismatic authority wanes as a revolutionary force after followers become increasingly interpellated. However, as Cedric Robinson and Roderick Ferguson observe, Weber's latter claim does not obtain in the West, where, under slavery and heterosexism, revolutionary impulses do not dull so easily.[7] Edwards corrects this tendency—to conceptualize charisma "simply as phenomenon or as an architectonic of authority"—examining it instead "as a discursive and performative terrain for the elaboration of black movements for social and political change."[8] In other words, Edwards analyzes the political and social circumstances of black life that compel black freedom struggles to perform charisma, while examining the sometimes debilitating consequences of these performances. Like *Exodus Politics*, Edwards's study is invested in analyzing everyday and noncharismatic exercises of resistance, defiance, and organization that attempt to unhinge oppressive institutions, policies, and practices.

African American literature and social thought not only have challenged the authority of charisma, but also have called into question discourses that frame the charismatic leader as a political messiah. In *Black Messiahs and Uncle Toms: Social and Literary Manipulations of a Religious Myth* (1982), the historian Wilson Jeremiah Moses argues that black messianism has dominated black sociopolitical thought since slavery. From the antebellum period through the Garvey movement and into the mid-twentieth-century civil rights movement, black messianism has shaped the contours of black leadership and black civil rights agendas and has circumscribed black literary production. According to Wilson, the civil rights movement engendered sociological and psychocultural shifts that led artists and critics to reevaluate the political efficacy of messianism.

While Moses believes that "black messianic movements are clearly destined to continue well into the twenty-first century," he warns that the "secularization of black leadership" and "the loss of direction experienced by black America since the deaths of Malcolm X and Martin Luther King" "threaten the persistence of traditional forms."[9] Even as leadership becomes more "secularized" and the "black church" is no longer imagined to be the primary site of black political organization and culture, Wilson suggests that messianism will persist as the form of leadership black people desire. Yet by suggesting that the "traditional" form of messianism will not endure the political shifts that the civil rights movement caused, Wilson prompts the question: What ideologies would messianism have to eschew, or embody, in order to be a productive force for black political organization, activism, and advancement?

I have argued in this book that it may not be possible to reconceive messianism in a way that would promote the long-term achievement and preservation of civil rights, while recognizing the complicated nature of black leadership and political mobilization. My readings of *Miss Pittman*, *Meridian*, *Corregidora*, and *Dreamer* return to fundamental questions: How can messianism empower communities if the longevity of a movement is tied to the leader's life span? Can models that require formal leadership simultaneously cultivate empowered, self-sustainable communities? Does messianism assume a hierarchical relationship between the leader and the community, and will that hierarchy be replicated in a hierarchy of concerns, with those of dominant community members taking priority? *Exodus Politics* clarifies the paradoxical propositions these questions raise, while contending that even reimagined forms of messianism may not be compatible with civil rights attainment.

Black Politics: The Long Civil Rights Movement and American Myths

While the election of Barack Hussein Obama as the forty-fourth president of the United States was historic because the win secured his position as the first African American man to serve in America's highest political office, the implications this election has had for black political activity resound throughout American culture. His election, first presidential term, and reelection have invoked the civil rights movement, engendering debates about the symbolic and material significance of "the age of Obama" to the movement overall.[10] Obama's election and presidency have become discursive sites to articulate and rearticulate, stage and restage, affirm and contest, ideologies about black politics, postracialism, and civil rights. The questions that have emerged include: Did Obama's election fulfill Dr. King's dream?[11] Should a black president promote a separate black politics for black communities?[12] Is "the age of Obama" a postracial era?

Regardless of how one responds to these questions, their persistence brings up important historical and contemporary contexts for understanding the relationship between civil rights, black politics, and black leadership. That a black man would be elected president four decades after the pinnacle of the civil rights movement's legislative accomplishments signifies a tectonic shift in American race relations. This shift, however, has not dislodged the material effects the history of race has produced. As Kenan's epigraph proposes, contemporary race relations are not "so easily defined as the ongoing black-against-white conflict." From Reconstruction to the present, black-white race relations have been structured by the exclusion, suppression, and/or incorporation (often meaning co-optation) of black political activity. Before the 1950s and 1960s, Jim and Jane Crow segregation seemed immovable and race relations doomed for failure. Yet while the civil rights movement has changed America's racial climate, analysts of black life and politics cannot ignore, minimize, or otherwise take for granted the enduring significance of slavery, Reconstruction, and Jim and Jane Crow segregation. The legacies of these historical epochs continue to structure African Americans' cultural production, political thought, and life opportunities.

In *Sites of Slavery: Citizenship and Racial Democracy in the Post–Civil Rights Imagination* (2012), Salamishah Tillet argues that "one of the fundamental paradoxes of post–civil rights American politics" is "African Americans' formal possession of full legal citizenship and their inherited burden of civic estrangement."[13] Tillet means that African Americans "have been marginalized or underrepresented in the civic myths, monuments, narratives, icons, creeds, and images of the past that constitute, reproduce, and promote an American national identity."[14] *Exodus Politics* articulates the problem of African American exclusion, particularly in terms of the persistence of inequality, despite the improvements in black life and opportunities that phase one of the civil rights movement made possible. Obama's election, as he himself has portrayed it and as the American cultural imaginary has interpreted it, straddles the paradox that Tillet theorizes: Obama draws upon the icons and myths that Tillet identifies to write African American civic participation into the national myths, but he does not call into question the problematic aspects of these mythologies.

Obama's inaugural speech, for example, invokes the principles of the Declaration of Independence and the Constitution, documents that were crucial in cementing African Americans' statuses as noncitizens, as the means to reverse the symbolic and material exclusion of African Americans from America's institutions: "This is the meaning of our liberty and our creed— why men and women and children of every race and every faith can join in celebration across this magnificent mall, and why a man whose father less than 60 years ago might not have been served at a local restaurant can now stand before you to take a most sacred oath[.] So let us mark this day with remembrance, of who we are and how far we have traveled."[15] The "our" is both American and African American in that it inserts African Americans, as racialized subjects, as a part of America's founding principles, thereby giving them access to "creeds" that "promote an American national identity." Furthermore, Obama acknowledges the role of the civil rights movement in affording him the opportunity to serve as president. By ending the Jim and Jane Crow segregation that might have prohibited his father from "being served at a local restaurant," and that certainly would have prevented black people from voting and holding elected offices, the civil rights movement helped to democratize American society. Obama thus frames his position on the stage at the National Mall within a narrative of American progress that identifies the civil rights movement as responsible for enfranchising African Americans. Not only has the movement literally granted African Americans the right to vote alongside other markers of full citizenship; it has also improved race relations.

If, as Winfrey declares, Obama may be read as a political messiah, his messianic role partly stems from the idea that his election also symbolizes a new chapter in America's race relations. In this capacity, Obama also functions as a charismatic leader, someone who, as Edwards contends, "in moments of crisis . . . is to provide a practical schema for sweeping change as well as to serve as a fantastic locus of projections of hope, wholeness, national identity, and renewal."[16] Situating his speeches within the contexts of black political performances that rely on the fiction of charisma to reveal "an idealized narrative of liberation rooted in history," Edwards explains the broader cultural repository from which Obama has drawn.[17] Yet as she argues (and I readily concur), this tradition warrants further interrogation because the ideologies it encodes are counterproductive to liberatory politics. To that end, Obama's own rhetoric further contextualizes why pundits, conservatives, scholars, public intellectuals, and everyday people alike have interpreted this election as a new chapter in American history: racial politics does not rely solely on the old wars of white against black. One danger of becoming postracial in the post–civil rights era, or post–civil rights in the postracial era, is that both propositions ignore how the language of "post-" renders invisible instances in which civil rights have not been attained and race continues to matter.

While Obama reads his election as a sign of the racial progress that the civil rights movement made possible, this success also has been interpreted as evidence par excellence that Americans live in a post–civil rights and postracial society where "race" does not matter. By treating the exception— Obama—as representative of black people's endless possibilities, postracialists obfuscate the pervasive cultural and material realities of black disenfranchisement. While those who proclaim a postracial era argue that the civil rights movement fundamentally changed the structure of inequality for the better, Melvin Oliver and Thomas Shapiro's *Black Wealth / White Wealth: A New Perspective on Racial Inequality* (2006), Cornel West's foreword to Michelle Alexander's *The New Jim Crow: Mass Incarceration in the Age of Colorblindness* (2010), and Manning Marable's *Race, Reform, and Rebellion: The Second Reconstruction and Beyond in Black America, 1945–2006* (2007) have maintained that the civil rights movement, while improving black middle-class life, left the black poor and working class worse off than they had been before. As my analyses of *Dreamer* and *Meridian* clarify, the changing complexity of racial disenfranchisement in the absence of de jure segregation requires new conceptual and practical models for engaging the reality of civil rights injustices. The contemporary political climate in which the election of Barack Obama as president can be read as the removal, and not the restructuring, of disenfranchisement complicates the development of black political alliances.

Observing the nation's diminished capacity to engage problems surrounding race and civil rights injustices in light of Obama's election, David Eng notes: "Today we inhabit a political moment when the disparities of race— not to mention sex, gender, and class—apparently no longer matter; they neither signify deep structural inequities nor mark profound institutional emergencies. Our historical moment is overburdened by the language of colorblindness—especially with the election of our nation's first African American President—the one marked by the erosion of a public language for discussing race and racism."[18] While Obama's insistence on a unified community might also contribute to the "erosion of a public language," society cannot allow the rhetoric of postracialism and color blindness to obscure inequality's persistence. Rather, communities must trace how inequality takes new forms, despite social practices and customs that attempt to veil them. As the African American literary texts that *Exodus Politics* examines demonstrate, phase two of the civil rights movement found itself responding to this challenge as commitments to civil rights justice waned and as discrimination became more difficult to prove.

Lawrie Balfour also argues that the idea of color blindness erodes the potential for Americans to capitalize on the equality that the civil rights movement demanded because the notion denies the ongoing significance of race in structuring political and cultural access. Although "widespread acceptance of the *principle* of racial equality represents genuine progress," "resistance, particularly among white Americans, to mechanisms designed to implement the principle points to the limits of that progress. Despite tremendous gains, recent appeals for a national dialogue about race and the difficulty of engaging in such a dialogue signal the failure of the American people 'to rise above . . . itself' simply by declaring race to be irrelevant to citizenship."[19] Although Obama's election has reconstituted debates on race, racism, color blindness, and even multiculturalism, this important conversation—one in which many scholars, public intellectuals, supporters, and antagonists have engaged—is only part of what seems to be at stake in the significance of Obama's election as it relates to discourses on civil rights, black nationalism, and black politics.

Rather than signaling that black people collectively possess the same access to the opportunities that assisted Obama's ascendancy, the election magnifies the widening division that exists between the equality of opportunity that the legislative and congressional acts of the 1950s and 1960s bestowed in theory and the reality of continued inequality. If color-blind and postracial discourses elide how structural inequality and disparity truncate the opportunities available to African Americans, so too does Obama's handling of these issues.[20] As David Ikard and Martell Teasley lament, "Obama steers the discourse of racial empowerment toward romanticized and symbolic domains and away from hardcore strategies to obliterate the structural barriers that continue to hamper black upward mobility and fortify poverty."[21] The development of solutions that diminish inequality can happen only when political models reflect on how civil rights issues, black leadership models, and black politics have changed in the wake of phase one of the civil rights movement.

Obama's election, then, does not fulfill the goal of equality that drove the civil rights movement; it only marks another beginning, as law professor and political scientist Kareem Crayton rightly notes: "Electing a black candidate for the nation's highest office may certainly be part of the formula for black political power, but it cannot substitute for the enactment of substantive policies that respond to the long overdue calls for racial justice. On this score, the Obama political story largely remains a work in progress."[22] What is left undone is the political work to ensure that the theoretical equality of opportunity translates into an equality of outcome.

The scholarly and public conversations about color blindness and postracialism that have surrounded Obama's election have been exhaustive. I recall them here to situate "the age of Obama" in the context of a question that *Exodus Politics* has argued warrants more scholarly attention: How has the civil rights movement reconstituted the discursive terrain of black politics, black leadership, and civil rights in the decades that followed the movement's milestones? A long historical framework becomes necessary to understand the civil rights movement in both its historical and its contemporary contexts. Cornel West is therefore right to argue that "the sixties is not a chronological category which encompasses a decade, but rather a historical construct or heuristic rubric that renders noteworthy historical processes and events intelligible."[23] If America is in a post–civil rights era, the prefix *post-* signals that communities must change their leadership strategies if they are to address civil rights inequities that have taken new forms in the wake of the achievements of the civil rights movement.

African American Literature and Exodus Politics

Exodus politics has been a vexed political strategy at best and a counterproductive one at worst. African Americans strategically deployed exodus politics during the nineteenth century primarily because it afforded them both a "nation language" and a "political strategy" by which to insert themselves into the American body politic. Exodus politics, however, has not kept up with the political changes and social upheavals that have occurred since the nineteenth century. Both African American literature and "long civil rights movement" historiography demonstrate how the elision of gender, sexual, and social class differences among African Americans undermines exodus politics' best intentions for empowerment by (re)producing its paradoxes. African American literary and cultural modes of expressivity—from the African American spiritual "Go Down Moses" to Toni Morrison's *Paradise* (1998)—have engaged the paradoxes of exodus politics and thus exemplified how producers of African American culture conceptualize their art as affecting the discursive field of politics.

In the African American literary imagination that this book examines, the paradoxes of exodus politics manifest themselves in the leadership models that African Americans champion. They also emerge in the development of black political agendas that refuse to embrace and conceptualize cross-cutting issues as part of "[long] civil rights struggles." Late twentieth- and early twenty-first-century cultural trends nevertheless make it difficult for black leadership and civil rights discourses to recognize that differences among African Americans outweigh the putative "sameness" that aided the organization of mid-twentieth-century civil rights struggles; that the languages of color blindness and postracialism erode the equality of opportunity that the civil rights movement demanded; and that new Jim and Jane Crow-isms are reinstitutionalizing inequality. Under these conditions, neither black leadership nor civil rights discourses can afford to ignore difference or demand sameness. By treating black women's gender rights as "civil rights," *Corregidora,* in particular, makes cross-cutting issues central to contemporary black civil rights agendas. As chapter 3 has shown, the text provides innovative ways for black leadership and civil rights discourses to recalibrate and reconceptualize strategies to address civil rights issues in the contemporary moment.

In the aftermath of the civil rights movement, African American literary texts have repeatedly taken leadership and civil rights discourses as points of departure, building upon a long-standing tradition in African American letters that situates literature as an important cultural site for formal and informal political activity. In this way, writers of contemporary African American literature make two critical interventions in civil rights historiography: first, they conceptualize civil rights intersectionally and foreground cross-cutting issues as the main source of black politics and political mobilization; second, they embrace leadership models that are more egalitarian than the ones that exodus politics offers. Through these interventions, they reveal to black communities how to further long-term black enfranchisement, thereby imploding the paradoxes of exodus politics that have long vitiated the long civil rights movement.

Notes

Introduction

1. West, *Race Matters*, 56.

2. In "Toward a True Black Liberation Theology," Horace Griffin argues against the biblical and theological justifications for homophobia by historicizing homophobia, heteronormativity, and sexism as important cultural frameworks that shape biblical and theological understandings. Irene Monroe's "When and Where I Enter" offers a similar critique of heterosexism but emphasizes the cultural manifestations of sexism more than the biblical and theological contexts. Michael Eric Dyson's "When You Divide the Body and Soul, Problems Multiply" is perhaps one of the most persuasive critiques of the philosophical, theological, and cultural ideologies that reproduce homophobia and disenfranchise black lesbian, gay, bisexual, and transgendered people. Each of these scholars makes compelling arguments for why gay rights are civil rights while proposing useful ways to embark upon a paradigm shift to conceptualize them as such.

3. See Moynihan, *Negro Family*.

4. The black feminist notion of intersectionality foregrounds how one's multiple subject positions constantly intersect and interact and affect one's political and cultural opportunities and outcomes. It rejects the notion that race and gender, for example, are separable, or that race is more important than gender or vice versa. Instead, it considers how multiple identities are always already being constituted by each other. Although Kimberlé Crenshaw coined this term in a legal context in the 1990s, earlier work by Frances Beale on black women's "double jeopardy" and by Deborah King on "multiple consciousness" expresses the same concept (Crenshaw, "Mapping the Margins"; Beale, "Double Jeopardy"; D. King, "Multiple Jeopardy").

5. Scott, *Extravagant Abjection*, 8.

6. B. Smith, "Toward a Black Feminist Criticism," 410.

7. Ibid., 417.

8. See Cheryl Clarke, "Lesbianism."

9. Abdur-Rahman, *Against the Closet*, 2.

10. Ibid., 9.

11. See Carbado, "Introduction," esp. 1–3.

12. See Patricia Hill Collins's theory of the new racism in *Black Sexual Politics*.

13. Steve Estes's *I Am a Man!* compellingly explains how gender, and manhood in particular, shaped civil rights movement discourses. This work importantly foregrounds the implicit ways that gender, and masculinism more specifically, intersected with race and sexuality to articulate the struggle for civil rights.

14. See Giddings, *When and Where I Enter*, and Robnett, *How Long? How Long?*

15. See Williams, *Sisters in the Wilderness*; Monroe, "When and Where I Enter"; and Douglas, *Sexuality and the Black Church*.

16. See Mueller, "Ella Baker."

17. See James, *Transcending the Talented Tenth*, to see her admonition against elevating literature to this status.

18. Iton, *In Search of the Black Fantastic*, 6.

19. Monteith, "Revisiting the 1960s," 234.

20. Ibid., 234.

21. Hall's call for a "long" periodization echoes the arguments made in Lawson, *Running for Freedom* (1991), Marable, *Black Leadership* (1998), Joseph, "Waiting till the Midnight Hour" (2000), and Payne, *I've Got the Light of Freedom* (1995) insofar as collectively these historians desire to "make civil rights harder" by dismantling the notion in American history that the classical phase was the movement's essence. Although they do not use the term *long*, their conceptualization of the civil rights movement in "phases" addresses the larger claim that Hall maintains. This "phasing" not only reflects the historical shift in the movement's strategies, philosophies, and goals as it transitioned from agitation to implementation but, more importantly, emphasizes the fact that legislative achievements were only an initial component of a more expansive set of corrective actions necessary to ensure that African Americans would enjoy their civil rights and liberties.

22. Here I am referring to Lorraine Hansberry's play *A Raisin in the Sun* (1959), which invokes Harlem Renaissance poet Langston Hughes's poem "Harlem" as its point of departure to examine the limits (symbolic and material) of residential integration in Chicago.

23. The idea here is that the rhetoric of equality has been used to shift the focus from institutional racism to personal responsibility in order to explain the disparities that exist between African Americans and whites. Hall, in "Long Civil Rights Movement," draws attention to this point, but other cultural critics such as Michael Eric Dyson in *Is Bill Cosby Right?* have examined how this formulation obfuscates the institutional barriers that persist to obstruct civil rights justice.

24. Metress, "Making Civil Rights Harder," 140.

25. Ibid., 141. In *Neo-segregation Narratives*, Brian Norman suggests further theorizations that should take place about segregation's representation in African American literature. I am gesturing toward a theorization of the formal features that should constitute "a long civil rights movement" narrative. Although the four questions that frame this study might be a starting point, such an interrogation would investigate more specific tropes to generate and/or respond to those questions.

26. In "Site of Memory," esp. 68–72, Morrison argues that African American literature that returns to the subject slavery attempts to fill in the "interiority" that literary and historical conventions often omitted from slave narratives. As a writer, she is interested in uncovering historiographical truths, which can be differentiated from "facts." Morrison argues that these truths supplement historical narratives and that literary texts provide insights into history that sometimes eludes "historical" texts.

27. Iton, *In Search of the Black Fantastic*, 8.

28. Jarrett, *Representing the Race*, 4.

29. Ibid., 4.

30. Ellison quoted in Watts, *Heroism and the Black Intellectual*, 49.

31. Building upon the work of civil rights historian Belinda Robnett, this project considers bridging activities as "leadership" in order to unsettle the problematic and sometimes arbitrary distinction often made between "leadership" (formal leadership) and "activism" (bridge leadership). Doing so, as chapter 1 explains, is important particularly to democratize the politics of gender and sexuality as they pertain to leadership during the civil rights movement. Because the majority of the formal leaders were men, while the bridge leaders were women whose "leadership" was classified as secondary and less important "activist" work, any corrective historiography must trouble this division.

32. Jarrett, *Representing the Race*, 7. For Reed, according to Jarrett, blurring this distinction erroneously attributes more power to cultural forces than Reed argues they have. See A. Reed, *W. E. B. Du Bois*.

33. Ibid., 9.

34. Warren, *What Was African American Literature?*, 5.

35. V. Smith, foreword to *Sarah Philips*, xi.

36. Here I am referring to Hurston's *Moses, Man of the Mountain* and Baldwin's *Go Tell It on the Mountain*, both of which I examine later in this introduction.

37. According to Nora in "Between History and Memory," "Lieux de memoire (sites of memory) are simple and ambiguous, natural and artificial, at once immediately available in concrete sensual experience and susceptible to the most abstract elaboration. Indeed, they are lieux in three senses of the word—material, symbolic, and functional. Even an apparently purely material site, like an archive, becomes a lieu de memoire only if the imagination invests it with a symbolic aura" (295). In my formulation, I suggest that African American writers are combining the material, symbolic, and functional in their treatments of the civil rights movement as a way to reconceptualize the movement's multiple significations.

38. *Exodus Politics* diverges from Melissa Walker's *Down from the Mountaintop* (1991) in that it is not a comprehensive survey of how black women's texts use the historical referents of where the struggle for racial justice has been to argue where it is going. While the past informs contemporary and future issues of civil rights, I am more concerned with a larger philosophical inquiry about the categories of civil rights and leadership. I diverge from Dubey's *Black Women Novelists* (1991) by locating the paradoxical liberation-oppression dyad in civil rights discourses, focusing specifically on leadership and activism, and frustrating periodizations that draw a strict line between the civil rights and black power movements. Finally, I diverge from Rolland Murray's *Our Living Manhood* (2007) by calling into question the degree to which black men, too, countered notions of black masculinity that attempted to inscribe

166 / NOTES TO INTRODUCTION

them in problematic discourses as they related to civil rights, black leadership, and black political activity.

39. Edwards, *Charisma*, xv.

40. Ibid.

41. Ibid.

42. In my forthcoming essay entitled "A Triple-Twined Re-appropriation: Womanist Theology and Gendered-Racial Protest in the Writings of Jarena Lee, Frances E. W. Harper, and Harriet Jacobs," I argue that Harper is invested in patriarchal leadership but that she foregrounds the role of women by illuminating the important role Moses's mother plays in his becoming a leader.

43. Wright, "Blueprint for Negro Writing," 99; Valkeakari, *Religious Idiom*, 2, 3.

44. Ibid., 3–4.

45. In *Breaking the Silence* (2007), Ikard's analysis of *Go Tell It on the Mountain* emphasizes how the black church's cultural significance further complicates Florence's willingness and ability to contest its patriarchal leanings because doing so would marginalize her within this particular community. See chapter 2, "Black Patriarchy and the Dilemma of Black Women's Complicity in James Baldwin's *Go Tell It on the Mountain*," esp. pp. 67–69.

46. Ferguson, *Aberrations in Black*, 82–93.

47. In *Faithful Vision* (2006), James Coleman provides a reading of *Go Tell It on the Mountain* that stands apart from the majority of criticism in that he maintains that Baldwin celebrates religion itself but highlights how the characters have problems relating with each other. His reading of *Go Tell It on the Mountain* insists that "*Go Tell It on the Mountain* moves inevitably toward the anguished mystery of existence, particularly African American life, and the implication that God must be that mystery; the mystery of God is the saving Word that one can know only by faithfully giving up the self to the spiritual experience of the power and benevolence of God" (44). While Coleman is right that the characters have problems relating to each other, his reading underestimates the degree to which Baldwin is indicting religion for its role in antagonizing these relationships. See the first half of chapter 2, "The Centrality of Religious Faith: Communal Acceptance, Textual Ambiguity, and Paradox," 43–59.

48. Murray, *Our Living Manhood*, 24.

49. Edwards, "Moses, Monster of the Mountain," 1085.

50. Edwards, *Charisma*, 102.

51. Ibid., 102.

52. McDowell, "Foreword," xiii.

53. B. Johnson, "Moses and Intertextuality," 15–29.

54. Albert Raboteau is one of many theologians who have argued that enslaved African Americans believed that God was on the side of the oppressed and saw God as a Liberator. Their formulations resist the notion that African Americans passively accepted their conditions and were otherworldly, focusing more on freedom in heaven and not in America. See Raboteau, *Slave Religion* (1978). Specifically regarding these issues in black American spirituals, Cone advances a similar argument about their content in "Black Spirituals."

55. Walzer, *Exodus and Revolution*, 4.

56. Hurston, "Author's Note," in *Moses, Man of the Mountain*, xxiv.

57. Glaude, *Exodus!*, 6.

58. Williams, *Sisters in the Wilderness*, 149–50. Although I discuss other black theologians including Albert Raboteau and James Cone, the main church historian I am thinking of here is Gayraud Wilmore; see his *Black Religion and Black Radicalism*.

59. Ibid., 150.

60. Ferguson, *Aberrations in Black*, 117–18.

61. Douglas, *Sexuality and the Black Church*, 96.

62. Ibid., 97.

63. I am referring to the popular notion that black men are in danger of becoming extinct, metaphorically, as their exclusion from educational and employment arenas and their overrepresentation in the criminal system have made their existence precarious. See Patricia Dixon's concepts of institutional deprivation and decimation in *African American Relationships*.

64. Monroe, "When and Where I Enter," 126.

65. Jacquelyn Grant makes a similar point years earlier in "Black Theology and the Black Woman," where she argues that in an attempt to reclaim their manhood black liberation theologians have not called into question the normative uses of scripture as they relate to women and sexism.

66. Glaude, *Exodus!*, 12.

67. Peterson, *Doers of the Word*, 18,

68. Foster, introduction to *Written by Herself*, 4.

69. Stewart, "Religion," 30; Stewart, "Farewell Address," 71.

70. Also see Truth's "When Women Get Her Rights" for a more specific articulation of Truth's vision for political equality.

71. C. Johnson, "Conversation with Charles Johnson," 234.

1 / "Is He the One?"

1. According to Tom Carter, who interviewed Ernest Gaines for *Essence* magazine in 1975, *The Autobiography of Miss Jane Pittman* had sold nearly one million copies (850,000 in paperback and 26,000 in hardback). The sales for this book far outnumbered those for his previous works (Gaines, "Ernest Gaines" [Carter interview], 80). Additionally, as Jerome Tarshis reports from his interview with Gaines for the *San Francisco Magazine* in 1975, the cinematic production of the text increased the accessibility of the novel to people who viewed CBS television network's adaptation, even though Gaines was rarely mentioned in the publicity or Emmy Awards that were won (Gaines, "Ernest Gaines" [Tarshis interview], 72). Both of these factors contributed to the widespread consumption of *The Autobiography of Miss Jane Pittman*.

2. Several African American novels come to mind, including Margaret Walker's *Jubilee* (1966), Ishmael Reed's *Mumbo Jumbo* (1972), Alice Walker's *The Third Life of Grange Copeland* (1970), and Toni Morrison's *Song of Solomon* (1977), which represent the range of historical issues that became sites of memory in African American literature during this time period.

3. See Andrews, "We Ain't Going Back There"; Byerman, "'Slow-to-Anger' People"; Giles, "Revolution and Myth"; Hicks, "To Make These Bones Live"; and Jackson's "*Jane Pittman* through the Years."

4. See Franklin and Meier, *Black Leaders*; Lewis, *King*; Oates, *Let the Trumpet Sound*.

5. Cohen, *Boundaries of Blackness*, 8–9.

6. While black feminism and black studies have secured more of a place in the academy, black queer studies, as E. Johnson and Henderson's *Black Queer Studies* (2007) demonstrates, has only recently begun to be institutionalized within the academy. All of these disciplines, from varying angles, and to different extents, challenge essentialist notions of black identity.

7. See Neal, "Some Reflections" and "Black Arts Movement," Calvin Hernton, "Sexual Mountain," and Fuller, "Towards a Black Aesthetic," for a general overview of the prevailing definitions that dominated black aesthetic discourses. For an exemplary explanation of how black women writers challenge the prescriptiveness of the black aesthetic, see Dubey, *Black Women Novelists*.

8. For the male critics' views on how black women writers were portraying black men, see Hogue, the chapter "History, the Feminist Discourse" in *History and the Other*; Watkins "Sexism, Racism"; Addison Gayle, quoted in Roseann Bell's "Judgment"; and Ishmael Reed, quoted in Alexander and Wright, "Race, Sex, and Class," as well as black feminist critics Deborah McDowell ("Family Matters") and Valerie Smith ("Gender"). The men's antagonism stemmed not only from black aestheticians' notions of how black literature should represent black people but also from an ideological difference, in that black women were concerned with interrogating the realities of their lives which included oppression by black heteropatriarchy. They were not, as black male critics accused, "male bashing."

9. I would instead argue that the narrative struggles to foreground the women's voices and that Miss Jane's life story at times competes with the male narratives, which can predominate. For criticism regarding the feminine voice, see Doyle, "Tales within Tales," Babb, "From History to Her-Story," and Gaudet's "Miss Jane and Personal Narrative" and "Black Women."

10. Byerman, "'Slow-to-Anger' People," 108.

11. Here Gaines's work complements that of his contemporary Toni Cade Bambara, who argues in "On the Issue of Roles" that social transformation begins with a radical ideological reprogramming of the self and that black people's investment in traditional gender roles and norms undermines black liberation, creating antagonistic relationships between black men and black women and diminishing the capacity to develop cooperative coalitions that can tackle concerns that are specific to each group.

12. See, e.g., Morris, *Origins of the Civil Rights Movement*, which treats male formal leadership as the primary catalyst for engendering the masses to participate in the movement.

13. Robnett, *How Long? How Long?*, 18.

14. Ibid., 13.

15. Ibid., 19.

16. Peter Ling, "Gender and Generation," 101.

17. Giddings's *When and Where I Enter* (1983), Crawford, Rouse, and Woods's *Women in the Civil Rights Movement* (1993), Ling and Monteith's *Gender and the Civil Rights Movement* (2004), and Whitt's *Short Stories of the Civil Rights Movement* (2006) are just a few of the scholarly texts that explore the transformative role of women's leadership during the long civil rights movement.

18. Hussen, "'Black Rage' and 'Useless Pain,'" 316.

19. Byerman, "'Slow-to-Anger' People," 120.

20. Gaines, "Interview with Ernest Gaines" [Lowe interview], 303.

21. Andrews, "We Ain't Going Back There," 149.

22. See Kelley, *Hammer and Hoe*. The quotation is from Robnett, *How Long? How Long?*, 8.

23. DuBois, "Souls of Black Folk."

24. Benston, "I Yam What I Am," 5.

25. Benston argues that in the 1960s, with the rise of black consciousness, African American literature becomes especially concerned with the process of naming. He identifies Jay Wright as an exemplary poet whose work examines the process and significance of naming. According to Benston, "To know your name, Wright feels, implies knowing your genealogy; self-definition is more generous, less aggressive, when it comes from a sense of continuity" (10). Accordingly, names connect individuals to their direct familial line, and by extension, to their racial communal line. For a more in-depth analysis of Wright's conceptualization of names, see Benston, "I Yam What I Am," 9–11.

26. Babb, "From History to Her-Story," 82.

27. When the soldier renames Jane, he tells her not only that Ticey is a slave's name but also that "his girl" back home is also named Miss Jane. This moment in the text is problematic, illuminating how this moment of empowerment objectifies Miss Jane. The allusion to the soldier's "girl" articulates the double objectification, by race and gender, that Miss Jane experiences under slavery and will continue to experience after Emancipation. This moment, nevertheless, remains significant for reasons that Babb argues and also because, as I argue, it awakens in Miss Jane a consciousness that is at least doubly coded, that is, racialized and gendered.

28. Black feminists, for example, have praised Sojourner Truth's 1851 speech, "Ain't I a Woman," delivered at the women's rights convention in Akron, Ohio, as expressing the intersection of racial, gender, and class politics that black women faced in antebellum America.

29. Doyle, "Tales within Tales," 136.

30. Washington, "Introduction," xvii.

31. For an engaging review of how ineptly high school history textbooks have handled the subject of black history, see Loewen, *Lies My Teacher Told Me*, and Anderson, "Secondary School History Textbooks."

32. K. Gaines, *Uplifting the Race*, 129.

33. Logan describes the period from the end of Reconstruction through the turn of the twentieth century as the "nadir" or lowest point in race relations that the nation had experienced since Reconstruction, explaining how the cultural phenomena I cite contribute to the increasing problems between African Americans and white Americans. See *Negro in American Life*.

34. See Richardson, *Black Masculinity*, for a discussion of how these multiple contexts articulate black masculine discourses and how black masculine discourses articulate themselves through and against these contexts.

35. Truth, quoted in *Rise and Fall of Jim Crow*, program 1, *Promises Betrayed*.

36. Reddy, *Freedom with Violence*, 21.

37. Ibid., 20.

38. Frederick Douglass, quoted in *Rise and Fall of Jim Crow*, Program 1, *Promises Betrayed*.

39. In *Charisma*, Edwards provides a cogent reading of the gender politics of the Million Man March in her discussion of the Million More March, which celebrated the ten-year anniversary of the Million Man March. As Edwards demonstrates, both the first and second marches framed black political enfranchisement as a project for men, and Farrakhan's gender formulations were staged by the presence and absence of black women (ix–xiv).

40. Cone, *Martin and Malcolm and America*, 273.

41. Mitchem, *Introducing Womanist Theology*, 109. Eulogizing these four children, King referred to them as "martyred heroines of a holy crusade," suggesting that "the girls' deaths might redeem Birmingham, the South, and even America itself" (153). See Miller, *Voice of Deliverance*.

42. Papa, in "His Feet on Your Neck," argues that Gaines rejects Anglo-Protestantism because it symbolizes white oppression (187). This argument, however, ignores the prevalence of Anglo-American dominant themes, including Miss Jane's "white Christology" when she "gets religion." While Gaines challenges some of the prevailing ideologies in Afro-Protestantism, Papa's contention that Gaines rejects this tradition does not hold against the evidence *Miss Pittman* provides to the contrary.

43. Whitted, *A God of Justice?*, 11.

44. Whereas the book ends with Miss Jane and other community members pledging their allegiance to still go to the courthouse, the movie shows Miss Jane actually "demonstrating": both whites and blacks watch her walk to the courthouse, drink from the water fountain, return to the pickup truck, and leave without incident. The movie thus connects Miss Jane to the male characters who serve as the public figureheads of civil rights activism.

45. Doyle, "Tales within Tales," 151.

2 / "The Refusal of Christ to Accept Crucifixion"

1. In many respects, the civil rights movement and the Black Power movement share similar goals of improving the material conditions of African Americans. The year 1966 is often cited as designating the beginning of Black Power, when Stokely Carmichael first used the phrase, and the year 1968, when King died, is often used to mark the end of the civil rights movement. But a long civil rights movement historical framework, such as Walker is concerned with, breaks down this distinction between the beginning of one movement and the end of another.

2. Quoted in Baker, *Betrayal*, 38.

3. See Hamilton, "Federal Law."

4. Rustin, "From Protest to Politics: The Future of the Civil Rights Movement" [1965], in *Time on Two Crosses*, 112. In this same essay, Rustin argues that the removal of legal barriers informed three trends that were central to the changing face of the civil rights movement: "a shifting focus of the movement in the South; the spread of the revolution to the North; and the expansion of the movement's base in the Negro community" (111). For Rustin, these changes necessitated establishing a power base within communities that would hold institutions accountable for achieving the fact of equality. In many ways, the bridge leadership Walker depicts engages in a similar project.

5. Moynihan, *Negro Family*, 3.

6. See, e.g., J. Collins, "'Like a Collage,'" on Walker's "distinction between the non-violence of the civil rights movement and the militancy of the Black Power movement" (175).

7. T. Davis, "History's Place Markers," 195.

8. See Danielson, "Alice Walker's *Meridian*"; Hendrickson, "Remembering the Dream"; Stein, "*Meridian*"; Yoon, "Gendering the Movement"; Dubey, *Black Women Novelists*, ch. 7, "'A Crazy Quilt': The Multivalent Pattern of *Meridian*"; and Melissa Walker, *Down from the Mountaintop*, ch. 6, "In the Wake of the Movement."

9. T. Davis, "History's Place Markers," 195.

10. Nadel, "Reading the Body," 155.

11. Emmett Till was murdered for allegedly whistling at a white woman in Money, Mississippi. Although the sheriff in Money had ordered the casket not to be opened, Till's mother demanded to see her son's corpse. Upon witnessing his mutilation, she decided that the world ought to see what white racists had done to her son. In addition to the thousands of people who viewed the body in Chicago, on September 15, 1955, *Jet* magazine brought that image into even more homes by publishing it. For a comprehensive study of the different aspects of this case, see Metress, *Lynching of Emmett Till*.

12. Metress and Pollack, *Emmett Till in Literary Memory*, 4.

13. See Barker, "Visual Markers," esp. 464–66.

14. Marable, *Race, Reform, and Rebellion*, 146–47.

15. Walters and Smith, *African American Leadership*, 225.

16. Lipsitz, *Possessive Investment in Whiteness*.

17. M. King, *Why We Can't Wait*, 166.

18. Marable, *Race, Reform, and Rebellion*, 91.

19. Ibid., 91.

20. Smith, quoted in Giddings, *When and Where I Enter*, 297.

21. A. Walker, "Civil Rights Movement," 121.

22. Wall provides a cogent overview of the multiple audiences that Walker addresses through this essay, including the white media and black nationalists. See *Worrying the Line*, 217–20.

23. B. Bell, *Afro-American Novel*, 262–63.

24. A. Walker, "Civil Rights Movement," 125.

25. B. Bell, *Afro-American Novel*, 263.

26. Dubey, *Black Women Novelists*, 134.

27. Melissa Walker, *Down from the Mountaintop*, 170.

28. Barnett's "'Miscegenation,' Rape," explores the tensions between race, gender, and sexuality manifested in *Meridian*'s portrayal of a black man's rape of a white woman. Employing Valerie Smith's notion of split affinities, Barnett argues that Walker contests hegemonic notions of gender via the feminist movement and race via the black nationalist and civil rights movement to challenge narrow notions of "allegiance." The essay compellingly situates Walker's discussion not only in the contemporary context but in a larger historical trajectory of black and white relations.

29. Hendrickson, "Remembering the Dream," 114.

30. In "History and Genealogy," Butler-Evans asserts that "racial history is marginalized here [in *Meridian*], noted only in the fact that Meridian is a civil rights worker," to suggest that racial and gender identities can be separated. This reading, as I suggest throughout, is problematic for the reasons I have outlined.

31. Berlant, "Race, Gender, and Nation," 211.

32. Danielson, "Alice Walker's *Meridian*," 323.

33. Christian, *Black Feminist Criticism*, 243.

34. See Standley, "Role of Black Women"; Robnett, "Women in the Student Non-violent Coordinating Committee."

35. Quoted in Mueller, "Ella Baker," 58. For a comprehensive study of Baker, see Ransby's *Ella Baker*.

36. Baker quoted in Standley, "Role of Black Women," 194.

37. In 1966, SNCC voted to expel white activists from its organization, reflecting not only racial tensions within the group but larger organizational and philosophical problems. My reading here does not intend to present SNCC as a problem-free organization; rather, it suggests that SNCC's guiding principle of participatory democracy provided a vision of leadership that, unlike those of several other organizations, imparted many of the values and ideas that would propel the civil rights movement forward and would undermine the paradoxes of exodus politics.

38. Mueller describes Ella Baker as a key founder and practitioner of participatory democracy in order to unsettle historiographical accounts that center the Students for a Democratic Society (SDS) as originating this concept. For the definition quoted here, see "Ella Baker," 52–53; for broader historical context, also see 53–55.

39. Marable, *Race, Reform, and Rebellion*, 79.

40. Steigerwald, *Sixties*, 48.

41. Hamer, *Speeches of Fannie Lou Hamer*, xviii–xxi.

42. Steigerwald, *Sixties*, 49.

43. Byerman, "Gender and Justice," 97. Cotten's "Womanist Interventions" shows how ideology and materialism intersect in *Meridian*'s notion of civil rights justice and thereby also contests Byerman's conclusions.

44. Yoon, "Gendering the Movement," 199.

45. Wallace, *Black Macho*, challenges how the image of the strong black woman has been problematically used to enforce the racial and gender oppression of black women.

46. Willis, "Walker's Women," 93.

47. A. Walker, "Alice Walker," 180.

48. Ruskin, "Bridge Poem."

49. Ibid.

50. Ibid.

51. Danielson, "Alice Walker's *Meridian*," 325.

3 / "The Important Thing Is Making Generations"

1. Farah Jasmine Griffin's "Conflict and Chorus" exemplifies the conversation I am entering in that she posits that the 1970s witnessed a proliferation of black women's writing, inaugurated by Toni Cade Bambara's *The Black Woman: An Anthology*, that illuminated the intersections of civil rights and women's rights in black women's freedom struggles. This trend extended beyond fictive texts to include theoretical essays and autobiographical ones as well.

2. Hall, "Long Civil Rights Movement," 1253.

3. Morrison, "Toni Morrison on a Book She Loves," 110.

4. In *Sex and Racism in America*, Hernton employs this phrase to argue that racism is sexually charged and that contemporary laws against interracial marriage, for example, reflect how racism and sexism (and I would add heterosexism) are intertwined. Slavery itself, predicated on ideas of racial inferiority that were constantly sexualized, demonstrates, as black queer studies argues, how black civil rights denials operated through racial, sexual, gender discourses simultaneously.

5. Boutry, "Black and Blue"; Athey, "Poisonous Roots"; Dubey, *Black Women Novelists*, 74–75.

6. In *Monstrous Intimacies*, Sharpe's compelling analysis of *Corregidora* demonstrates how Brazil's institution of a Free Womb Law, which set parameters under which children of enslaved women could be sold and regulations under which owners would have to provide for those children if they did not free them, helped begin the emancipation of black women and their descendants. Yet slave owners found ways to skirt the law so that black women's and their descendants' rights would continue to be abrogated (39–41).

7. Roberts, *Killing the Black Body*, 6.

8. See Irigaray, *Sex Which Is Not One*.

9. Davis, "Women and Capitalism," 157.

10. Spillers, "Mama's Baby, Papa's Maybe," 76.

11. K. Gaines, *Uplifting the Race*, 12.

12. Rich, *Of Woman Born*, 34.

13. Athey, "Poisonous Roots," 263.

14. Weinbaum, *Wayward Reproductions*, 7.

15. Ibid., 7.

16. Holloway, *Private Bodies, Public Texts*, 31.

17. Dubey, *Black Women Novelists*, 74

18. Verge, "Revolutionary Vision," 103.

19. Dubey, *Black Women Novelists*, 74.

20. Athey, "Reproductive Health," 3.

21. Ibid., 6.

22. President Obama's health care legislation has been subjected to an inordinate amount of scrutiny for a variety of reasons; the requirement for employers to pay for women's birth control and the possibility that women might use their health insurance to finance an abortion have intensified the debate.

23. See Kapsalis, "Mastering the Female Pelvis," for a complete discussion of Sims's exploitation of enslaved black women's sexuality and how that practice, however changed, continues today.

24. Athey, "Reproductive Health," 6.

25. Bambara, "Pill," 205.

26. Ibid., 206.

27. See Douglass, "I Am a Radical Woman Suffrage Man."

28. Williams, *Sisters in the Wilderness*, 128–29.

29. See Sharpe, "Costs of Re-membering," and Coser, "Dry Wombs of Black Women."

30. S. Con. Res. 26: A Concurrent Resolution Apologizing for the Enslavement and Racial Segregation of African Americans, 111th Cong., 2009–10, text as of June 18, 2009 (referred to House Committee), www.govtrack.us/congress/bills/111/sconres26/text.

31. Ibid.

32. M. Dixon, "Singing a Deep Song," 239.

33. Wall, *Worrying the Line*, 120.

34. Rather than provide a comprehensive examination of this body of scholarship, I illuminate here some of the key formulations about the blues that recur throughout the scholarship to ground my specific discussion of the genre and the performances in the context of exodus politics, civil rights, and leadership. For thoroughly engaging critical genealogies of blues scholarship, see the chapter "Trouble in Mind" in Wall, *Worrying the Line*; the chapter "Gayl Jones's *Corregidora* and Reading" in Sharpe, *Monstrous Intimacies*; and the chapter "A New World Song" in Dubey, *Black Women Novelists*.

35. Chapman, *Prove It on Me*, 6.

36. See Margolick's "Performance as a Force for Change," which portrays Holiday as a performer who was not cognizant of her song's political significance, thereby siding with critics who viewed her as incapable of apprehending the meaning of the song.

37. Hardack, "Making Generations," 653.

38. Coser, "Dry Wombs of Black Women," 134.

39. Abdur-Rahman, *Against the Closet*, 124.

40. DuCille, *Skin Trade*, 73.

41. See Rushdy, "Relate Sexual to Historical"; Griffiths, *Traumatic Possessions*; Simon, "Traumatic Repetition."

42. In "Love and the Trauma," Li argues that Ursa's knowledge of her mother's private memory demonstrates "how the resistance of one generation becomes the trauma of another" (132). Furthermore, she maintains that this awareness incites Ursa's ability to empathize with her mother and that this empathy helps Ursa not only to develop a better relationship with her mother but also to heal herself.

43. Davis, *Blues Legacies and Black Feminism*, 41.

44. Ward, *Just My Soul Responding*, 339.

45. Ibid., 290–91, 290.

46. Ibid., 300.

47. Here I am referring to Simone's own admission that she wanted her musical performances to influence the black freedom struggles, that she was consciously making music to upset the status quo. See Simone, *I Put a Spell on You*, for a more thorough discussion.

48. Feldstein, "I Don't Trust You Anymore," 1351.

49. Jones, "Interview with Gayl Jones" [Rowell interview], 45.

50. Rushdy, "Relate Historical to Sexual," 276.

51. Dubey, *Black Women Novelists*, 84.

52. Richard Hardack's "Making Generations," Goldberg's "Living the Legacy," and S. Robinson's "*Corregidora*" all argue that (hetero)sexuality is a complex female desire for black women to exercise in patriarchal societies. Building on Teresa De Lauretis's formulation of "space off," the marginalized "elsewhere" outside hegemonic discourse, Sally Robinson argues that "by having Ursa's discourse oscillate between a repetition of her mother's stories, and a narrative of her own experience, Jones constructs a tale that demonstrates the ways in which the specificity of Corregidora's mastery gets translated into the present, in the form of a heterosexual contract based on man's complete mastery over, and ownership of, women's bodies. In order for Ursa to represent herself as subject, she must become adept at reading normative representations

of the 'self' that is required by the master narratives of white patriarchal cultures" (150). Although Robinson's assertion particularly addresses Ursa's relationship with her husband, Mutt, it is relevant to her task as bridge leader because her role as wife affects her understanding of her role as leader as much as her roles as daughter and granddaughter do.

53. See Henderson, "Speaking in Tongues."

54. Davis, *Blues Legacies and Black Feminism*, 137.

55. Ibid., 137.

56. According to Davis: "In contrast to the condemnatory and censuring character of Christianity, it knows few taboos. As a cultural form that has long been a target of racist-inspired marginalization, the blues categorically refrains from relegating to the margins any person or behavior. Because the blues realm is open to discourse on every possible subject affecting the people who created it, it need not banish religion. Rather, what it rejects is religion's manner of defining the blues as an inferior expression of an inferior people. The openness of the blues realm—its repudiation of taboos of all sorts—is rendered possible by virtue of the fact that the blues always decline to pass judgment" (133).

57. Boutry, "Black and Blue," 108.

58. As Hardack argues, even oral sex is always figured as heteronormative. He explains, oral sex "is always represented as fellatio and never lesbian or even heterosexual cunnilingus; Ursa cannot imagine a discourse or desire outside the binaries of reproductive sexuality" ("Making Generations," 646). Hardack's reading not only further contextualizes how Jones deals with Cat's lesbianism as well as Ursa's response to it but explains why Robinson views the act of oral sex as reinforcing problematic discourses; Robinson explains, "Although Ursa recognizes Mutt's vulnerability, metaphorically rendered by the threat of castration, this scene locks the male and female agents into the circular pattern of a master/slave dialectic with no hope for escape" (164). While *Corregidora* challenges some aspects of heterosexuality and patriarchy, it ultimately rearticulates several of its feminist discourses through those same discourses.

59. See Cognard-Black, "I Said Nothing."

60. Dubey, *Black Women Novelists*, 77; Wade-Gayles, *No Crystal Stair*, 175.

61. Holland, *Raising the Dead*, 116–18.

62. Here, I reiterate a previous point I argue about the degree to which solely hatred characterized Great Gram's feelings toward Corregidora, and this perspective is crucial as the narrative ends with Ursa reuniting with Mutt, understanding in her quest for black women's rights that her relationship with him need not be antagonistic. Also, in one interview, Jones suggests that for Ursa and Mutt to have the tenderness they possess at the end of the novel they need to have experienced some brutality. Jones shares, "Although the main focus of *Corregidora* is on the blues relationships or relationships involving brutality, there seems to be a growing understanding, working itself out, of what is required to be genuinely tender" (Jones, "Interview with Gayl Jones" [Tate interview], 147). In another interview, Jones echoes her notion that the blues "talks about the simultaneity of good and bad, as feeling, as something felt" (Jones, "Gayl Jones" [Harper interview], 700).

4 / "We All Killed Him"

1. DuBois, "Souls of Black Folk," 10.

2. Lopez, *White by Law*, 7.

3. Ibid., 8.

4. Harris, *Price of the Ticket*, xi–xii.

5. Ibid., xi–xii.

6. Abdur-Rahman, *Against the Closet*, 134.

7. West, *Race Matters*, 45–46.

8. Wright's realist novel highlights how economic determinism circumscribes African Americans' opportunities even in the North, where, because of de facto segregation, African Americans remain disadvantaged.

9. Wright, "Ethics of Living Jim Crow."

10. C. Johnson, "Lessons from Fictionalizing King."

11. Dyson's *I May Not Get There With You* rereads King outside his status as a cultural icon to understand that "man" who was behind the movement. Monteith observes a similar trend in the critical moves in King studies in her essay "Revisiting the 1960s."

12. Hall, "Long Civil Rights Movement."

13. Monteith, "Revisiting the 1960s," 215. In "Human Dimension," an interview with Charles Mudede, Charles Johnson contends that without a knowledge of King's orienting philosophies, his overarching theology, and his personhood one cannot know the "true" King or understand him in the context of the civil rights movement (239). In "Site of Memory," Morrison argues that fictive texts that revisit slavery often explore the psychological dimensions of enslaved people's experience that were necessarily omitted from autobiographical narratives of slavery because of the social mores and political contexts in which the authors wrote. Fictive imaginings, however, were not bound by these conventions and therefore could explore critical dimensions of enslaved experience. Although not a neo–slave narrative, *Dreamer* similarly seeks King's interiority in ways that biographies have not.

14. See Hall, "Long Civil Rights Movement," 1237–39, for a thorough discussion of the attempts the New Right made in the North and South to quell black civil rights.

15. Marable, *Race, Reform, and Rebellion*, 215.

16. Hall, "Long Civil Rights Movement," 1234.

17. Slessarev, *Betrayal of the Urban Poor*, 10–11.

18. Ibid.

19. Marable, *Race, Reform, and Rebellion*, 203.

20. Abdur-Rahman, *Against the Closet*, 134.

21. Literary and cultural critic Marc Conner, for example, contends that *Dreamer*, unlike the *Oxherding Tale*, foregrounds Christianity because "his previous philosophical explorations have proven insufficient, or in need of supplement"; in contrast, John Whalen-Bridge argues that the text's exploration of Christianity draws the readers' attention to the parallels between Christianity and Buddhism. Conner, "At the Numinous Heart"; Whalen-Bridge, "Waking Cain."

22. Conner, "At the Numinous Heart," 153.

23. Here I am referring to Sedgwick's notion that in patriarchal societies women become exchange units that men use to demonstrate their superiority to other men. Women matter insofar as they prove a man's status. The absence of women in *Dreamer* confirms this point, underscoring their true alleged insignificance in nation building. See Sedgwick, *Epistemology of the Closet*.

24. C. Johnson, "Conversation with Charles Johnson" [Nash interview]; Byrd, *I Call Myself an Artist*; Selzer, *Charles Johnson in Context*, 216.

25. In *Why We Can't Wait,* particularly ch. 8, "The Days to Come," 149–82, King outlines a plan for implementation and argues that no one leader can be said to have orchestrated the racial movement. He understands, as Miss Jane suggests, that people move the leaders. Yet this understanding doesn't necessarily translate into practice and governance.

26. Byrd, *Charles Johnson's Novels,* 150.

27. King, *Why We Can't Wait,* 160.

28. Murray, "Time of Breach," 15.

29. Byrd, *Charles Johnson's Novels,* 154.

30. King, *Why We Can't Wait,* 145.

31. Monteith, "Revisiting the 1960s," 222.

32. Ibid., 222.

33. Garrow, *Bearing the Cross*; Branch, *At Canaan's Edge.*

34. C. Johnson, "Conversation with Charles Johnson," 234.

35. Lewis, *King,* 316.

36. Finley, "Open Housing Marches," 5.

37. Byrd, *Charles Johnson's Novels,* 148.

38. Garrow, *Bearing the Cross,* 512

39. In *"I'm Not a Racist, But . . ."* Blum argues that we need a more nuanced vocabulary to distinguish between racially coded acts and racism per se. Although Blum would argue that a policy such as "Last one hired, first one fired" is not racist per se, he would concede that it has racial implications based on the history of race (8–15).

Epilogue

1. Crowley and Johnson, "Oprah Winfrey Tells Iowa Crowd."

2. Ibid.

3. Edwards, *Charisma,* 3.

4. Ibid., 33.

5. Ibid., 12.

6. Specifically, Edwards takes as points of departure the formulations of charisma in Rudolf Sohm's *Outlines of Church History* (1892), Walton's *Watch This!* (2009), and Weber's *Economy and Society* (1968) to trace the trajectory of charisma's most common deployments in socio-theological and socio-theological-political cultural contexts. Edwards lays this foundation to explain how black charismatic authority diverges from these ideas and disrupts their normativity.

7. See Ferguson, *Aberrations in Black*; C. Robinson, *Terms of Order.*

8. Edwards, *Charisma,* 18.

9. Moses, *Black Messiahs,* 15.

10. In *Beyond Black and White,* Marable identifies two important goals of the civil rights movement, suggesting that ending Jim Crow segregation was one component of a multifaceted process needed to integrate African Americans into America's institutions. If "the eradication of all legal barriers to blacks' gaining full access to civil society, economic exchange, and political institutions" constituted white America's first responsibility in ensuring African Americans had *access* to the democratic republic's opportunities, the removal of these obstructions to political institutions would result in "an increase in the numbers of African-Americans representing their race in both real and symbolic positions of authority within the state." While Marable's second

claim perhaps too narrowly identifies a unified set of black political interests in what has become, as the epigraph reminds us, "a fractal world of politics and economies," it does underscore that integration is necessary but not sufficient for the attainment of civil equity. More to the point, Marable suggests that black authority within the state, beyond its symbolic function, would promote agendas (however fractured and varied) that would be designed to improve black life (19).

11. In "Racializing Obama," Marable maintains that claims that Obama's election is the fulfillment of King's dream ignore all the evidence of the continued inequality African Americans face, which has made the Dream a nightmare. His examples accord with the larger argument I offer throughout this book about the persistence of civil rights inequities.

12. For a comprehensive analysis of this issue, see Harris, *Price of the Ticket.*

13. Tillet, *Sites of Slavery*, 3.

14. Ibid., 3.

15. Obama, *Inaugural Address 2009*, 13.

16. Edwards, *Charisma*, 187.

17. Ibid., 18.

18. Eng, *Feeling of Kinship*, 3.

19. Balfour, *Evidence of Things Not Said*, 5.

20. Abolition of segregation and outright discrimination did not necessarily yield tangible and massive results for African Americans. For instance, even though African Americans may not be discriminated against for a certain job, the fact that they still earn less than their white counterparts in the same job bespeaks larger historically situated problems that the theoretical promise of equality did not necessarily address. The effects of these phenomena persist.

21. Ikard and Teasley, *Nation of Cowards*, 30.

22. Crayton, "You May Not Get There with Me," 206.

23. West, "Paradox of African American Rebellion," 22.

Bibliography

Abdur-Rahman, Aliyyah. *Against the Closet: Black Political Longing and the Erotics of Race.* Durham: Duke University Press, 2012.

Alexander, Don, and Christine Wright. "Race, Sex, and Class: The Clash over *The Color Purple.*" *Women and Revolution* 34 (Spring 1998): 20.

Anderson, James D. "Secondary School History Textbooks and the Treatment of Black History." In *The State of Afro-American History: Past, Present, and Future,* edited by Darlene Clark Hine, 253–74. Baton Rouge: Louisiana State University Press, 1986.

Andrews, Williams. "We Ain't Going Back There: The Idea of Progress in *The Autobiography of Miss Jane Pittman.*" *Black American Literature Forum* 11, no. 4 (1977): 146–49.

Athey, Stephanie. "Poisonous Roots and the New World Blues: Rereading Seventies Narration and Nation in Alex Haley and Gayl Jones." *Narrative* 7, no. 2 (1999): 169–93.

———. "Reproductive Health, Race, and Technology: Political Fictions and Black Feminist Critiques, 1970s–1990s." *Sage Race Relations* 22, no. 1 (1997): 3–27.

Babb, Valerie. "From History to Her-Story: *The Autobiography of Miss Jane Pittman.*" In *Ernest Gaines,* 76–96. Boston: Twayne, 1991.

Baker, Houston. *Betrayal: How Black Intellectuals Have Abandoned the Ideals of the Civil Rights Era.* New York: Columbia University Press, 2008.

Baldwin, James. *Go Tell It on the Mountain.* New York: Bantam Dell, 2005.

———. *No Name in the Street.* New York: Dial Press, 1972.

Balfour, Lawrie. *The Evidence of Things Not Said: James Baldwin and the Promise of American Democracy.* Ithaca: Cornell University Press, 2001.

Bambara, Toni Cade, ed. *The Black Woman: An Anthology.* New York: Washington Square Press, 2005.

———. "On the Issue of Roles." In *The Black Woman: An Anthology,* edited by Toni Cade Bambara, 123–25. New York: Washington Square Press, 2005.

———. "The Pill: Genocide or Liberation?" In *The Black Woman: An Anthology,* edited by Toni Cade Bambara, 203–12. New York: Washington Square Press, 2005.

———. *The Salt Eaters.* New York: Vintage Books, 1992.

Barker, Deborah E. "Visual Markers: Art and Mass Media in Alice Walker's *Meridian.*" *African American Review* 31, no. 3 (1997): 463–79.

Barnett, Pamela E. "'Miscegenation,' Rape, and 'Race' in Alice Walker's *Meridian.*" *Southern Quarterly: A Journal of the Arts in the South* 39, no. 3 (2001): 65–81.

Beale, Frances. "Double Jeopardy: To Be Black and Female." In *Words of Fire: An Anthology of African American Feminist Thought,* edited by Beverly Guy-Sheftall, 146–56. New York: New Press, 1995.

Bell, Bernard. *The Afro-American Novel and Its Tradition.* Amherst: University of Massachusetts Press, 1987.

Bell, Roseann. "Judgment: Addison Gayle." In *Sturdy Black Bridges: Visions of Black Women in Literature,* edited by Roseann Bell, Bettye Parker, and Beverly Guy-Sheftall, 210–16. Garden City, NY: Anchor Books, 1979.

Benston, Kimberly. "I Yam What I Am: Naming and Unnaming in Afro-American Literature." *Black American Literature Forum* 16, no. 1 (1982): 3–11.

Berlant, Lauren. "Race, Gender, and Nation in *The Color Purple.*" In *Alice Walker: Critical Perspectives Past and Present,* edited by Henry Louis Gates and K. A. Appiah, 211–38. New York: Amistad Press, 1993.

Blum, Lawrence. *"I'm Not a Racist But . . .": The Moral Quandary of Race.* Ithaca: Cornell University Press, 2002.

Boutry, Katherine. "Black and Blue: The Female Body of Blues Writing in Jean Toomer, Toni Morrison, and Gayl Jones." In *Black Orpheus: Music in African American Fiction from the Harlem Renaissance to Toni Morrison,* edited by Saadi Sidawe. New York: Garland, 2000.

Branch, Taylor. *At Canaan's Edge: America in the King Years, 1965–68.* New York: Simon and Schuster, 2006.

Butler-Evans, Elliott. "History and Genealogy in Walker's *The Third Life of Grange Copeland* and *Meridian.*" In *Alice Walker: Critical Perspectives Past and Present,* edited by Henry Louis Gates and K. A. Appiah, 105–25. New York: Amistad Press, 1993.

Byerman, Keith. "Gender and Justice: Alice Walker and the Sexual Politics of Civil Rights." In *The World Is Our Culture: Society and Culture in Contemporary Southern Writing,* edited by Jeffrey J. Folks and Nancy Summers Folks, 93–106. Lexington: University Press of Kentucky, 2000.

———. "A 'Slow-to-Anger' People: *The Autobiography of Miss Jane Pittman* as

Historical Fiction." In *Critical Reflections on the Fiction of Ernest J. Gaines*, edited by David Estes, 107–22. Athens: University of Georgia Press, 1994.

Byrd, Rudolph. *Charles Johnson's Novels: Writing the American Palimpsest.* Bloomington: Indiana University Press, 2005.

———. *I Call Myself an Artist: Writings by and about Charles Johnson.* Bloomington: Indiana University Press, 1999.

Carbado, Devon. "Introduction: Where and When Black Men Enter." In *Black Men on Race, Gender, and Sexuality: A Critical Reader*, edited by Devon Carbado, 1–13. New York: NYU Press, 1999.

Carby, Hazel. "It Jus Be's Dat Way Sometime: The Sexual Politics of Women's Blues." In *Feminisms: An Anthology of Literary Theory and Criticism*, edited by Robyn R. Warhol and Diane Price Herndl, 746–58. New Brunswick: Rutgers University Press, 1991.

Chapman, Erin. *Prove It on Me: New Negroes, Sex, and Popular Culture in the 1920s.* New York: Oxford University Press, 2012.

Christian, Barbara. *Black Feminist Criticism: Perspectives on Black Women Writers.* New York: Pergamon Press, 1985.

Clarke, Cheryl. "Lesbianism: An Act of Resistance." In *Words of Fire: An Anthology of African-American Feminist Thought*, edited by Beverly Guy-Sheftall, 242–52. New York: New Press, 1995.

Cognard-Black, Jennifer. "'I Said Nothing': The Rhetoric of Silence and Gayl Jones's *Corregidora*." *NWSA Journal* 13, no. 1 (2001): 40–60.

Cohen, Cathy. *The Boundaries of Blackness: AIDS and the Breakdown of Black Politics.* Chicago: University of Chicago Press, 1999.

Coleman, James. *Faithful Vision: Treatment of the Sacred, Spiritual, and Supernatural in Twentieth-Century African American Fiction.* Baton Rouge: Louisiana State University Press, 2006.

Collins, Janelle. "'Like a Collage': Personal and Political Subjectivity in Alice Walker's *Meridian*." *CLA Journal* 44, no. 2 (2000): 161–88.

Collins, Patricia Hill. *Black Sexual Politics: African Americans, Gender, and the New Racism.* New York: Routledge, 2004.

Cone, James. "Black Spirituals: A Theological Interpretation." In *African American Religious Thought: An Anthology*, edited by Cornel West and Eddie S. Glaude Jr., 775–89. Louisville, KY: Westminster John Knox Press, 1993.

———. *God of the Oppressed.* San Francisco: HarperSanFrancisco, 1975.

———. *Martin and Malcolm and America: A Dream or a Nightmare.* Maryknoll, NY: Orbis Books, 2005.

Conner, Marc. "At the Numinous Heart of Being: *Dreamer* and Christian Theology." In *Charles Johnson: The Novelist as Philosopher*, edited by Marc Conner and William Nash, 150–67. Jackson: University Press of Mississippi, 2007.

Cooper, Anna Julia. "Womanhood a Vital Element in the Regeneration and Progress of a Race." In *A Voice from the South*, 9–47. New York: Oxford University Press, 1988.

Coser, Stelmaris. "The Dry Wombs of Black Women: Memories of Brazilian Slavery in *Corregidora* and *Song for Anninho*." In *Bridging the Americas: Literature of Paule Marshall, Toni Morrison, and Gayl Jones*, 120–63. Philadelphia: Temple University Press, 1995.

Cotten, Angela L. "Womanist Interventions in Historical Materialism." In *Cultural Sites of Critical Insight: Philosophy, Aesthetics, and African American and Native American Women's Writings*, edited by Angela L. Cotten and Christa Davis Acampora. Albany: SUNY Press, 2007.

Crawford, Vicki L., Jacqueline Rowe, and Barbara Woods. *Women in the Civil Rights Movement: Trailblazers and Torchbearers, 1941–1965*. Bloomington: Indiana University Press, 1993.

Crayton, Kareem. "You May Not Get There with Me: Obama and the Black Political Establishment." In *Barack Obama and African American Empowerment: The Rise of Black America's New Leadership*, edited by Manning Marable and Kristin Clarke, 195–207. New York: Palgrave Macmillan, 2009.

Crenshaw, Kimberlé. "Mapping the Margins: Intersectionality, Identity Politics, and Violence against Women of Color." *Stanford Law Review* 43 (1991): 1241–99.

Crowley, Candy, and Sasha Johnson. "Oprah Winfrey Tells Iowa Crowd: Barack Obama Is 'the One.'" *Cnn.com*, December 8, 2007. www.cnn.com/2007/POLITICS/12/08/oprah.obama/.

Danielson, Susan. "Alice Walker's *Meridian*, Feminism, and the 'Movement.'" *Women's Studies: An Interdisciplinary Journal* 16, nos. 3–4 (1989): 317–30.

Davis, Angela. *Blues Legacies and Black Feminism: Gertrude Ma Rainey, Bessie Smith, and Billie Holiday*. New York: Vintage Books, 1999.

———. "Women and Capitalism: Dialectics of Oppression and Liberation." In *The Black Feminist Reader*, edited by Joy James and T. Denean Sharpley-Whiting, 146–82. Malden, MA: Blackwell, 2000.

Davis, Thadious M. "History's Place Markers in Memory: 1954 and 1999." In *What Democracy Looks Like: A New Critical Realism for a Post-Seattle World*, edited by Amy Schrager Lang and Cecelia Tichi, 193–204. New Brunswick: Rutgers University Press, 2006.

Dixon, Melvin. "Singing a Deep Song: Language as Evidence in the Novels of Gayl Jones." In *Black Women Writers (1950–1980): A Critical Evaluation*, edited by Mari Evans, 236–48. Garden City, NY: Anchor-Doubleday, 1984.

Dixon, Patricia. *African American Relationships, Marriages and Families: An Introduction*. New York: Routledge, 2007.

Douglas, Kelly Brown. *Sexuality and the Black Church: A Womanist Perspective*. Maryknoll, NY: Orbis Books, 1999.

Douglass, Frederick. "I Am a Radical Woman Suffrage Man." In *Traps: African American Men on Gender and Sexuality*, edited by Rudolph Byrd, 37–45. Bloomington: Indiana University Press, 2001.

Doyle, Mary Ellen. "Tales within Tales: The Autobiography of Miss Jane

Pittman." In *Voices from the Quarters: The Fiction of Ernest J. Gaines*, 130–53. Baton Rouge: Louisiana State University Press, 2002.

Dubey, Madhu. *Black Women Novelists and the Nationalist Aesthetic*. Bloomington: Indiana University Press, 1991.

DuBois, W. E. B. "The Souls of Black Folk." In *Three Negro Classics*, edited by John H. Franklin, 207–389. New York: Avon Books, 1999.

DuCille, Ann. *Skin Trade*. Boston: Harvard University Press, 1996.

Dyson, Michael Eric. *I May Not Get There with You: The True Martin Luther King, Jr.* New York: Free Press, 2000.

——. *Is Bill Cosby Right? Or Has the Black Middle Class Lost Its Mind?* New York: Basic Civitas Books, 2005.

——. "When You Divide the Body and Soul, Problems Multiply." In *The Michael Eric Dyson Reader*, edited by Michael Eric Dyson, 219–37. New York: Basic Civitas Books, 2004.

Edwards, Erica. *Charisma and the Fiction of Black Leadership*. Minneapolis: University of Minnesota Press, 2012.

——. "Moses, Monster of the Mountain: Gendered Violence in Black Leadership's Gothic Tale." *Callaloo* 31, no. 4 (2008): 1084–1102.

Eng, David. *The Feeling of Kinship: Queer Liberalism and the Racialization of Intimacy*. Durham: Duke University Press, 2010.

Estes, Steve. *I Am a Man! Race, Manhood, and the Civil Rights Movement*. Chapel Hill: University of North Carolina Press, 2005.

Feldstein, Ruth. "I Don't Trust You Anymore: Nina Simone, Culture, and Black Activism in the 1960s." *Journal of American History* 91, no. 4 (2005): 1349–79.

Ferguson, Roderick. *Aberrations in Black: Toward a Queer of Color Critique*. Minneapolis: University of Minnesota Press, 2004.

Finley, Mary. "The Open Housing Marches: Chicago, Summer '66." In *Chicago 1966: Open Housing Marches, Summit Negotiations, and Operation Breadbasket*, edited by David Garrow, 1–47. Brooklyn, NY: Carlson, 1989.

Foster, Frances Smith, ed. *Written by Herself: Literary Production by African American Women, 1796–1892*. Bloomington: Indiana University Press, 1993.

Franklin, John Hope, and August Meier, eds. *Black Leaders of the Twentieth Century*. Urbana: University of Illinois Press, 1982.

Fuller, Hoyt. "Towards a Black Aesthetic." In *Within the Circle: An Anthology of African American Literary Criticism from the Harlem Renaissance to the Present*, edited by Angelyn Mitchell, 199–206. Durham: Duke University Press, 1994.

Gaines, Ernest. *The Autobiography of Miss Jane Pittman*. New York: Bantam Books, 1972.

——. "Ernest Gaines." Interview by Tom Carter. In *Conversations with Ernest Gaines*, edited by John Lowe, 80–85. Jackson: University Press of Mississippi, 1995.

——. "Ernest Gaines." Interview by Jerome Tarshis. In *Conversations with*

Ernest Gaines, edited by John Lowe, 80–85. Jackson: University Press of Mississippi, 1995.

———. "An Interview with Ernest Gaines." Interview by John Lowe. In *Conversations with Ernest Gaines*, edited by John Lowe, 297–328. Jackson: University Press of Mississippi, 1995.

Gaines, Kevin. *Uplifting the Race: Black Leadership, Politics, and Culture in the Twentieth Century*. Chapel Hill: University of North Carolina Press, 1996.

Garrow, David. *Bearing the Cross: Martin Luther King, Jr., and the Southern Christian Leadership Conference*. New York: William Morrow, 1986.

Gaudet, Marcia. "Black Women: Race, Gender, and Culture in Gaines' Fiction." In *Critical Reflections on the Fiction of Ernest J. Gaines*, edited by David Estes, 139–57. Athens: University of Georgia Press, 1994.

———. "Miss Jane and Personal Narrative: Ernest Gaines' *The Autobiography of Miss Jane Pittman*." *Western Folklore* 51 (1992): 23–32.

Giddings, Paula. *When and Where I Enter: The Impact of Black Women on Race and Sex in America*. New York: Perennial, 2001.

Giles, James. "Revolution and Myth: Kelley's *A Different Drummer* and Gaines' *The Autobiography of Miss Jane Pittman*." *Minority Voices* 1, no. 2 (1977): 39–48.

Glaude, Eddie. *Exodus! Religion, Race, and Nation in Early Nineteenth-Century Black America*. Chicago: Chicago University Press, 2000.

Goldberg, Elizabeth. "Living the Legacy: Pain, Desire, and Narrative Time in Gayl Jones' *Corregidora*." *Callaloo* 26, no. 2 (2003): 446–72.

Grant, Jacquelyn. "Black Theology and the Black Woman." In *Black Theology: A Documentary History, 1966–1979*, edited by Gayraud Wilmore and James Cone, 418–33. Maryknoll, NY: Orbis Books, 1979.

Griffin, Farah Jasmine. "Conflict and Chorus: Reconsidering Toni Cade's *The Black Woman: An Anthology*." In *Is It Nation Time? Contemporary Essays on Black Power and Black Nationalism*, edited by Eddie S. Glaude Jr., 113–29. Chicago: University of Chicago Press, 2002.

Griffin, Horace. "Toward a True Black Liberation Theology: Affirming Homoeroticism, Black Gay Christians, and Their Love Relationship." In *Loving the Body: Black Religious Studies and the Erotic*, edited by Dwight N. Hopkins and Anthony B. Pinn, 133–55. New York: Palgrave Macmillan, 2004.

Griffiths, Jennifer. *Traumatic Possessions: The Body and Memory in African American Women's Writing and Performance*. Charlottesville: University of Virginia Press, 2010.

Hall, Jacquelyn Dowd. "The Long Civil Rights Movement and the Political Uses of the Past." *Journal of American History* 91, no. 4 (2005): 1233–63.

Hamer, Fannie Lou. *The Speeches of Fannie Lou Hamer: To Tell It Like It Is*. Edited by Maegan Brooks and Davis Houck. Jackson: University Press of Mississippi, 2011.

Hamilton, Charles. "Federal Law and the Courts in the Civil Rights Movement."

In *The Civil Rights Movement in America*, edited by Charles Eagles, 97–117. Jackson: University Press of Mississippi, 1986.

Hansberry, Lorraine. *A Raisin in the Sun*. New York: Random House, 1959.

Hardack, Richard. "Making Generations and Bearing Witness: Violence and Orality in Gayl Jones's *Corregidora*." *Prospects: An Annual Journal of American Cultural Studies* 24 (1999): 645–61.

Harper, Frances Ellen Watkins. "Moses: A Story of the Nile." In *A Brighter Coming Day: A Frances Ellen Watkins Harper Reader*, edited by Frances Smith Foster. New York: Feminist Press at the City University of New York, 1990.

Harris, Frederick. *The Price of the Ticket: Barack Obama and the Rise and Decline of Black Politics*. New York: Oxford University Press, 2012.

Henderson, Mae. "Speaking in Tongues: Dialogics, Dialectics, and the Black Woman Writer's Literary Tradition." In *African American Literary Theory: A Reader*, edited by Winston Napier, 348–68. New York: NYU Press, 2000.

Hendrickson, Roberta M. "Remembering the Dream: Alice Walker, *Meridian* and the Civil Rights Movement." *MELUS* 24, no. 3 (1999): 111–28.

Hernton, Calvin. *Sex and Racism in America*. New York: Anchor, 1982.

———. "The Sexual Mountain and Black Women Writers." *Black American Literature Forum* 18, no. 4 (1984): 139–45.

Hicks, Jack. "To Make These Bones Live: History and Community in Ernest Gaines's Fiction." *Black American Literature Forum* 11, no. 1 (1977): 9–19.

Hogue, Lawrence. *Discourse and the Other*. Durham: Duke University Press, 1986.

Holland, Sharon P. *Raising the Dead: Readings of Death and (Black) Subjectivity*. Durham: Duke University Press, 2000.

Holloway, Karla. *Private Bodies, Public Texts: Race, Gender, and a Cultural Bioethics*. Durham: Duke University Press, 2011.

Hughes, Langston. "Harlem." In *The Collected Poems of Langston Hughes*, edited by Arnold Rampersad and David Roessel, 424. New York: Knopf, 1994.

Hurston, Zora Neale. *Moses, Man of the Mountain*. New York: HarperCollins, 1991.

Hussen, Aida. "'Black Rage' and 'Useless Pain': Affect, Ambivalence, and Identity after King." *South Atlantic Quarterly* 112, no. 2 (2013): 303–18.

Ikard, David. *Breaking the Silence: Toward a Black Male Feminist Criticism*. Baton Rouge: Louisiana State University Press, 2007.

Ikard, David, and Martell Teasley. *Nation of Cowards: Black Activism in Barack Obama's Post-racial America*. Bloomington: Indiana University Press, 2012.

Irigaray, Luce. *The Sex Which Is Not One*. Ithaca: Cornell University Press, 1985.

Iton, Richard. *In Search of the Black Fantastic: Politics and Popular Culture in the Post–Civil Rights Era*. New York: Oxford University Press, 2008.

Jackson, Blyden. "*Jane Pittman* through the Years: A People's Tale." In *American Letters and the Historical Consciousness: Essays in Honor of Lewis P.*

Simpson, edited by Gerald Kennedy and Daniel Fogel, 255–73. Baton Rouge: Louisiana State University Press, 1987.

Jacobs, Harriet. *Incidents in the Life of a Slave Girl, Written by Herself.* Edited by Kwame Appiah. New York: Modern Library, 2000.

James, Joy. *Transcending the Talented Tenth: Black Leaders and American Intellectuals.* New York: Routledge, 1997.

Jarrett, Gene. *Representing the Race: A New Political History of African American Literature.* New York: NYU Press, 2010.

Johnson, Barbara. "Moses and Intertextuality: Sigmund Freud, Zora Neale Hurston, and the Bible." In *Poetics of the Americas: Race, Founding, and Textuality*, edited by Barnard Cowan and Jefferson Humphries, 15–29. Baton Rouge: Louisiana University Press, 1997.

Johnson, Charles. "A Conversation with Charles Johnson." Interview by William Nash. In *Passing the Three Gates: Interviews with Charles Johnson*, edited by Jim McWilliams, 214–35. Seattle: University of Washington Press, 2004.

——. *Dreamer.* New York: Simon and Schuster, 1998.

——. "The Human Dimension: An Interview with Writer-Philosopher Charles Johnson." By Charles Mudede. In *Passing the Three Gates: Interviews with Charles Johnson*, edited by Jim McWilliams, 236–45. Seattle: University of Washington Press, 2004.

——. "Lessons from Fictionalizing King." *Seattle Times*, spring 1998, http://seattletimes.nwsource.com/mlk/legacy/Johnson_intro.html.

——. *Oxherding Tale.* New York: Plume, 1995.

Johnson, E. Patrick, and Mae Henderson, eds. *Black Queer Studies: A Critical Anthology.* Durham: Duke University Press, 2007.

Jones, Gayl. *Corregidora.* Boston: Beacon Press, 1986.

——. "Gayl Jones: An Interview." By Michael Harper. *Massachusetts Review* 18, no. 4 (1975): 692–715.

——. "An Interview with Gayl Jones." Interview by Charles Rowell. *Callaloo* 16 (1982): 32–53.

——. "An Interview with Gayl Jones." Interview by Claudia Tate. *Black American Literature Forum* 13, no. 4 (1979): 142–48.

Joseph, Peniel. "Waiting till the Midnight Hour: Reconceptualizing the Heroic Period of the Civil Rights Movement, 1954–1965." *Souls* 2, no. 1 (2000): 6–17.

Kapsalis, Terri. "Mastering the Female Pelvis: Race and the Tools of Reproduction." In *Skin Deep, Spirit Strong: The Black Female Body in American Culture*, edited by Kimberly Wallace-Sanders, 263–300. Ann Arbor: University of Michigan Press, 2002.

Keizer, Arlene. *Black Subjects: Identity Formation in the Contemporary Narrative of Slavery.* Ithaca: Cornell University Press, 2004.

Kelley, Robin D. G. *Hammer and Hoe: Alabama Communists during the Great Depression.* Chapel Hill: University of North Carolina Press, 1990.

Kenan, Randall. *The Fire This Time.* Hoboken, NJ: Melville House, 2007.

King, Deborah. "Multiple Jeopardy, Multiple Consciousness: The Context of Black Feminist Ideology." In *Words of Fire: An Anthology of African American Feminist Thought,* edited by Beverly Guy-Sheftall, 146–56. New York: New Press, 1995.

King, Martin Luther, Jr. "I Have a Dream." In *I Have a Dream—40th Anniversary Edition: Writings and Speeches That Changed the World,* edited by James Melvin Washington, 101–6. New York: HarperCollins, 1992.

———. "Remaining Awake during a Great Revolution." In *I Have a Dream—40th Anniversary Edition: Writings and Speeches That Changed the World,* edited by James Melvin Washington, 276–78. New York: HarperCollins, 1992.

———. *Why We Can't Wait.* Boston: Beacon Press, 2010.

Lawson, Steven. *Running for Freedom: Civil Rights and Black Politics in America since 1941.* New York: McGraw-Hill, 1991.

Lee, Andrea. *Sarah Phillips.* Boston: Northeastern University Press, 1993.

Lee, Jarena. *Religious Experience and Journal of Mrs. Jarena Lee, Giving an Account of Her Call to Preach the Gospel.* Philadelphia: P. S. Duval, 1849.

Lewis, David. *King: A Biography.* Urbana: University of Illinois Press, 1978.

Li, Stephanie. "Love and the Trauma of Resistance in Gayl Jones's *Corregidora.*" *Callaloo* 29, no. 1 (2006): 131–50.

Ling, Peter. "Gender and Generation: Manhood at the Southern Christian Leadership Conference." In *Gender and the Civil Rights Movement,* ed. Peter J. Ling and Sharon Monteith, 101–30. New Brunswick: Rutgers University Press, 2004.

Ling, Peter J., and Sharon Monteith, eds. *Gender and the Civil Rights Movement.* New Brunswick: Rutgers University Press, 2004.

Lipsitz, George. *The Possessive Investment of Whiteness: How White People Profit from Identity Politics.* Philadelphia: Temple University Press, 1998.

Loewen, James W. *Lies My Teacher Told Me: Everything Your American History Textbook Got Wrong.* New York: New Press, 1995.

Logan, Rayford. *The Negro in American Life and Thought: The Nadir, 1877–1901.* New York: Dial Press, 1954.

Lopez, Ian. *White by Law: The Legal Construction of Race.* New York: NYU Press, 2006.

Marable, Manning. *Beyond Black and White: Transforming African-American Politics.* New York: Verso, 1995.

———. *Black Leadership.* New York: Columbia University Press, 1998.

———. *Race, Reform, and Rebellion: The Second Reconstruction and Beyond in Black America, 1945–2006.* Jackson: University Press of Mississippi, 2007.

———. "Racializing Obama: The Enigma of Postblack Politics and Leadership." In *Barack Obama and African American Empowerment: The Rise of Black America's New Leadership,* edited by Manning Marable and Kristin Clarke, 1–12. New York: Palgrave Macmillan, 2009.

Margolick, David. "Performance as a Force for Change: The Case of Billie Holiday and 'Strange Fruit.'" *Cardozo Studies in Law and Literature* 11, no. 1 (1999): 91–109.

McDowell, Deborah. "Foreword: Lines of Descent/Dissenting Lines." In *Moses, Man of the Mountain*, by Zora Neale Hurston, vii–xxiv. New York: HarperCollins, 1991.

———. "Reading Family Matters." In *Changing Our Own Words: Essays on Criticism, Theory, and Writing by Black Women*, edited by Cheryl Wall, 75–97. New Brunswick: Rutgers University Press, 1989.

McGuire, Danielle. *At The Dark End of the Street: Black Women, Rape and Resistance—A New History of the Civil Rights Movement from Rosa Parks to the Rise of Black Power*. New York: Knopf, 2010.

Metress, Christopher, ed. *The Lynching of Emmett Till: A Documentary Narrative*. Charlottesville: University of Virginia Press, 2002.

———. "Making Civil Rights Harder: Literature, Memory, and the Black Freedom Struggle." *Southern Literary Journal* 40, no. 2 (2008): 138–50.

Metress, Christopher, and Harriet Pollack, eds. *Emmett Till in Literary Memory and Imagination*. Baton Rouge: Louisiana State University Press, 2008.

Miller, Keith D. *Voice of Deliverance: The Language of Martin Luther King, Jr. and Its Sources*. New York: Maxwell Macmillan International, 1992.

Mitchell, Angelyn. *The Freedom to Remember: Narrative, Slavery, and Gender in Contemporary Black Women's Fiction*. New Brunswick: Rutgers University Press, 2002.

Mitchem, Stephanie. *Introducing Womanist Theology*. Maryknoll, NY: Orbis Books, 2002.

Monroe, Irene. "When and Where I Enter, Then the Whole Race Enters with Me: Que(e)rying Exodus." In *Loving the Body: Black Religious Studies and the Erotic*, edited by Dwight Hopkins and Anthony Pinn, 121–31. New York: Palgrave Macmillan, 2004.

Monteith, Sharon. "Revisiting the 1960s in Contemporary Fiction: 'Where Do We Go from Here?'" In *Gender and the Civil Rights Movement*, edited by Peter Ling and Sharon Monteith, 215–38. New Brunswick: Rutgers University Press, 2004.

Morris, Aldon. *The Origins of the Civil Rights Movement: Black Communities Organizing for Change*. New York: Free Press, 1984.

Morrison, Toni. *Beloved: A Novel*. New York: Vintage International, 2004.

———. *Paradise*. New York: Penguin Group, 1999.

———. "The Site of Memory." In *What Moves at the Margins*, edited by Carolyn Denard, 65–80. Jackson: University Press of Mississippi, 2007.

———. *Song of Solomon*. New York: Knopf, 1977.

———. *Sula*. New York: Knopf, 1973.

———. "Toni Morrison on a Book She Loves: Gayl Jones's *Corregidora*." In *What*

Moves at the Margins, edited by Carolyn Denard, 108–10. Jackson: University Press of Mississippi, 2007.

Moses, Wilson. *Black Messiahs and Uncle Toms: Social and Literary Manipulations of a Religious Myth*. University Park: Pennsylvania State University Press, 1982.

Moynihan, Daniel. *The Negro Family: The Case for National Action*. Washington, DC: Office of Policy Planning and Research, U.S. Department of Labor, 1965.

Mueller, Carol. "Ella Baker and the Origins of 'Participatory Democracy.'" In *Women in the Civil Rights Movement: Trailblazers and Torchbearers, 1941–1965*, edited by Vicki L. Crawford, Jacqueline Rowe, and Barbara Woods, 51–70. Bloomington: Indiana University Press, 1993.

Murray, Rolland. *Our Living Manhood: Literature, Black Power, and Masculine Ideology*. Philadelphia: University of Pennsylvania Press, 2007.

———. "The Time of Breach: Class Division and the Contemporary African American Novel." *Novel: A Forum on Fiction* 43, no. 1 (2010): 11–17.

Nadel, Alan. "Reading the Body: Meridian and the Archaeology of Self." In *Alice Walker: Critical Perspectives Past and Present*, edited by Henry Louis Gates and K. A. Appiah, 153–84. New York: Amistad Press, 1993.

Neal, Larry. "The Black Arts Movement." In *Within the Circle: An Anthology of African American Literary Criticism from the Harlem Renaissance to the Present*, edited by Angelyn Mitchell, 184–98. Durham: Duke University Press, 1994.

———. "Some Reflections on the Black Aesthetic." In *The Black Aesthetic*, edited by Addison Gayle Jr., 1–15. New York: Doubleday, 1972.

Nora, Pierre. "Between History and Memory: *Les Lieux de Memoire*." In *History and Memory in African American Culture*, edited by Genevieve Fabre and Robert O'Meally, 284–300. New York: Oxford University Press, 1994.

Norman, Brian. *Neo-segregation Narratives: Jim Crow in Post–Civil Rights American Literature*. Athens: University of Georgia Press, 2010.

Oates, Stephen. *Let the Trumpet Sound: The Life of Martin Luther King, Jr.* New York: Harper and Row, 1982.

Obama, Barack. *The Inaugural Address, 2009*. New York: Penguin Group, 2009.

Oliver, Melvin, and Robert Shapiro. *Black Wealth / White Wealth: A New Perspective on Racial Inequality*. New York: Routledge, 1995.

Papa, Lee. "His Feet on Your Neck: The New Religion in the Works of Ernest J. Gaines." *African American Review* 27, no. 2 (1993): 187–93.

Patterson, Robert J. "A Triple-Twined Re-appropriation: Womanist Theology and Gendered-Racial Protest in the Writings of Jarena Lee, Frances E. W. Harper, and Harriet Jacobs." *Religion and Literature*, forthcoming.

Payne, Charles. *I've Got the Light of Freedom: The Organizing Tradition and the Mississippi Freedom Struggle*. Los Angeles: University of California Press, 1995.

Peterson, Carla. *Doers of the Word: African American Women Speakers and Writers in the North (1830–1880)*. New York: Oxford University Press, 1995.

Raboteau, Albert. *Slave Religion: The "Invisible Institution" in the Antebellum South*. New York: Oxford University Press, 1978.

Ransby, Barbara. *Ella Baker and the Black Freedom Movement: A Radical Democratic Vision*. Chapel Hill: University of North Carolina Press, 2003.

Reddy, Chandan. *Freedom with Violence: Race, Sexuality and the US State*. Durham: Duke University Press, 2011.

Reed, Adolph. *W. E .B. DuBois and American Political Thought: Fabianism and the Color Line*. New York: Oxford University Press, 1997.

Reed, Ishmael. *Mumbo Jumbo*. New York: Scribner, 1996.

Rich, Adrienne. *Of Woman Born: Motherhood as Experience and Institution*. London: Norton, 1995.

Richardson, Riché. *Black Masculinity and the U.S. South: From Uncle Tom to Gangsta*. Athens: University of Georgia Press, 2007.

Roberts, Dorothy. *Killing the Black Body: Race, Reproduction, and the Meaning of Liberty*. New York: Vintage, 1999.

Robinson, Cedric. *The Terms of Order: Political Science and the Myth of Leadership*. Albany: State University of New York Press, 1980.

Robinson, Sally. "*Corregidora*: Black Female Subjectivity and the Politics of Heterosexuality." In *Engendering the Subject: Gender and Self-Representation in Contemporary Women's Fiction*. Albany: SUNY Press, 1991.

Robnett, Belinda. *How Long? How Long? African-American Women in the Struggle for Civil Rights*. New York: Oxford University Press, 1997.

———. "Women in the Student Non-violent Coordinating Committee: Ideology, Organizational Structure, and Leadership." In *Gender and the Civil Rights Movement*, edited by Peter J. Ling and Sharon Monteith, 131–68. New Brunswick: Rutgers University Press, 2004.

Rushdy, Ashraf. *Neo-Slave Narratives: Studies in the Social Logic of a Literary Form*. New York: Oxford University Press, 1999.

———. "Relate Sexual to Historical: Race, Resistance, and Desire in Gayl Jones's *Corregidora*." *African American Review* 34, no. 2 (2000): 273–97.

Ruskin, Donna Kate. "Bridge Poem" [1981]. In *This Bridge Called My Back*, 2nd ed., edited by Cherríe Moraga and Gloria Anzaldúa, xxi. New York: Kitchen Table, Women of Color Press, 1983. www.yorku.ca/lfoster/documents /TheBridgePoem_DonnaKateRuskin.html.

Rustin, Bayard. *Time on Two Crosses: The Collected Writing of Bayard Rustin*. Edited by Devon Carbado and Donald Weise. San Francisco: Cleis Press, 2003.

Scott, Darieck. *Extravagant Abjection: Blackness, Power, and Sexuality in the African American Literary Imagination*. Sexual Cultures. New York: NYU Press, 2010.

Sedgwick, Eve Kosofsky. *Epistemology of the Closet.* Berkeley: University of California Press, 1990.

Selzer, Linda. *Charles Johnson in Context.* Amherst: University of Massachusetts Press, 2009.

Sharpe, Christina. "The Costs of Re-membering: What's at Stake in Gayl Jones's *Corregidora.*" In *African American Performance and Theater History: A Critical Reader,* edited by Harry J. Elam Jr. and David Krasner, 306–27. Oxford: Oxford University Press, 2001.

———. *Monstrous Intimacies: Making Post-Slavery Subjects.* Durham: Duke University Press, 2010.

Simon, Bruce. "Traumatic Repetition: Gayl Jones's *Corregidora.*" In *Race Consciousness: African-American Studies for the New Century,* edited by Judith Fossett and Jeffrey Tucker, 93–112. New York: NYU Press, 1997.

Simone, Nina. *I Put a Spell on You: The Autobiography of Nina Simone.* Cambridge, MA: Da Capo Press, 1993.

Slessarev, Helene. *The Betrayal of the Urban Poor.* Philadelphia: Temple University Press, 1997.

Smith, Barbara. "Toward a Black Feminist Criticism." In *Within the Circle: An Anthology of African American Literary Criticism from the Harlem Renaissance to the Present,* edited by Angelyn Mitchell, 410–27. Durham: Duke University Press.

Smith, Valerie. "Gender and Afro-Americanist Literary Theory and Criticism." In *Speaking of Gender,* edited by Elaine Showalter, 50–65. New York: Routledge, 1989.

———. Introduction to *Sarah Phillips,* by Andrea Lee. Boston: Northeastern University Press, 1993.

Sohm, Rudolf. *Outlines of Church History.* New York: Hardpress, 2012.

Spelman, Elizabeth. *Inessential Women: Problems of Exclusion in Feminist Thought.* Boston: Beacon Press, 1988.

Spillers, Hortense. "Mama's Baby, Papa's Maybe: An American Grammar Book." In *The Black Feminist Reader,* edited by Joy James and T. Denean Sharpley-Whiting, 57–87. Malden, MA: Blackwell, 2000.

Standley, Anne. "The Role of Black Women in the Civil Rights Movement." In *Women in the Civil Rights Movement: Trailblazers and Torchbearers, 1941–1965,* edited by Vicki L. Crawford, Jacqueline Rowe, and Barbara Woods, 183–202. Bloomington: Indiana University Press, 1993.

Steigerwald, David. *The Sixties and the End of Modern America.* New York: St. Martin's Press, 1995.

Stein, Karen F. "*Meridian:* Alice Walker's Critique of Revolution." *Black American Literature Forum* 20, nos. 1–2 (1986): 129–41.

Stepto, Robert. *From behind the Veil: A Study of Afro-American Narrative.* Champaign: University of Illinois Press, 1991.

Stewart, Maria. "Mrs. Stewart's Farewell Address to Her Friends in the City of

Boston." In *Maria W. Stewart: America's First Black Woman Political Writer*, edited by Marilyn Richardson, 65–74. Bloomington: Indiana University Press, 1987.

———. "Religion and the Pure Principles of Morality, the Sure Foundation on Which We Must Build." In *Maria W. Stewart: America's First Black Woman Political Writer*, edited by Marilyn Richardson, 28–29. Bloomington: Indiana University Press, 1987.

Tillet, Salamishah. *Sites of Slavery: Citizenship and Racial Democracy in the Post–Civil Rights Imagination*. Durham: Duke University Press, 2012.

Truth, Sojourner. 'When Woman Gets Her Rights Man Will Be Right." In *Words of Fire: An Anthology of African-American Feminist Thought*, edited by Beverly Guy-Sheftall, 37–38. New York: New Press, 1995.

———. "Woman's Rights." In *Words of Fire: An Anthology of African-American Feminist Thought*, edited by Beverly Guy-Sheftall, 36. New York: New Press, 1995.

Valkeakari, Tuire. *Religious Idiom and the African American Novel, 1953–1998*. Gainesville: University Press of Florida, 2007.

Verge, Shane. "Revolutionary Vision: Black Women Writers, Black Nationalist Ideology, and Interracial Sexuality." *Meridians* 2, no. 2 (2002): 101–25.

Wade-Gayles, Gloria. *No Crystal Stair: Visions of Race and Gender in Black Women's Fiction*. Berea, OH: Pilgrim Press, 1984.

Walker, Alice. "Alice Walker." Interview by Claudia Tate. In *Black Women Writers at Work*, edited by Claudia Tate, 175–87. New York: Continuum Press, 1988.

———. "The Civil Rights Movement: What Good Was It?" In *In Search of Our Mothers' Gardens: Womanist Prose*, 119–29. New York: Harcourt Books, 1983.

———. *Meridian*. New York: Harcourt Books, 2003.

———. *The Third Life of Grange Copeland*. New York: Harcourt Brace Jovanovich, 1970.

Walker, Margaret. *Jubilee*. New York: Mariner Books, 1999.

Walker, Melissa. *Down from the Mountaintop: Black Women's Novels in the Wake of the Civil Rights Movement, 1966–1989*. New Haven: Yale University Press, 1991.

Wall, Cheryl. *Worrying the Line: Black Women Writers, Lineage, and Literary Tradition*. Chapel Hill: University of North Carolina Press, 2005.

Wallace, Michele. *Black Macho and the Myth of the Superwoman*. New York: Verso, 1999.

Walters, Ronald, and Robert Smith. *African American Leadership*. Albany: SUNY Press, 1999.

Walton, Jonathan. *Watch This! The Ethics and Aesthetics of Black Televangelism*. New York: NYU Press, 2009.

Walzer, Michael. *Exodus and Revolution*. New York: Basic Books, 1985.

Ward, Brian. *Just My Soul Responding: Rhythm and Blues, Black Consciousness, and Race Relations*. Berkeley: University of California Press, 1998.

Warren, Kenneth. *What Was African American Literature?* Cambridge, MA: Harvard University Press, 2011.

Washington, Mary Helen. "Introduction: The Darkened Eye Restored: Notes toward a Literary History of Black Women." In *Invented Lives: Narratives of Black Women, 1860–1900*, xv–xxxi. New York: Anchor Press, 1987

Watkins, Mel. "Sexism, Racism and Black Women Writers." *New York Times Book Review*, June 15, 1986, 36.

Watts, Jerry Gafio. *Heroism and the Black Intellectual: Ralph Ellison, Politics, and Afro-American Intellectual Life*. Chapel Hill: University of North Carolina Press, 1994.

Weber, Max. *Economy and Society: An Outline of Interpretive Sociology*. Berkeley: University of California Press, 1978.

Weinbaum, Alys. *Wayward Reproductions: Genealogies of Race and Nation in Transatlantic Modern Thought*. Durham: Duke University Press, 2005.

West, Cornell. Foreword to *The New Jim Crow: Mass Incarceration in the Age of Colorblindness*, by Michelle Alexander, ix–xii. New York: New Press, 2010.

———. "The Paradox of African American Rebellion." *Is It Nation Time? Contemporary Essays on Black Power and Black Nationalism*, edited by Eddie S. Glaude Jr., 22–38. Chicago: University of Chicago Press, 2002.

———. *Race Matters*. Boston: Beacon Press, 1993.

Whalen-Bridge, John. "Waking Cain: The Poetics of Integration in Charles Johnson's *Dreamer*." *Callaloo* 26, no. 2 (2003): 504–21.

Whitt, Margaret, ed. *Short Stories of the Civil Rights Movement*. Athens: University of Georgia Press, 2006.

Whitted, Qiana. *A God of Justice? The Problem of Evil in Twentieth-Century Black Literature*. Charlottesville: University of Virginia Press, 2009.

Williams, Delores S. *Sisters in the Wilderness: The Challenge of Womanist God-Talk*. Maryknoll, NY: Orbis Books, 1993.

Willis, Susan. "Walker's Women." In *Modern Critical Views: Alice Walker*, edited by Harold Bloom, 81–95. New York: Chelsea House, 1989.

Wilmore, Gayraud. *Black Religion and Radicalism: An Interpretation of the Religious History of African Americans*. Maryknoll, NY: Orbis Books, 1998.

Wright, Richard. "Blueprint for Negro Writing." In *Within the Circle: An Anthology of African American Literary Criticism from the Harlem Renaissance to the Present*, edited by Angelyn Mitchell, 97–106. Durham: Duke University Press, 1994.

———. "The Ethics of Living Jim Crow: An Autobiographical Sketch." In *Crossing the Danger Water: Three Hundred Years of African-American Writing*, edited by Deirdre Mullane, 557–66. New York: Anchor Books, 1993.

———. *Native Son*. New York: Harper Perennial, 1996.

Yoon, Seongho. "Gendering the Movement: Black Womanhood, SNCC, and Post–Civil Rights Anxieties in Alice Walker's *Meridian*." *Feminist Studies in English Literature* 14, no. 2 (2006): 179–207.

Index